THE

EUROPEAN UNION

EXPLAINED

THE
EUROPEAN UNION

EXPLAINED

THIRD EDITION

Andreas Staab

Institutions · Actors · Global Impact

Indiana University Press
Bloomington · Indianapolis

This book is a publication of

Indiana University Press
Office of Scholarly Publishing
Herman B Wells Library 350
1320 East 10th Street
Bloomington, Indiana 47405 USA

www.iupress.indiana.edu

Telephone orders   800-842-6796
Fax orders   812-855-7931

⧀ The paper used in this publication meets the minimum requirements
of the American National Standard for Information Sciences—Permanence
of Paper for Printed Library Materials, ANSI Z39.48-1992.

Manufactured in the United States of America

Cataloging information is available from the Library of Congress.

ISBN 978-0-253-00972-2 (pbk.)
ISBN 978-0-253-00976-0 (eb)

1 2 3 4 5   18 17 16 15 14 13

To Sophia and Luisa.
Europeans by birth and maybe even by choice.

Contents

Preface

The European Union (EU) today differs considerably from the integration project that began in the 1950s. Initially conceived as a way to safeguard peace and enable economic recovery among six Western European countries, the EU has developed into one of the world's most formidable trading blocs spanning much of the European continent. Its future, however, is very much in flux. The controversies over the ratification of the Lisbon Treaty and disagreements concerning policy reforms and how to finance them evoked fundamental disagreements over the future direction of the EU. The Eurozone's sovereign debt crisis brought economic hardships to many countries which prompted some analysts to conclude that Economic and Monetary Union had indeed been a step too far for European integration. Given the prospect of enlargement to the western Balkans and Turkey, a growing number of member state governments argue for less "Europe," while others view the events of recent years as compelling reasons for ambitious policy and institutional reforms.

Regardless of the outcome of this debate, the European Union represents a hugely influential vehicle for organizing Europe and constitutes a unique experiment of "deep" international cooperation. Economically, at least until the Eurozone crisis, it has boosted prosperity levels. Politically it has fostered the democratic transition of former fascist and communist dictatorships. It has helped to overcome the artificial division of Europe caused by the Iron Curtain and the Cold War, and has also assumed a global vanguard position in the fight against climate change. On the other hand, the EU has often been criticized for favoring big business over the economic and social needs of its citizens. Others accuse the EU of lacking transparency and accountability in its institutional processes, and some claim that European integration has led to the gradual erosion of national and cultural differences and traditions, while many citizens in countries affected by the financial meltdown that was caused by the sovereign debt crisis began to question the legitimacy and viability of the European project.

For these reasons the EU remains a highly intriguing subject, as it offers clear examples of the impact of politics on societies. The EU is not the European equivalent of the United States of America, but it is also much more than a traditional international organization. Throughout its existence, European leaders have continually been faced with far-reaching decisions: Which issues are better organized at the EU level and which should remain under the domain of national governments? Must member states give up parts of their national sovereignty for the sake of creating an ever closer union? To what extent should national differences prevail on how to organize a society's political, economic, social, and cultural spheres? From these perspectives, the past decades of the European integration project have given us valuable lessons in state building and the choices confronting political leaders and citizens.

This book offers a broad overview of the politics and policies of the European Union. Part 1 focuses on the key economic and political parameters but also the main actors and processes that have shaped the EU integration process, concluding with a discussion of enlargement that charts the development of the EU into a union of twenty-seven member states. Part 2 discusses the EU's institutional mechanisms and main actors, and part 3 deals with crucial policies and their impact on European societies and the wider world.

In recent years the EU has been the subject of a broad range of books and academic articles. To my knowledge, however, the overwhelming majority of publications are directed at an audience already tuned in to the language of political science and its related analytical and methodological concepts. Postgraduate and academic readership, in particular, seems to have a comprehensive library of materials on the EU. On the other hand, a number of publications portray the EU in a rather basic and rudimentary light. I was encouraged by the often positive feedback—not only from students but also from the "general public"—which the first and second edition received. It led me to the tentative conclusion that this book contributed to closing this gap, by offering an in-depth yet concise introduction to the European Union and its institutions and policies in a style accessible to undergraduate as well as high school students, indeed to any reader, young or old, academic or professional, with an interest in politics and history.

Since the publication of the second edition in the spring of 2011, the European Union has yet again undergone a remarkable transformation. The worldwide economic crises caused financial havoc for some members of the Eurozone and brought Economic and Monetary Union—one of the cornerstones of European integration of recent years—into disrepute. But shockwaves were not only felt in Ireland, Portugal, Spain, Italy, or Greece; the five countries most tragically affected.

Other Eurozone members and a host of EU actors frantically tried to bring the crisis under control in an attempt to place Economic and Monetary Union onto a firmer institutional and procedural footing. The speed and extent of the changes to EU governance, which emanated from the near-collapse of the Eurozone clearly merited an additional chapter. The third edition also offers updates on institutional developments, as well as on all other policy chapters. To provide a coherent understanding of the subject, I highlight a number of key issues surrounding the main areas of debate and controversy. For those seeking more advanced study, a list of publications organized according to the book's chapters is provided at the end.

Andreas Staab
London, July 2012

Acknowledgments

This book first took shape as a series of handouts designed for participants in seminars organized by EPIC—the European Policy Information Centre—which itself originated within the European Institute at the London School of Economics, where I taught until the summer of 2000. During that year a number of colleagues encouraged me to establish EPIC as an independent training agency and consultancy. Over the years we have been fortunate to work with civil servants, ministers, Supreme Court judges, businesspeople, and representatives from the nonprofit sector, as well as high school and university students from a number of EU accession and candidate countries. Thus the book has been shaped by the experiences of those for whom the EU is of practical relevance in their professional lives, as well as of individuals for whom Europe represents a panacea that may ultimately deliver political stability and economic prosperity.

Created for people for whom English is not their mother tongue, our courses, of necessity, were conducted in a style stripped of excessive academic jargon. It was Martin Lodge, a former colleague from the London School of Economics and a current EPIC associate, who suggested that the course handouts that accompany our seminars would be suitable for an undergraduate and indeed a nonacademic audience, and thus this book was born.

Several colleagues and friends of the EPIC family have offered much appreciated guidance and support, enabling me to narrow my own knowledge gaps and enhance my understanding of EU affairs. I am indebted to Martin Lodge, who added factual and analytical depth to the text. Charles Dannreuther was behind the conceptualization of the first chapter as well as the chapter on the environment.

Bruce Ross was a valuable sounding board regarding the intricacies of the Common Agricultural Policy, and Bob Hancké talked me through some of the intricacies of EMU. My thanks also go to the EPIC team, who had worked tirelessly with authorities in Bosnia and Herzegovina on the design and implementation of a rural development strategy. John Bedingfield, our team leader in Sarajevo, sadly passed away in 2011. His involvement in this project not only provided me with greater insight into the working mechanisms of the EU's Cohesion Policy but also helped me to understand a political situation in which the EU still has to and ought to assume a key responsibility. His expertise was outstanding, yet it was his interpersonal skills and the warm manner with which he related to staff and colleagues that were such a wonderful source of inspiration. He is sorely missed. John's deputy Ian Baker oversaw the completion of the project and is starting out with his own consultancy Catalys. Having delivered such a competent job for EPIC, I am sure he will go from strength to strength. My thanks also go to Sanela Klaric, our project coordinator, who put life and work into a much-needed perspective.

EPIC would not have survived, nor would this book have been written, without the help of partner organizations that supported us in running our training and consulting exercises. I am forever grateful to the British Council and especially Roy Cross, Andrew Hadley, Marina Ioannou, Elizabeta Jovanovska, Bob Ness, Peter Skelton, Monica Tantele, Dilek Behcetogullari and Sencan Yesilada. From the Croatian Ministry of Foreign Affairs, Tatjana Corlija, Dubravka Smolic and Sandra Trvtkovic deserve a special thank you. From the British Foreign and Commonwealth Office, Jonathan Allen, David Austin, Yilmaz Ahmetoglu, Philip Barton, Ambassador Edward Clay, Sabina Djapo, Matt Field, Richard Jones, Jill Morris, Ambassador Lyn Parker, and Ivana Vukov were great sources of support and encouragement. From the European Commission, former Ambassador Donato Chiarini deserves praise for never shying away from a debate about EU affairs, even if it meant that his employer was placed sometimes under uncomfortable scrutiny. Sinan Ertay from the Turkish delegation in Brussels reminded me of the transformative effect that prospective EU membership can have on a society. Dan Hannan, member of the European Parliament for the UK's Conservative Party, also deserves a special mention for providing constructive exchanges of ideas with a Eurosceptic. In return, his colleagues Nigel Farage and Roger Helmer, from the UK Independence Party, involuntarily reaffirmed my belief that giving up and sharing national sovereignty in Europe can still be in a country's national interest. Lastly, for constantly testing the accuracy and suitability of this material, I thank my American students, who spent a semester in London as part of their study abroad programs.

Acronyms

ACP	Asia, Caribbean, and Pacific
AFSJ	Area of Freedom, Security, and Justice
BAT	Best Available Technology
CARDS	Community Assistance for Reconstruction, Development, and Stabilization
CAP	Common Agricultural Policy
CCP	Common Commercial Policy
CEEC	Central and East European Countries
CEPOL	European Police College
CFSP	Common Foreign and Security Policy
CIS	Commonwealth of Independent States
COMECON	Council for Mutual Economic Assistance
COPA	Committee of Professional Agricultural Organization
COREPER	Committee of Permanent Representatives
DG	Directorate General
EAP	Environmental Action Plan
EBA	Everything But Arms
EBA	European Banking Authority
EBRD	European Bank for Reconstruction and Development

EC	European Community (merger of EEC, ECSC, and Euratom treaties)
EC	Economic Community (Pillar I of Maastricht Treaty
ECB	European Central Bank
ECHR	European Convention of Human Rights
ECM	European Common Market
ECOFIN	Council of Economic and Finance Ministers
ECSC	European Coal and Steel Community
ECU	European Currency Unit
EDC	European Defense Community
EEA	European Economic Area
EEA	European Environmental Agency
EEAS	European External Action Service
EEC	European Economic Community
EFTA	European Free Trade Association
EFSF	European Financial Stability Fund
EIOPA	European Insurance and Occupational Pensions Authority
ELO	European Liaison Officer
EMS	European Monetary System
EMU	Economic and Monetary Union
ENP	European Neighborhood Policy
ENPI	European Neighborhood and Partnership Instrument
EP	European Parliament
EPA	European Partnership Agreement
EPC	European Political Cooperation
EPI	Environmental Policy Integration
ERDF	European Regional Development Fund
ERF	European Refuge Fund
ERP	European Recovery Program
ESA	European Supervisory Authorities
ESM	European Stability Mechanism
ESRC	European Systems Risk Council
ESFS	European System of Financial Supervisors
ESF	European Social Fund

ETS	Emission Trading Scheme
EU	European Union
EULEX	European Union Rule of Law Mission in Kosovo
EUNAVFOR	European Union Naval Force Somalia Operation Atlanta
EUPOL COPPS	European Union Police Mission for the Palestinian Territories
EURATOM	European Atomic Energy Community
EUROJUST	European Judicial Unit
EUROMED	Euro-Mediterranean Partnership
EUROPOL	European Police Office
ESCB	European System of Central Banks
ESDP	European Security and Defense Policy
FRONTEX	European Agency for the Management of Operational Cooperation at the External Borders
FYROM	Former Yugoslav Republic of Macedonia
GAERC	General Affairs and External Relations Council
GATS	General Agreement on Trade in Services
GATT	General Agreement on Tariffs and Trade
GCC	Gulf Cooperation Council
GDP	Gross Domestic Product
GMOs	Genetically Modified Organisms
ICJ	International Court of Justice
ICTY	International Criminal Tribunal for the Former Yugoslavia
IGC	Intergovernmental Conference
IIF	Institute for International Finance
IMF	International Monetary Fund
IPA	Instrument for Pre-Accession
ISPA	Instrument for Structural Policies for Pre-Accession
JHA	Justice and Home Affairs
LTRO	Long-Term Repo Operation
MARRI	Migration, Asylum, Refugees Regional Initiative
MEP	Member of the European Parliament
NAP	National Allocation Plan
NATO	North Atlantic Treaty Organization
NGO	nongovernmental organization

NRC	NATO Russian Council
OCA	Optimum Currency Area
OECD	Organization for Economic Cooperation and Development
OEEC	Organization for European Economic Cooperation
OPEC	Organization of the Petroleum Exporting Countries
PHARE	Poland/Hungary Assistance for Reconstruction of Economies
PIIGS	Portugal, Ireland, Italy, Greece, Spain
QMV	Qualified Majority Voting
SAA	Stabilization and Association Agreement
SAP	Stabilization and Association Process
SAPARD	Special Program of Pre-Accession for Agriculture and Rural Development
SEA	Single European Act
SEM	Single European Market
SMEs	Small and Medium Sized Enterprises
SPUC	Society for the Protection of Unborn Children
TAIEX	Technical Assistance Information Exchange Instrument
TEU	Treaty on the European Union
TRIM	Trade Related Investment Issues
TRIPS	General Agreement on Intellectual Property Rights
TRNC	Turkish Republic of Northern Cyprus
UNMIK	United Nations Mission in Kosovo
VAT	Value Added Tax
VER	Voluntary Export Restraints
WEU	Western European Union
WTO	World Trade Organization

Tables

PART ONE

THE EVOLUTION OF THE

EUROPEAN UNION

1

Parameters of European Integration

Given the multitude of treaties, political actors, and policies, trying to gain an understanding of European integration can indeed be a daunting task. Coming to terms with the European Union is further complicated by often confusing official terminology with similar sounding names. What is the difference, after all, between the European Council, the Council of Europe, and the Council of the European Union? And exactly how does the European Community differ from the European Economic Community and the European Union? In answering these questions, this chapter introduces the key processes, actors, and developments that have shaped European integration ever since the start of the project in the 1950s. The key issues are the following:

1. *Policies, political actors, and political developments involved in supranational or intergovernmental integration.*
2. *The factors contributing to early European cooperation that were common to all West European states versus those relevant only in certain countries.*
3. *The Eurosclerosis of the 1970s that resulted from the Luxembourg Compromise in the 1960s.*

4. *The re-launch of European integration in the 1980s.*
5. *The 2001 Treaty of Nice and its goal of preparing the European Union for enlargement to Central and Eastern Europe.*
6. *The impact of the Lisbon Treaty of 2009 on the future development of the European Union.*

The Concept of European Integration

European integration is most frequently associated with the period after the end of the Second World War, as Western European states increasingly cooperated during various developmental stages of the European Union. But the concept of governing Europe actually has a far longer history. From the Roman Empire of Julius Caesar to Napoleon, Hitler, and Stalin, European history is marked by many attempts to organize the multitude of nations and ethnicities into a more or less coherent political entity with competing views of how the different states should be related and the degree to which autonomy and sovereignty should be preserved. Nonetheless, though the concept of an integrated Europe is not new, without question the European Union, the most recent vehicle for organizing Europe, has, to date, been a highly successful attempt at integration.

Minimalism versus Maximalism

With the end of the Second World War, debates over European integration again dominated the political agenda. Europe had just been through one of the most damaging and catastrophic events mankind had ever experienced, and there was a pressing need for an organizational vehicle that finally would be able to deliver peace and ultimately prosperity. The debates centered on two different views of European integration that would characterize many of the future discussions on the subject. The "maximalist" view called for a federal structure with the goal of establishing the United States of Europe, whereas the "minimalist" view envisioned a loose union based largely on trade relations between sovereign member states. The maximalists were personified by the Italian political philosopher Altiero Spinelli, and the minimalists were championed by the former prime minister of the United Kingdom Winston Churchill. Churchill's position developed from the perspective of a European country that did not endure fascist occupation and that emerged victorious from World War II. The UK could also look back on a strong democratic tradition, a powerful Commonwealth, and strong political and economic links with the United States. Borrowing heavily from the German philosopher Immanuel Kant and his work on "Perpetual Peace," Churchill, in a famous speech in Zurich in 1946, argued that one way of establishing peace would be to forge closer ties among the peoples of Europe

Table 1.1. Minimalism vs. Maximalism

Minimalism	Maximalism
• Winston Churchill	• Altiero Spinelli
• Safeguard peace through an economic union (Kant: trading nations do not go to war with one another)	• Economic ties alone are not enough to prevent conflict between nations
• Economic union only	• Economic and political union

through stronger trade relations. The prospect of war would then be greatly reduced, since any possible hostilities across borders would threaten one's potential trade partners and customers. Churchill, confusingly, termed this project the "United States of Europe," but in reality it was a watered-down version of what America's Founding Fathers had in mind (see Table 1.1).

Establishing peace along the lines of a trading union did not go far enough for Spinelli. After all, a loose economic union could not be expected to keep in check the rise of another dictator such as Hitler or Stalin. Hence Spinelli argued that only the combination of an economic and a political union could secure long-term peaceful conditions; he had even written a draft constitution for a federal Europe while imprisoned by Mussolini during the Second World War. Spinelli's supporters had often been accused of envisioning the end of the nation-state in Europe. But, in fact, Spinelli's view, which grew from the resistance movement in Nazi-occupied Europe where fascism had gravely undermined the nation-state, actually embraced European integration as essential to rescuing the nation-state after two devastating world wars and periods of economic and political instability.

Despite differences in their political objectives, both maximalism and minimalism—both Spinelli and Churchill—supported greater links between European states. With Europeans assessing the scale of devastation, support for European integration in the aftermath of World War II propelled the European Union (EU) into existence. However, the precise modalities of how the Union should be organized and, in particular, the degree of national sovereignty that should be surrendered for the sake of closer integration, remain to this date the essential issues regarding European integration.

Intergovernmentalism versus Supranationalism

At the beginning of the postwar European project, two concepts emerged about how integration could be implemented: supranationalism and intergovernmentalism. With supranationalism, institutions and policies supersede the power of their national equivalents. The European Court of Justice, for example, could issue verdicts that nullify and supersede verdicts reached by national courts. Similarly

Table 1.2. Concepts of European Integration

Intergovernmentalism	Supranationalism
• Integration through cooperation between national governments; no new institutions	• Integration by establishing new institutions and policies that rise above the national sovereignty of member states
• Example: EU foreign policy	• Example: Single European currency

supranational policies are implemented as political programs that replace their national equivalents. An example is Economic and Monetary Union (EMU), where the EU's single currency, the Euro, replaces national currencies (see Table 1.2).

Intergovernmentalism, in contrast, minimizes the creation of new institutions and policies, and conducts European integration through cooperation between national governments. This approach is illustrated in the realm of foreign policy. The EU does not have a foreign minister or a secretary of state, as there is no EU foreign policy worth speaking of, unless all the member state governments agree on an issue. In the case of the war in Iraq, the EU split into two camps, one supporting George Bush's military intervention and the other supporting continued inspections by the envoy of the United Nations Hans Blix. In light of these two opposing viewpoints a compromise simply could not be reached, which meant that the EU did not have a common foreign policy regarding Iraq. On the other hand, all member states condemned apartheid in South Africa in the late 1980s, and the EU as a whole imposed economic sanctions on that country.

The Impact of the Second World War

In the aftermath of World War II all European states had the staggering problem of reconstructing their economies, and the continent needed, above all, peace and stability. In Europe alone the war had left 15.6 million soldiers and 19.5 million civilians dead. Fifty million people were homeless, and cities and towns were in ruins. In Germany and Great Britain alone, 7 million homes were damaged or destroyed. Europe was facing mountainous challenges. The objective of any responsible government, therefore, was quite obvious: to establish relatively peaceful conditions that would enable the rebuilding of economies, and here, in particular, a largely destroyed infrastructure. The threat of famine was a real-life possibility. Rail networks and roads needed to be replaced; water, heating, and electricity restored; and houses rebuilt—all in the face of the additional problem of millions of refugees fleeing to the West from the advancing communist empire in Central and Eastern Europe. Against these monumental challenges, the first priority was to limit the possibility of a renewed conflict. A potential reemergence of hostilities, the advent of a new antagonistic regime, or military conflict, whether on the scale of a civil war or across borders, would have been catastrophic. But what to do?

The Treaty of Versailles in the aftermath of World War I had presented Europe with a bitter lesson: punishing the aggressors (Germany and Austria) with stifling reparation payments had contributed to the gradual implosion of the Weimar Republic and the eventual rise of fascism, which plunged the continent into another major crisis, only twenty years after the previous one presumably had been resolved. Perhaps a new approach of conciliation and integration would serve Europe better.

In this environment it seemed necessary for the United States to motivate the continent into action. To do so, the U.S. supplied more than $13 billion through the European Recovery Program (ERP), more commonly known as the Marshall Plan. This generous support is explained largely as an effort to block the spread of Soviet Communism to Western Europe. First and foremost, key policy makers in the U.S. feared a shift in political orientation in Europe toward the East and the Soviet Union and away from the United States. Many postwar national elections reflected a mood for change, favoring left-oriented parties that had gained significant support in France, Italy, Greece, and the United Kingdom. In addition, West European states appeared unable to provide food and other basic necessities in the period immediately after the war. The U.S. feared that this crisis could easily erupt into political instability, with communist and potentially even resurgent fascist movements able to gain the political support of a disillusioned electorate. The goal of Marshall Aid, therefore, was to cement the introduction of market-oriented and capitalist economic systems, which ultimately would establish links across the Atlantic and away from the Soviet Union. America's isolationist policies of the 1930s simply had not worked, as democratic European states, left to their own devices, were unable to contain the expansionist drive of fascism. Thus the Truman administration adopted a more proactive strategy in its foreign policy objectives.

American support provided a compelling financial incentive for cooperation that had not existed before. The result was the Organisation for European Economic Cooperation (OEEC), subsequently renamed the Organisation of Economic Cooperation and Development (OECD), which essentially was set up by the U.S. to ensure that the Marshall Plan money was distributed in an organized fashion. The OEEC also provided a framework in which European states were introduced to economic cooperation in an institutionalized setting and across national borders. The OEEC, then, was the forum where West European states prepared for the first attempts at supranational integration.

In 1949, shortly after the establishment of the OEEC, European states created the Council of Europe, which evolved from a congress held in the Dutch capital of The Hague the previous year and provided a framework of principles for the protection of human rights and key freedoms considered essential to a free and peaceful Europe. The Council of Europe has since become less influential, but it still plays a role through the institutional machinery that it established in the

European Court of Human Rights.[1] In the 1940s, however, the Council of Europe was important in promoting the concept of an integrated Europe, although one based on intergovernmentalism and on the autonomy of the nation-state.

The European Coal and Steel Community

The first impetus to supranational integration came mainly from France, especially from one man, Jean Monnet, a senior civil servant with a keen eye for political opportunity.[2] He had learned the advantages of economic planning in the U.S., and he applied the lessons with considerable success in the French planning system that he established after the war. Monnet had a straightforward and, because of its simplicity, ultimately brilliant idea. He envisioned that a supranationally regulated Europe-wide market in coal and steel was central to achieving sustained peace in Europe. The brilliance of this idea was that both commodities are essential for war: steel for the production of weapons and coal to provide energy for factories that could produce weapons. Monnet argued that an authority that was independent of national interests could greatly reduce the likelihood of war, at least war on the scale of the previous two world wars. He presented his concept to the French foreign minister Robert Schuman, whose plan (later called the Schuman Plan) specified exactly how a European Coal and Steel Community (ECSC) could be created and managed by a "Higher Authority" with "supranational powers." The Schuman Plan was not altogether altruistic, for it served the French national interest. Monnet's idea was conceived on the assumption that France would have access to the steel factories and coal reserves of the German Ruhr valley. In the end, France had to forsake this territorial aspiration as the Ruhr area was kept under German control. However, the incorporation of West Germany into the Marshall Plan meant that the French economy would grow in competition with West German industry rather than on the back of it. As a minor token to the French, the ECSC would at least secure French access to the resources of the Ruhr. At this historical juncture, however, the UK decided not to participate in the budding European project. The reason was, quite simply, that in 1945 the UK had elected a left-leaning Labour Party government that embarked on an ambitious economic program which included nationalization of the coal and steel sector. British Prime Minister Clement Atlee justifiably concluded that it would be impossible to supranationalize an industrial sector that only shortly before was subject to nationalization. This mundane historical development accounted for why the British did not jump on the European bandwagon. As it turned out later, the UK's rejection of the Schuman Plan set the tone for Britain's European policy ever since. Other European countries, however, responded enthusiastically to Monnet's vision; not only France and West Germany but also Italy, the Netherlands, Belgium, and Luxembourg signed up for the ECSC, thereby forming the nucleus of the "original six" that would eventually become the European Union of today.

Table 1.3. Summary of EU Treaties

Treaty	Signed	Entered into Force
European Coal and Steel Community (ECSC)	1951	1952
European Economic Community (EEC)	1957	1958
European Atomic Energy Community (EURATOM)	1957	1958
Single European Act	1986	1987
Treaty on the European Union (Maastricht Treaty)	1992	1993
Treaty of Amsterdam	1997	1999
Treaty of Nice	2001	2003
Lisbon Treaty	2007	2009

The ECSC was an important victory for Monnet, as it secured the principle of a supranational form of political organization. The Treaty of Paris in 1951, establishing the ECSC, set up the organizational blueprint for the future. The supranational High Authority was a small body, and thus it depended on the institutions of the member states. Also, on the insistence of Belgium, Luxembourg, and the Netherlands, an intergovernmental Council of Ministers was established to safeguard national interests, especially of smaller states. A supranational Court of Justice would enforce the law, and the citizens of Europe were very loosely involved through a supranational Assembly of National Representatives (see Table 1.3).

Toward a European Defence Community (EDC)

The Korean War from 1950 to 1953 broadened the scope of European integration beyond the simple coal and steel union. The war was widely perceived as a potential precursor to World War III, prompting the U.S. to request military assistance from Europe, arguing, in particular, that a coherent defense of democracy in Europe and the rest of the world would be well advised to take advantage of West Germany's industrial strength. President Truman declared that Germany's military capacities ought to be reintegrated into a wider regional setting. At first France balked at Truman's idea, given the fresh memories of the fatal consequences of Hitler's military might and the prospect of German rearmament. But a new plan emerged, again developed by Monnet, but this time presented by French Prime Minister Pleven: the plan would allow the remilitarization of Germany but only within the organizational setup of a European Defence Community (EDC), which would be controlled by a supranational authority in a way similar to the integration of West German reindustrialization under the ECSC. Even more important, discussions between the states concerning the EDC also led to a proposal for a European Political Community, under which related issues of foreign policy could also be decided. At this stage it seemed that a supranational United States of Europe, with a unified military umbrella and a unified foreign policy, was indeed likely.

But the proposals had stretched the idea of European integration to its limit. Although the six negotiating states of the ECSC signed the Treaty on the EDC in 1952, the final proposal failed to be ratified by the French parliament. Thus much of the impetus for the European Political Community evaporated. Defense cooperation between states was later developed under the weaker Western European Union (WEU),[3] which essentially only provided a consultative forum for the founding members of the ECSC and the UK. The incorporation of such nationally sensitive political areas as foreign policy and defense into a supranational European organizational structure was too ambitious a leap to federalism at such an early stage. In the end, after the integration of West German forces into the North Atlantic Treaty Organization (NATO) in 1955, the idea of a European security umbrella had finally lost momentum.

Toward an Economic Community

Monnet resigned in 1954, primarily so that he could maintain the impetus for European integration at a distance from the exposure that the failure of the EDC had thrust upon him. This marked the end of what had been an extremely successful partnership between Monnet and French Foreign Minister Schuman. But Monnet had not given up on European integration just yet. In the Belgian Prime Minister Paul Henri Spaak he found an important new ally to pursue the goal of a federal Europe. At an ECSC meeting in the Italian resort of Messina, Monnet and Spaak restarted the European project through the establishment of a committee chaired by Spaak that would investigate the possibility of further integration in other areas. The support of the six ECSC member states to set up such a committee was an indication that, despite the failures of the EDC, a strong desire remained to pursue the European project.

The member states were relatively noncommittal at the conference and left Spaak a degree of flexibility as to how the process of integration should be pursued. Spaak seized this opportunity by arguing for the integration of the European atomic industry in an organization to be called EURATOM (European Atomic Energy Community).[4] In addition to the original six, EURATOM also envisioned the inclusion of Britain, and representatives from London were invited to attend the meeting at Messina. But the UK wanted only very limited integration in the form of a free trade area. Such a position was untenable in the view of the other states, and the UK left the Messina conference before it had even finished, thereby leaving Britain with only a peripheral role in the European project.

But although an agreement on atomic industry was reached, economic integration was more problematic. France, in particular, still feared the emerging industrial and economic might of its historical enemy, Germany. The French government insisted that a sudden exposure of the country's industrial sector to the competitive forces of a European market would be catastrophic for France's economic growth and employment. In the end, French acceptance of the common market was secured by creating a Common Agricultural Policy (CAP) from which France would reap substantial benefits.

Given the disproportionate political power that the agricultural sector wielded in the French National Assembly, the CAP proposition seemed too good to miss. The introduction of the CAP in the proposed European Economic Community (EEC) therefore strongly contributed to the acceptance of the Treaty in France, but the accord was also welcomed by agricultural interests in other member states.

The Treaties of Rome, signed in March 1957, established the EEC and EURATOM. The EEC Treaty was the more significant of the two in both content and structure, and its principles were extremely ambitious. Article 2 stated that the EEC would "promote throughout the Community a harmonious development of economic activities, a continuous and balanced expansion, an increase in stability, an accelerated raising of the standard of living and closer relations between the states belonging to it." This statement made it clear that the EEC would not remain simply a loose, consultative economic forum. On the contrary, the EEC Treaty provided core principles that would form the basis for the extension of its powers in the future. In particular, the establishment of the European Common Market (ECM) was envisioned to be achieved through the realization of the four economic freedoms: the free movement of goods, capital, services, and persons across borders and beyond national regulations.[5]

The Intergovernmental Assertion of the 1960s

The optimism that surrounded the European project was bolstered by Europe's rapid economic growth between the 1950s and the early 1960s. Between 1955 and 1964, for example, West Germany's GDP rose by 40.3 percent. Against the backdrop of progress in Rome in 1957 and in Paris in 1951, the first strong challenge to the European integration project came as a surprise. The political figure central to these developments was the French president Charles de Gaulle. De Gaulle's leading role in organizing the resistance movement against Nazi-occupied France had given him the status of a national hero and subsequently propelled him to the French Presidency of the Fifth Republic in December 1958. De Gaulle was not anti-Europe and, in fact, had supported the EEC early in his Presidency, most notably the establishment of the CAP. Nonetheless, de Gaulle was willing to challenge the smooth progress of European integration by blocking Britain's first EEC membership application of 1961, arguing that the UK did not have a true "European vocation" and was, in fact, merely an "American Trojan horse," meaning that Britain would simply act as a champion of U.S. government policy.[6]

By 1967 de Gaulle's attitude toward the UK had not changed, and once again he vetoed Britain's second application to the EEC, citing the same reasons that he had four years earlier. De Gaulle was also skeptical of any institutional developments that might undermine the national sovereignty of France. For him, a union—whether political or purely economic—was only viable if the national interests of the member states could be safeguarded at all times. It is safe to say that de Gaulle personified the intergovernmentalists.

De Gaulle found a further nemesis in Walter Hallstein, the acting president of the European Commission.[7] Hallstein thought that it would only be appropriate for the EEC, as a union of democracies, to introduce some form of majority voting in its institutions and, in particular, in the Council of Ministers. De Gaulle opposed majority rule, even though the Treaty of Rome had provided for its introduction at the end of a transitional period. But de Gaulle was extremely critical of this idea, as this would open the gate for a majority of countries to be able to overrule France, should it be in the minority. Hallstein's idea also would have strengthened the position of the supranational bureaucracy of the EEC, the European Commission, as proposals by this institution would have required only a majority but not all of the member states to oppose it.

To protest Hallstein's proposition, de Gaulle recalled all French ministers from Brussels, resulting in the "empty chair crisis," which started in mid-1965 and continued until the summit meeting in Luxembourg of all European partners in January 1966. The term "crisis" was justified. The EEC was momentarily incapacitated, as any proposals required the unanimous support of all six member states. The summit in Luxembourg reached a compromise (the "Luxembourg Compromise") which resolved that,

> Where, in the case of decisions which may be taken by majority vote on a proposal from the Commission, very important interests of one or more of the member states are at stake, the Members of the Council will endeavor, within a reasonable time, to reach solutions which can be adopted by all the Members of the Council while respecting the mutual interests and those of the Community.

The member states therefore had agreed in principle to a system of majority voting. But if, at any stage, a member state felt that its national interest might be threatened, the voting would simply switch back to unanimity. The logical outcome of this was that unanimous voting remained the norm, but at least the European partners agreed, in principle, to advance their cooperation in a supranational manner through majority voting. Also, any single country could still veto a proposal by the European Commission. This meant that the pace of European integration was now firmly controlled by member states. The empty chair crisis may have been removed, but the compromise reached had a far-reaching impact, fundamentally altering the delicate balance of powers between the Commission and the member states that had been built into the treaties of Rome and Paris.

The Political Spring of 1969: The Hague Summit

Throughout the Western world, the 1960s witnessed far-reaching social and political changes. In the United States the Civil Rights movement, the murders of the Kennedy brothers and Martin Luther King Jr., as well as growing resentment and protest over the country's involvement in the Vietnam War led to antagonistic and occasionally explosive political discourse, in marked contrast to the comparatively harmonious 1950s. In the U.S., widespread student protests against the Vietnam War in the spring of 1968 vividly demonstrated that a new political dawn was on the horizon. In Europe, from London to Amsterdam, Berlin, and Paris, younger generations grew increasingly critical of the political elites of the 1960s who, some felt, represented a former era more closely associated with World War II.[8] But the turbulent events of the 1960s also helped to reignite the dormant European project. The initial impetus came from France itself. The student upheavals of 1968 had seriously damaged the French economy, forcing a devaluation of the franc. After ten years in office de Gaulle resigned and was replaced by George Pompidou, a long-standing member of the Gaullist party, who nevertheless had little desire to challenge the integration process. Given the state of his country's economy, Pompidou saw the economic welfare of France inextricably linked to the EEC. A further contributing factor was the emergence of West Germany as Europe's economic powerhouse,[9] raising concerns over that country's potential economic domination over its European partners. Finally, the EEC had emerged as a highly attractive vehicle for organizing Europe and, in addition to the UK, Denmark and Ireland became increasingly impatient to join the community.

In the end the summit in The Hague addressed three major issues concerning integration that can be summarized as "deepening, widening, and completing." "Deepening" investigated the possibility of cooperation in more than just economic fields, for instance, in foreign policy. More important, deepening referred specifically to West Germany; given this country's economic might, the European leaders agreed to look further into the possibility of an economic and monetary union, including a single European currency that could integrate the German economy more effectively into a wider European setting. The goal was to prevent the West German government, and the monetary policies of its independent central bank, the Bundesbank, from having detrimental consequences for other countries.[10]

"Widening" simply referred to accepting Denmark, Great Britain, and Ireland as new member states. Accession of the three countries was completed in 1973. "Completing" forced the European Community (EC),[11] as it was called by then, to look closely at past treaty achievements and to assess whether these had been put into practice. In particular, the establishment of a European Common Market, which had been a goal of the Treaty of Rome in 1957, when it established the free movement of goods, services, capital, and people, was still far from a political and economic reality and, instead, was obstructed by different national regulations and standards.

Still and all, the summit in The Hague offered a brief window of supranationalism after an intergovernmental interlude dominated by the Luxembourg Compromise. The principles of deepening, widening, and completing indeed represented a bold agenda: to propel the European Community further, with new members and new policies based on a more solid and coherent foundation.

The Eurosclerosis of the 1970s

The term "sclerosis" refers to a medical condition involving constrictive processes that hinder movement, and indeed, after the optimism surrounding The Hague summit in the 1970s, the member states paid little attention to European integration or to finding common solutions to shared problems. The early 1970s, moreover, were indeed tumultuous internationally. U.S. President Richard Nixon abandoned the Bretton Woods system, which, since its inception in 1944, had provided for fixed exchange rates. Nixon argued that the dollar was overvalued and that a freely traded U.S. currency would boost American exports. Nixon was right, as West European currencies, most notably the British pound and the German Deutschmark, rose in value relative to the dollar. In addition, Libya's leader, Colonel Muammar Gaddhafi, in 1973 convinced his fellow Arab leaders to decrease the production of oil. The Organization of the Petroleum Exporting Countries (OPEC) repeated the trick again in 1979, and on both occasions the costs for Western businesses and consumers increased significantly.

The first oil crisis, combined with the effects of the dollar crisis of 1971, plunged Western European economies into a recession, albeit by today's standard a relatively mild one. The unemployment rate of Europe's biggest economy, West Germany, rose from 1 percent in early 1973 to a high of 5.1 percent in August 1975. Ever since the early 1950s Western Europe gradually had become accustomed to continuous economic growth. For nearly the previous twenty-five years Western Europeans were safe in the knowledge that every year the economic well-being of their societies was improving. In light of this comfortable state of mind, the downturn of the 1970s was a shock that caused widespread concern.

After the euphoria of 1969, one might have assumed that the European Community would seek common solutions to common problems. After all, every member state was affected by the fall of the U.S. dollar, the rise of the price of oil, and the subsequent economic recession. The culmination of the dollar crisis in 1971 forced the EC to consider how its national economies could operate without the stability in exchange rates that was guaranteed by linkage to the U.S. dollar. The relevance of economic and monetary cooperation and even the introduction of a single European currency were suddenly much more relevant. But attempts to create an Economic and Monetary Union (EMU) were disbanded by 1973, to be replaced by a much looser commitment that merely asked national governments to keep the values of their currencies within a narrow range of one another.[12] The Werner Committee, which had been set up to assess the possibility of European monetary integration, was faced with an array of obstacles. The Committee stated that the institutional implications of enlargement were inextricably linked to institutional reform in the EC. For reasons of democratic legitimacy, Werner argued that the creation of a European Central Bank—a key requirement for EMU—would have to be accountable to the European Parliament. But such a sweeping institutional reform was just too much for an already overloaded agenda that included the pressures of integrating Denmark, Ireland, and the United Kingdom. In addition, there were already many different conflicting ideas about the larger problem of merging the national economies into a single European one, and the member states could not agree on the EMU project.

Thus, even beyond the ambitious EMU, the advancement of the overall European project came to a sudden standstill. Although the OPEC crisis triggered economic recession across the EC, the member states had little incentive to promote economic cooperation on a European level, as each state was struggling to maintain its own economic prosperity. This shortsightedness limited the scope for developing longer-term strategies or more ambitious projects to merely symbolic gestures of protracted negotiations. The inability of the European Commission to provide leadership in this environment led to summit meetings in the informal but highly influential European Council. The French president Giscard d'Estaing, who had replaced Pompidou in 1974, launched informal summit meetings in 1975, thereby further increasing the role of the member states in the policy-making process. Just as the Luxembourg Compromise had limited the role of the European Commission in advancing integration through specific policy proposals, now the evolution of summitry undermined the Commission's role in setting the strategic agenda.

Another strain on progress toward integration was the accession of the UK. After two previous failures, British Prime Minister Edward Heath had been keen to ensure that this time the UK would join successfully. His attitude can be summed up as "get in now, worry about the problems later," a tactic that would keep the European Community busy solving the problems for years to come. The question of the UK's financial contributions, for example, caused much controversy. The EC spent a great deal of its budget on agriculture, and since farming had relatively little importance in the UK, accession made that country the second biggest net contributor. Although a new regional policy aimed at developing poorer areas somewhat compensated Britain for the lack of subsidies it received from the EC's agricultural policy, the issue of UK contributions would provide ammunition for anti-European politicians in the UK well into the next decade.

Although the European Court of Justice made some important decisions during the 1970s, the decade was dominated by member-state politics, a policy-making system that was paralyzed by its own complexity and the inability of the main actors to develop sufficient momentum to launch new policy initiatives. The term "sclerosis," the inability to move, is therefore an apt description of the European condition at this time.

A New Direction for European Integration in the 1980s

After the inactivity of the 1970s the dawn of a new decade coincided with internal and external developments that reinvigorated the European project. Japan and the United States were about to embark on a period of significant economic growth, which forced European leaders to streamline their markets in order to improve their international competitiveness.[13] The 1980s also saw a further round of enlargement of the European Community. Three former fascist dictatorships—Portugal, Spain, and Greece—all sought to anchor their young democracies within a community of stable political systems. Despite the weak economic infrastructure of Greece, that country's accession in 1981 was handled quite speedily. A little more difficult was the accession of the two Iberian candidates. Specifically, negotiations over Spain's membership were complicated by concerns expressed in Italy and France, both of which offered the same agricultural products as Spain and feared a significant drop in income for their own farmers once Spanish competitors were also allowed to offer their produce to European consumers. Not until 1986 did Portugal and Spain join the Community. But despite some difficult negotiations, this southern expansion confirmed that the EC had established itself as a highly attractive vehicle for organizing Europe.

Another reinvigorating development was that much-needed institutional reforms had started to have an impact on the European scene. For the first time direct elections were held to the European Parliament in 1979. Although this institution was included in the Treaty of Rome, Members of the European Parliament (MEPs) were previously appointed by national governments. Although 1979 did not see increased powers for Parliament, which only had an advisory legislative function, it did have two important effects. First, it gave a much-needed degree of legitimacy to the European Community that had been lacking before. This in turn attracted political actors who had previously not found the European Parliament an attractive proposition. New people with greater political ambitions and capabilities gave the Community a new dynamic and added a further source of political pressure to reinvigorate the European project.

On another internal level, in 1979 we witnessed the arrival of UK Prime Minister Margaret Thatcher, who saw the grand opportunity that a more unified European market could offer Britain. After all, it is more profitable to sell one's products to potentially 340 million European consumers than to only 60 million Brits. Like her counterpart Ronald Reagan, she was an advocate of neoliberal policies and pursued an intensive privatization program. Companies in which the British government had at least part ownership were sold to the public sector, including British Airways and British Telecom. Thatcher was also adamant about keeping the UK's budget under tight monetary control, resulting in drastic cuts in welfare spending. She was often portrayed as the "Euroskeptic" par excellence. It is true that her abrasive confrontational style was not well received by her European partners. She criticized European institutions for being too bureaucratic and costly, and she passionately fought many proposals that might have undermined British national sovereignty. But the image of the feisty lady, banging her handbag on the negotiating tables of Brussels, ought to be at least slightly rectified. As a politician who advocated the principle of the free market, an enlarged European free market was too good an opportunity to let pass.

All these internal and external factors were conducive to a change in direction. Now it fell to the leader of the European bureaucracy, Commission President Jacques Delors, to elevate the Community to a new level, which he did by spurring the implementation of the Single European Market (SEM)—the free movement of goods, services, capital, and labor—through precise steps. Delors had been the finance minister of France under a socialist government, and he combined three unique qualities which, taken by themselves, would already have been quite impressive. First, he was a cunning diplomat and negotiator, always well prepared and briefed before summit meetings. Delors often managed to forge alliances in secret, and he had proactive control of the EC's agenda and more than once acted as a masterful puppeteer controlling the European heads of government. His clashes with Thatcher became the stuff of legends.

Second, Delors was a very skillful bureaucrat. Based on an in-depth report by Delors's fellow commissioner, Lord Cockfield, the Community finally agreed, in 1985, to realize the Single Market, which the Treaty of Rome, thirty years earlier, had already agreed to do. Delors, however, turned that theoretical objective into practical reality by drafting 270 precise measures, which, once implemented by the member states, would guarantee the four freedoms. Delors even had the courage to impose a six-year deadline on the implementation, after which the member states would be subject to fines by the European Commission. An especially impressive feature of the Cockfield Report was a timetable that was not only realistic but also sufficiently transparent to ensure that the necessary pressure from the Commission could be maintained. Lastly, Delors was a visionary who adopted a commonsensical approach to the future of the European project, and questioned which policies would have been better organized at the supranational rather than the national level. For instance, the environment is essentially supranational; clouds and rivers, and therefore pollution, do not recognize borders. With this in mind, Delors was able to convince national leaders to set up a European environmental policy. Further evidence that supranational efforts were needed was provided by the technological innovations emanating from Japan and the United States; because individual European countries were unable to keep pace with those countries in these areas, Delors argued for transnational cooperation in scientific research and technology—this ultimately resulted, for instance, in the development of the Airbus.

The Single European Act

The Single European Act (SEA), signed by the member states in 1986, marked a dramatic departure from the intergovernmentalism that dominated the previous seventeen years. At last, the spirit of The Hague, in 1969, resulted in concrete treaty commitments. The SEA linked the re-launching of European integration with institutional reform and a range of new policy responsibilities, a strategy that would maintain the momentum of the invigorated European Community for years to come. The key characteristics of the SEA can be seen in terms of these policy areas and institutional reforms and their political consequences.

The main policy area of the SEA was the Single European Market initiative, with its famous 1992 deadline, which reasserted the free movement of goods, services, capital, and labor, and meant, of course, the removal of national quotas and tariffs. Still, the SEM went further than any previous attempts at establishing a single European market. This time the SEM was concerned with removing nontariff barriers that distorted trade through different product specifications or purchasing agreements. This would finally secure the four freedoms outlined in the Treaty of Rome. In addition, completely new policy areas involved cohesion (the reduction of economic and social inequalities between rich and poor regions), research and technology, and European Political Cooperation (EPC), a forum to discuss foreign policy. The Single European Act, with its SEM initiative and impressive range of new policy fields, certainly moved toward accomplishing the two key goals of completing and deepening, which had been the objective of The Hague summit of 1969 (see Table 1.4).

The main elements of institutional reform were primarily concerned with the introduction of a system of majority voting. Though majority voting was initially restricted to issues connected to the completion of the Single European Market, it nonetheless represented a significant departure from an era dominated by the Luxembourg Compromise. It also significantly increased the status of the EC's bureaucratic apparatus (the European Commission), because individual member states were no longer able, single-handedly, to block legislative proposals emanating from that organization. Second, the role of the European Parliament was increased. Although members of the EP had been directly elected since 1979, their legislative function was severely curtailed, given that they were only consulted once the Commission had already drafted and proposed new laws. The SEA, however, introduced the so-called cooperation procedure through which the EP was now allowed to play a role in amending legislation, albeit only on a limited number of issues. In addition, the assent procedure required the approval of a majority of MEPs in cases where the European Community incorporated new member states

Table 1.4. The Single European Act, 1986

- New policies:
  - Research and Technology
  - Single Market Deadline for 1992
  - European Political Cooperation
- Institutional reform:
  - More power to the EP
  - Qualified majority voting

or concluded international agreements. Although the powers of the EP still paled in comparison with other democratic assemblies, the SEA nonetheless was seen as an important improvement in the democratic features of the Community.

The political consequences were also significant, as the existence of the SEA demonstrated that Europe was now an important area of real political activity. The interaction between national ministries and departments, on the one hand, and the European bureaucracy in Brussels, on the other, had intensified as new legislative proposals drafted by the Commission ran their course. Also, with the rise of the SEM, interest groups began to pay more attention, and subsequently the number of lobby groups present in Brussels skyrocketed. Finally, the SEA created the largest and wealthiest market in the world, and it gave the Community a much greater weight at the international level. In particular, the Uruguay Round, which started in 1986 and aimed to set up global free trade, was heavily influenced by the Europeans who negotiated as a single, unified economic actor.

A New World Order in the 1990s

Throughout the history of European integration, internal reforms often were the political responses to major external events. By far the most important event was the collapse of communism in Central and Eastern Europe between 1989 and 1991. One by one the former communist satellite states of Hungary, Czechoslovakia, Poland, Romania, Bulgaria, and East Germany shed their authoritarian past and held free elections. Nascent democratic regimes in these states sought closer cooperation with the rest of Europe. In December 1991 the old Soviet Union ceased to exist and was replaced by a loose so-called Commonwealth of Independent States (CIS). These political developments posed severe challenges for the European Community. With the old Warsaw Pact gone, a security vacuum emerged, and no one could safely predict whether the transitions to democracy and capitalism in Central and Eastern Europe would be successful. The worst-case scenario could have been a return to autocratic forms of government. Furthermore, after years of communist rule, democratic practices and institutions, as well as a pluralistic civil society, needed to be established in countries with little history of democracy.

Hence Western European states had to prepare themselves for such possible security threats as drugs and human trafficking, organized crime, or widespread migratory movements, and to seek institutional mechanisms to address these problems.

The collapse of communism, however, also brought more immediate concerns for the Community in the shape of German unification. In economic terms, the fall of the Berlin Wall resulted in the unification of the West European champion and the champion of the communist trading bloc, the Council for Mutual Economic Assistance, or COMECON. Despite both the significant financial costs of unification and the run-down state of the East German industrial infrastructure, European leaders, most notably French President François Mitterrand, felt that an already economically dominant West Germany would become even more capable of further dominating the European economy. Mitterrand saw further European integration as a safeguard against such dominance, and he strongly pushed for closer economic and monetary integration.

It therefore came as no surprise that, only five years after the SEA, the Community embarked on another amendment to its treaties. But in the run-up to the summit in the Dutch town of Maastricht in December 1991, a number of opposing views on the future direction of European integration began to swell the political agenda. Arguing for a more supranational path, Commission President Jacques Delors published a report in 1989 on the benefits of economic and monetary union. In a similar vein the report by Commissioner Paolo Cecchini, in 1988, had analyzed the costs of what he called a non-Europe that would fail to integrate to greater degrees. Margaret Thatcher, meanwhile, was increasingly skeptical of the ambitions of the Brussels bureaucracy, and in her famous speech at the College of Europe in Bruges in 1988 she refocused the debate on the limits of European integration by arguing for the safeguarding of national sovereignty and independence.[14] She stressed that "willing and active cooperation between independent and sovereign states is the best way to build a European Community."

Disagreement over the precise path of future integration among the European political elite was now mirrored by the public. In order for a treaty to be ratified, each member state had to approve of it; depending on national constitutional requirements, this could be done either by a parliamentary act (the most common form) or by referendum (as used, for instance, in Denmark and Ireland). After finally agreeing on the Maastricht Treaty—officially called the Treaty on the European Union—Mitterrand decided to hold a referendum, even though ratification by the French parliament would have been sufficient. Mitterrand argued that the popular approval which a clearly won referendum could offer would carry more symbolic weight and would encourage ratification in other countries. There was one flaw in his calculation, however; until the 1990s European integration was largely an elitist project, with only rare interaction between politicians and the general public. The policies of the Single European Act of 1986, with its establishment of the Single Market, and to an even greater extent the policies of this new Treaty, with its proposed introduction of a single currency, had a much more tangible effect on the lives of European citizens. Many reacted with skepticism, borne not necessarily out of opposition to the European idea but simply out of a lack of information. The referendum in France just produced a "yes" vote by the narrowest of margins. With a 70 percent turnout in September 1992, the referendum was approved by only 51 percent. Thus instead of an affirmation of France's pro-European stance, the referendum turned into a disastrous public-relations exercise.

In Denmark, ratification of the Maastricht Treaty was rejected outright in a referendum in June 1992. Obviously the entire ratification process was in jeopardy. The Danish government therefore negotiated an opt-out clause for Maastricht's most controversial policy—the single European currency—and at another referendum, in May 1993, the Danes finally gave their approval.

Britain experienced similar political turmoil when John Major, who replaced Thatcher as prime minister in 1990, decided not to hold a referendum. The parliamentary act of approval turned out to be a troublesome affair that split his ruling Conservative Party. Major was also forced to negotiate an opt-out clause both for the single currency and for the social charter that established certain workers' rights throughout Europe. In the end only a watered-down version of the treaty for the UK and Denmark placed the ratification train back on track.

The Treaty on the European Union (Maastricht Treaty)

Against the backdrop of these conflicts over the future of European integration, the Treaty on the European Union (TEU) represented a compromise that was actually less coherent than the previous SEA treaty of 1986. Of course, responses needed to be found to new internal and external challenges, but these had to finely balance intergovernmental concerns over a potential loss of the member states' national sovereignty and supranational aspirations for an increasingly unified Europe.

The TEU was unique and far-reaching in content and structure. First, the European Community gave itself a new name—the European Union—reflecting the closer nature of the member states' relationships with one another. The TEU also referred for the first time to citizenship values and gave Europeans, at least those who were citizens of an EU member state, uniform rights. This attempt to address the Union's lack of democratic credibility was complemented by a number of institutional innovations. The legislative powers of the European Parliament were increased through a new method for drafting legislation called the co-decision procedure.[15] The EP was also told to appoint an ombudsperson so that EU citizens could challenge administrative decisions taken by any EU institution. Another independent institution—the Committee of the Regions—was created to include subnational, regional voices in the EU's legislative process; this Committee had to be consulted whenever a regional issue appeared on the agenda.

Even more significant, the TEU completely elevated new policy fields to the European level, away from the exclusive authority of the member states. Although Maastricht did not replace previous treaties but only amended them, these

Table 1.5. The Maastricht Treaty, 1992

Pillar I Economic Community	Pillar II Common Foreign and Security Policy	Pillar III Justice and Home Affairs
Economic and Monetary Union,Single Market, agriculture	Unified international diplomacy Common Defense Policy	Asylum, immigration Police cooperation, customs
Qualified majority voting	Unanimous agreements	Unanimous agreements
Supranationalism	Intergovernmentalism	Intergovernmentalism

amendments were indeed far-reaching. The TEU was organized as three pillars. First and foremost was Pillar I, also called the Economic Community, containing previous treaties and their revisions but also important new policies, most notably the single currency and Economic and Monetary Union (EMU). The second pillar introduced a Common Foreign and Security Policy (CFSP). The third addressed cooperation in the fields of Justice and Home Affairs (JHA), including such issues as police cooperation, immigration, asylum, and internal security matters. The most important difference between the three pillars was that decisions in Pillars II (CFSP) and III (JHA) would be made through intergovernmental negotiations between member states, whereas the largely economic Pillar I retained and extended supranational policy making (see Table 1.5).

The most significant innovation was, undoubtedly, the decision to merge national macroeconomic policies in an Economic and Monetary Union. Essentially EMU envisaged not only a single currency but also a single monetary policy, such as one interest rate, for all participating countries. Obviously EMU would relieve companies trading across borders and cross-border travelers the cost of exchanging currencies. This also meant that national central banks could no longer fine-tune their economies by adjusting interest rates in response to changing economic climates. In the Maastricht Treaty the member states agreed both to a timetable for implementing EMU by 1999 and to a number of European institutions to manage the transition.

The CFSP of Pillar II provided a framework enabling member states to present a unified presence in international diplomacy. Because foreign and security policies are often regarded as vital bastions of a country's national sovereignty, this was indeed a very ambitious undertaking. It bears repeating that joint diplomatic action was not based on majority voting but on unanimous agreement by all member states, which greatly reduced the scope of diplomacy. As was seen in the Iraq crisis in the spring of 2003, EU member states could not agree on a common approach to dealing with Saddam Hussein, which simply meant that, on that occasion, one could not speak of a common policy response. Finally, the CFSP built a framework for developing a common defense policy through the Western European Union

(WEU)[16] that would "elaborate and implement decisions and actions of the Union which have defence implications" (Article J4 TEU).

The third pillar, representing Justice and Home Affairs, provided guidelines for coordinating various ad hoc arrangements concerning asylum, drug trafficking, or customs. JHA, as did the CFSP, offered member states a chance to develop joint actions in these fields but, again, only through unanimity.

Without question, the institutional reforms and policy innovations dramatically changed the face of the European project. But this push for closer integration came at a high price. Because of severe public concern in Denmark and Britain, the ratification process could only be safeguarded by offering these countries the option to withdraw from EMU (Denmark and Britain) and from the social charter (Britain only).[17] As a result, the notion of European solidarity, of a one-size-fits-all Europe, was now gone. Instead, Maastricht introduced the concept of a Europe à la carte—albeit in a mild form—where member states rejected policies that were not in line with their own national political agenda. The provision of the opt-out clauses accommodated differences between member states, and thus highlighted the serious differences between European governments concerning the future of the EU.

Another result was that the European project turned from an elitist undertaking driven by individual political leaders into a hotly debated issue that was now part of the political mainstream. The referenda in France and Denmark offered ample evidence for this. In the UK the Maastricht debate had split the ruling Conservative Party, as well as the public. In Germany, often portrayed as one of the continent's main driving forces for European integration, the general population harbored serious doubts over whether it was a good idea to give up the beloved Deutschmark for some supranational coins and notes. The responses by European citizens to the Maastricht Treaty effectively placed a limit on the speed and extent of integration that the populace of the member states would tolerate. Any further treaty amendments, therefore, had to be less ambitious and more intent on ironing out some of the institutional and policy shortcomings that still undermined the Union.

The Treaty of Amsterdam

The Amsterdam Treaty, agreed to by the EU's political leaders on 17 June 1997 and signed on 2 October of that year, was the culmination of two years of discussions and negotiations about the goal of a citizens' Europe, the role of the European Union on the international stage, improvements in the institutions' operations, and the prospect of enlarging the Union. Specific issues addressed were economic globalization and its impact on jobs, the fight against terrorism, international crime and drug trafficking, ecological problems, and threats to public health. The Treaty finally entered into force in April 1999.

Table 1.6. The Treaty of Amsterdam, 1997

- The Schengen Agreement incorporated in the Treaty
- Cooperation between police forces, customs
- Coordinated strategy for employment
- High Representative for Common Foreign and Security Policy

A few years earlier, in 1995, the Union had welcomed three more members: Austria, Finland, and Sweden, which had been neutral countries, siding neither with NATO nor the Warsaw Pact. But with the demise of the latter, the rationale for staying outside the EU was no longer valid. The existing EU hugely welcomed this expansion of its club, which was not surprising given the prosperity levels of the candidates, which added much-needed funds to the Union's coffers. Specifically the Amsterdam Treaty focused on fundamental rights such as gender equality, nondiscrimination, and data privacy. It included a new section on visas, asylum, and immigration, as well as police and judicial cooperation in criminal matters. The free movement of people was considerably strengthened by the decision to integrate the previously bilateral Schengen Agreement, which abolished border controls between signatory countries (see Table 1.6).[18]

The Treaty of Amsterdam brought a crucial clarification of the concept of European citizenship.[19] It also included a chapter on the coordination of national employment policies, as well as emphasizing a stronger commitment to tackle social exclusion. Further, four years after Maastricht had introduced the CFSP, the Amsterdam treaty established the post of High Representative to give the EU's foreign policy greater prominence and coherence. As for institutional reforms, the treaty gave the European Parliament a considerable boost by broadening the use of the co-decision procedure in which the EP had a veto power on all legislative proposals. After the crisis over the ratification of Maastricht, the EU clearly tried to use the Amsterdam treaty to win over Europe's citizens through four prime measures:

- placing employment and citizens' rights at the heart of the Union
- allowing Europeans to move freely and live in a secure environment
- giving Europe a message and a voice in the world
- providing effective institutions for an enlarged EU

But this ambitious public-relations exercise had a mixed reception. As in the case of EMU, the bilateral Schengen Agreement again granted opt-outs for the UK, Ireland, and Denmark, and thereby created further asymmetry within the EU. Also, the post of High Representative for the CFSP, which was occupied by the Spaniard Javier Solana, did not give the EU the expected stronger voice in the world. With several members of the European Commission already active on the international stage (most notably the commissioners responsible for trade, agriculture, external relations, and enlargement), this new post only raised a puzzling question: Who represents the EU abroad? Furthermore, a coordinated strategy on employment may have sounded laudable, but such promises were dismissed as impractical given the increasing pressures of globalization to which Europe's economies had to adjust as well as the neoliberal approaches of a number of EU member states. Finally, the treaty did not create the institutions needed to integrate the former communist countries of Central and Eastern Europe. The EU itself acknowledged that the reforms were merely a step toward more effective institutions but were not the ultimate answer. Institutional questions, therefore, were subsequently addressed more vigorously during the next round of negotiations that culminated in the Treaty of Nice (see below). Nonetheless, the concept of a European citizenship and the (albeit limited) integration of fundamental rights principles gave the EU a new direction; the EU was now headed toward a more coherent and complete polity that significantly departed from the mainly economic outlook of the Rome and Paris treaties.

The Treaty of Nice

The third treaty amendment in the space of less than ten years (and the fourth amendment since the Eurosclerosis of the 1970s) was negotiated in Nice in December 2000. Under the chairmanship of the French president Jacques Chirac, the member states devoted this summit to preparing the Union for the challenges of enlargement. Thus institutional and democratic reform was high on the agenda.

European leaders recognized that the composition and responsibilities of the EU institutions that had been adopted in the 1950s by the six founding member states had become outdated by 2000, when the EU had received the applications of Estonia, Latvia, Lithuania, Poland, the Czech Republic, Slovakia, Hungary, Slovenia, Malta, Cyprus, Bulgaria, and Romania, and was about to expand to twenty-seven members. Yet, apart from the introduction of direct elections to the European Parliament in 1979, there had been no major institutional reform. Clearly, in Nice, the old EU-15 realized that the organization was in much need of major institutional reform. The Intergovernmental Conference (IGC),[20] which preceded the Nice meeting, had to come up with a vision of how the Union could function effectively with an expanded membership. Without going into too much detail,[21] Nice limited the size of the European Parliament to 732 members, while also placing a ceiling on the number of commissioners (a maximum of 27). After acrimonious and lengthy negotiations, the summit also agreed to a new voting formula for the Council of Ministers, which acts as the intergovernmental forum of the member states with the main responsibility of approving legislation. Apart from these institutional changes, the EU also tried to silence its critics by addressing democratic shortcomings, specifically the lack of a fundamental rights agenda (see Table 1.7).

Prior to the summit in Nice, a group of constitutional experts had drafted the Charter on Fundamental Rights and recommended that it be included in the

Table 1.7. The Treaty of Nice, 2001

- **Changes**
  1. European Parliament capped at 732 MEPs
  2. Council of Ministers: more policies that will be decided under majority voting by using a new voting system
  3. Commission: maximum 27 members
  4. Commission president can fire commissioners and change their portfolios
- **Aspects Not Addressed**
  1. Fundamental rights charter still not part of EU law
  2. Unanimity voting remained in such policy areas as tax, cohesion, CFSP, JHA

EU treaty structure. The Charter sets out the civil, political, economic, and social rights of EU citizens under six headings: dignity, freedom, equality, solidarity, citizens' rights, and justice. These rights were based on the fundamental rights and freedoms recognized by the European Convention for the Protection of Human Rights and Fundamental Freedoms, as well as on the constitutional traditions of EU countries.

Although the Charter was viewed favorably by most member states, UK Prime Minister Tony Blair refused to permit the Charter to be enforceable under EU law or to allow the European Court of Justice to base its rulings on it. Nonetheless, the EU took significant steps to address undemocratic practices. Prompted by Austria's far-right Freedom Party becoming a coalition partner in the Austrian government, and by the subsequent wave of Austria's diplomatic isolation, the EU adopted a clear procedure on how to deal with member states that departed from the democratic track. The Council of Ministers, with a majority comprised of four-fifths of its members, and with the approval of the European Parliament, could now declare that a clear danger existed of a member state committing a serious breach of the fundamental rights or freedoms on which the Union was founded. The Council could then issue "appropriate recommendations" to that member state, although Nice explicitly shied away from allowing a member state to be expelled from the Union.

Nonetheless, given the daunting challenge of extending the Nice Treaty into Central and Eastern Europe, the treaty could not be considered a success. President Jacques Chirac, as the leader of the host country, was severely criticized for insufficiently organizing the summit, and his forceful, if not arrogant, approach to diplomacy caused much consternation in London, Berlin, and other European capitals. First, the haggling over the specific voting majorities in the Council of Ministers caused frustration, prompting critics to describe it as a bargaining approach more suited to a flea market than to intergovernmental decision making. Second, the exclusion of the Human Rights Charter from enforceable EU law further emphasized that the EU was primarily an economic union, with only secondary interest in political and social rights. Third, calls for a clearer delineation of power between member states and Brussels, and between national parliaments and the European Parliament, were not addressed. Finally, it seemed doubtful whether the Nice summit prepared the EU sufficiently for expansion. Important issues that were not addressed included the budget and, above all, reform of the financially wasteful agricultural policy. Such crucial matters were postponed to another IGC that would then include representatives from the ten new member states that joined in 2004.[22]

Quo Vadis EU: The Lisbon Treaty of 2007 and the Sovereign Debt Crisis

An important step toward reforming the EU, especially its institutions, would have been the ratification of a constitution. Over a period of eighteen months, between 2002 and 2003, the so-called Convention for Europe[23] managed to draft a supposed Constitution for Europe. Representatives at the Convention were drawn from a wide range of backgrounds, including national and EU parliamentarians, members of civil society, and government representatives. For this draft to become EU law, ratification by every member state would have been necessary. In most countries this would have been done through simple parliamentary approval, but others decided to hold a referendum on the issue. The initial text put forward by the Convention did not meet the approval of Spain and Poland, since both benefited greatly from the Treaty of Nice which gave them disproportionately powerful voting rights in the Council of Ministers. Italy's prime minister Silvio Berlusconi, whose government had the Presidency of the EU in the second half of 2003, failed to agree on a compromise, and it was up to Berlusconi's successor, Irish Prime Minister Bertie Ahern, to pick up the pieces. After some acrimonious debates, during which Jacques Chirac and Tony Blair clashed on several points, a compromise was reached.

Alas, negative referenda in France and the Netherlands in May 2005 meant that this treaty revision did not become effective. Chris Patten, former Commissioner for External Relations (1999–2004), even described the constitutional process as "dead as a dodo." But this did not mean that the EU was without any legal foundation, as it simply continued to rely on the Treaty of Nice and the decisions reached there. With the accession of Bulgaria and Romania in 2007, calls for institutional reforms again were voiced from several member states. Indeed, the underlying rationale had not changed but instead had become even more precarious: an institutional setup designed for six countries in the 1950s could hardly cope with the political reality of an ever expanding club now comprised of twenty-seven members.

Table 1.8. The Treaty of Lisbon, 2007

- **Institutional Changes**

  1. Extended involvement of the European Parliament: ordinary legislative procedure (former co-decision procedure now the norm)

  2. More qualified majority voting in the Council of Ministers

  3. New voting procedure in the Council of Ministers (double majority system)

  4. New President of the European Council

  5. New High Representative of the Union for Foreign Affairs and Security Policy

- **Organizational Aspects**

  1. Elimination of the three-pillar system

  2. Legally binding Charter of Fundamental Rights

  3. One-third of national parliaments can force legislative reconsideration

  4. European Court of Justice has authority to rule over Justice and Home Affairs issues

  5. Citizen Initiative: petition with one million signatures triggers legislative proposal

---

During the German Presidency in the first half of 2007, Chancellor Angela Merkel was pressing for a new treaty before the EU could even contemplate further enlargement rounds. At that stage the EU had received applications from Croatia, the Former Yugoslav Republic of Macedonia, and, most controversially, from Turkey. At a summit meeting in June 2007 the EU agreed on a new treaty; though it was called a Reform Treaty (or Lisbon Treaty, based on the capital where the treaty was signed in December 2007), it was actually a stripped-down version of the Constitution (a term, incidentally, that was dropped altogether) and contained some of the improvements already envisioned by the proposed Constitution. As with all the other treaties, this new agreement was subject to approval by all member states. But a negative referendum in Ireland in June 2008 cast severe doubt over the ratification process. It was not until a much-improved information campaign by the Irish government and a more serious political debate that a second referendum in October 2009 assured that the Lisbon Treaty had cleared its final hurdle and entered into force on 1 December 2009.

As we can see from Table 1.8, changes to the way the EU functions mostly affect institutional mechanisms. Lisbon therefore represented the culmination of years of debates on how to prepare for further enlargement without sacrificing the Union's capability as an efficient polity, while also safeguarding such democratic principles as equality and transparency. A much needed step in this direction was the reform of the voting system in the Council of Ministers. The awkward Nice formula had now been replaced by a much more comprehensive mechanism which requires 55 percent of the member states representing 65 percent of the EU population to approve of legislative proposals that emanate from the Commission.[24] In addition, qualified majority voting was also extended to new policy areas. Now only defense and taxation still require the approval of all member states.

Regarding the summit, a new office of President of the European Council was created to offer more coherence and consistency. Previously summits were organized on a rotating basis, so placing the responsibility for hosting and chairing the get-togethers of the heads of government within one position seemed a significant improvement. The former Belgian prime minister Herman van Rompuy, who assumed this new role in January 2010, however, was not actually the president of Europe. The post is mainly administrative and gives little chance of strategic direction.[25]

The Commission was also subject to institutional innovation. With the ambitiously worded "High Representative of the Union for Foreign Affairs and Security Policy," the Lisbon Treaty aimed to bring under one umbrella those portfolios that have an external dimension, including foreign affairs, but also trade, agriculture, or the environment. As a consequence, this new post replaced the High Representative for Common and Security Policy (which in itself was only created a decade earlier at the Treaty of Amsterdam). The High Representative was placed within the supranational Commission, and thereby gave the first incumbent, Baroness Catherine Ashton, much-needed administrative support.[26]

Responding to criticism of a democratic deficit in the EU, Lisbon also improved the standing of the European Parliament. The EP is now an equal partner to the Council of Ministers when approving legislation under the new so-called ordinary legislative procedure, giving it the right to veto but also to amend legislation. In line with powers granted to national parliaments, the EP now also has to approve the budget in its entirety, an essential improvement of the democratic legitimacy of the EU. However, one criticism voiced against the EP—that of an assembly that is too large—has not been addressed in a satisfactory manner, and the number of MEPs has risen to 754 by 2011.[27]

But the Lisbon Treaty went beyond institutional changes. Gone was the categorization of activities into three pillars, which was introduced at Maastricht; now we can simply refer to this European integration project as the European Union. In a bid to meet further criticism of insufficient democratic legitimacy, the member states also agreed to give national parliaments a mildly stronger voice in the way legislation is passed at the EU level. Hereafter every national parliament would receive proposals for new EU legislation directly from the Commission. Should one-third of national parliaments voice concerns, the proposals would be sent back for review by the Commission. If, after this, a majority of national parliaments still oppose the proposal, and national governments or the European Parliament also disagree, then the proposal would be struck down. Although this change in procedures does not necessarily mean that national parliaments have the ability to block EU legislation outright, it certainly provides for a closer dialogue between Brussels and national capitals.

Arguably the most controversial innovation of Lisbon was the integration of a legally binding Charter of Fundamental Rights which gives the European Court of Justice the power to judge on human rights abuses and overrule national courts in this domain. Alas, as with the Maastricht Treaty, some member states secured opt-outs, thereby adding further asymmetry to what was once a uniform EU, and, moreover, the charter is not applicable to Poland and the UK.[28] Beyond human rights, Ireland, Denmark, and the UK secured opt-outs for asylum, visa, and immigration, with Britain deciding on a case-by-case basis whether to join EU initiatives in these fields. Lisbon added a powerful vehicle of direct democracy. Now, a petition of one million signatures forces the Commission to formulate a legislative proposal which is then voted upon by the European Parliament and the Council of Ministers.

But despite this impressive number of changes, some issues that ought to have been remedied were not addressed at Lisbon. Treaty changes still have to be ratified by all member states, sometimes through a national referendum (such as in Ireland and Denmark) but most often through approval by national parliaments. Obviously, with this system, the EU always has to confront the potential danger of being held hostage by one member state that simply refuses to ratify. This, of course, runs counter to the democratic principle of majority rule. At the Convention, the Commission therefore argued for the introduction of a ⅚ majority in the European Council for treaty changes to mainly economic policies. Alternatively a member state could be given a deadline (say one year) during which it either has to renegotiate, ask for an opt-out for specific policies, or simply leave the EU). The Convention, as well as the Lisbon Treaty, has failed to discuss any of these issues.

The last twenty-five years have seen frequent and far-reaching changes to the EU's constitutional makeup. In quick succession, the Single European Act (1986), the Maastricht Treaty (1992), and the Amsterdam (1997), Nice (2003), and Lisbon (2007) treaties aimed to adjust the EU to new internal and external developments that required a departure from the relatively rudimentary setup of the 1950s. It is no wonder that an exasperated UK Prime Minister Gordon Brown stated, in 2007, that the Lisbon Treaty will be the last of its kind for quite a while. But the EU has not reached an end point just yet. One might want to glance at Lisbon's treaty provision of "enhanced cooperation." According to this clause, at least one-third of EU member states (i.e., in 2009, nine countries) may work together more closely on justice and home affairs issues without needing the support of other member states as long as the latter are not affected by any such measures. The clause has the potential to add more asymmetry to an already diverging EU, with some member states wishing for more integration and others for less.

More worryingly, economic and financial developments in the aftermath of the credit crunch of 2008 and 2009 brought the legitimacy of European integration—of securing peace and prosperity across the continent— into question. In Central and Eastern European countries (CEEC), membership in the EU had sparked a consumer spending and building bubble that burst once the world economy entered a recession. With collapsing global demand, exports began to stagnate, foreign investment dried up, and unemployment figures increased dramatically.

Even worse, in the immediate aftermath of joining the EU, banks in the region, which were largely owned by western financial institutions, had started to issue mortgages in Euros although none of the CEEC had joined the single currency at this stage. With some domestic currencies in free fall against the Euro, a number of homeowners found it difficult to meet their mortgage commitments and banks (in east and west) were all of a sudden loaded with bad debt. Intervention by the EU and the International Monetary Fund somewhat softened the economic pain and modest growth returned to the region by 2010, albeit on the back of unemployment figures that stubbornly stayed at high levels. This prompted many people in the accession countries to take a more critical look at EU membership, which did not always deliver the promised land of higher incomes and standards of living.

In the Eurozone, public debt levels in Portugal, Ireland, Italy, Greece, and Spain (the so-called PIIGS) reached unsustainable levels. In those countries, hazardous economic models became the norm, which relied on cheap money granted by low Euro interest rates that sparked a consumer and building boom. Once credit started to dry up, the public finances of the PIIGS tumbled like a house of cards. Greek Prime Minister George Papandreou admitted in 2009 that previous governments had returned falsified accounts, which managed to disguise the financial malaise for many years. European leaders and their citizens watched in disbelief as the crisis spread from Greece to other countries as international money markets started to scrutinize the under-performers of the Eurozone and charged punitive interest rates in light of rapidly diminishing prospects for a solution. Since the beginning of Economic and Monetary Union (EMU) in 1999, the EU had turned a blind eye to the tax and spending patterns of some members, and made no attempt to insist on the implementation of EMU's Stability Pact which after all prescribed strict rules on the levels of debt a Eurozone country was allowed to accumulate. The shocking lesson that came out of the sovereign debt crisis was the realization that the Eurozone was far from being an optimum currency area (OCA) and that the economic disparities between the richer North and the poorer South might be too pronounced for a single currency to work. EU leaders who agreed to EMU in the Maastricht Treaty had sacrificed economic and financial prudence on the altar of a political ambition that aimed to create an "ever-closer union." After ignoring EMU's fundamental flaws for so long, it was the next generation of politicians who had to try to fix a policy that might have been unsuitable for European integration in the first place. Without doubt, the single currency was the most ambitious endeavor that the EU had ever embarked upon. But it prompted the eruption of the biggest crisis that the continent had experienced since the end of the second World War; a crisis which brought economic and financial hardship to many Europeans and the momentary loss of moral authority of the European project. The EU and the member state governments will have to work hard to regain the trust of their citizens which they so carelessly squandered.

2

Enlargement

During the 1950s and 1960s the emerging European Union was only one of several alternatives for fostering cooperation among European states. The European Free Trade Association (EFTA), at one stage, had more members than the European Union had.[1] But when Britain first applied for membership to the European Economic Community in 1961, it became clear that the EU was indeed highly attractive, especially because the development of a unified market promised expanding trade relations. Over subsequent years, one European state after the other handed in its application, and we can now safely claim that the EU has become the primary vehicle for organizing Europe. But expanding the membership has also been attractive to existing member states. Not only did enlargement offer more markets, it also increased stability and security on the continent, and some member states, such as the UK and Denmark, welcomed enlargement as a way to water down ambitions for greater political integration.

After a brief history of the successive enlargement rounds of the EU, this chapter offers insights into why and how the EU has integrated new members, especially the ambitious 2004 round that expanded the Union in one sweep from fifteen to twenty-five members. This is followed by a discussion of future enlargements and an analysis of how the EU might be able to cope with an ever expanding membership. The key issues surrounding enlargement are the following:

1. *What explains the speed of enlargement?*
2. *How does the European Union enlarge?*
3. *What are the costs and benefits of enlargement for the EU as well as for the candidate countries?*
4. *Where will enlargement end?*
5. *Should Turkey join the EU?*

History of Enlargement

The first round of enlargement could have happened as early as 1961, had it not been for the then French president Charles de Gaulle. The French leader vigorously opposed Britain's membership application on the grounds that British interests in the Community were mainly in the field of trade and market access, with no firm commitments to other policies, most notably agriculture. Hence Britain's first application was turned down, as was the second in 1967. Twice de Gaulle put his foot down, declaring that the UK lacked a true European vocation. When George Pompidou succeeded de Gaulle in 1969, however, progress on the British application was swift. Battling against a skeptical public, which found both the successor to its empire—the Commonwealth—as well as close relations with America more appealing than membership in the EC, UK Prime Minister Edward Heath nonetheless managed to convince his ruling Conservative Party of the growing importance of European trade partners for British industry. He effectively used the argument that EU economies had continuously outperformed their British counterpart, which meant that the UK had fallen further and further behind the continent in terms of prosperity. As for Denmark and Ireland, their applications were always connected to that of the UK, since both countries had strong trade relations with Britain (see Table 2.1).

With the first round of enlargement, then, the Union changed in a number of ways: the special relationship between Britain and the United States gave the EU a stronger global link; the accession of Ireland provided for the inclusion of an economically backward state, where economic performance and development lagged far behind the union's average; and the acceptance of Denmark and the UK meant that the EU, for the first time, had to confront a higher degree of skepticism toward European integration, particularly political union, than had previously existed among the original six founding states.

The second enlargement, in 1981, involved Greece and repeated the Ireland experience almost a decade earlier in that Greece was another economically backward country joining the community to boost trade and the country's standard of living. In contrast to Ireland, however, the EU had to address the political

Table 2.1. Chronology of Enlargement

Year	Membership Count	Countries
1951	Original six	West Germany, France, Italy, Belgium, Luxembourg, the Netherlands
1973	9	Britain, Ireland, Denmark
1981	10	Greece
1986	12	Portugal, Spain
1995	15	Sweden, Finland, Austria
2004	25	Malta, Cyprus, Estonia, Latvia, Lithuania, Poland, Hungary, Czech Republic, Slovakia, Slovenia
2007	27	Bulgaria, Romania
2013	28	Croatia
beyond	36*	Macedonia, Turkey, Albania, Iceland, Serbia, Bosnia and Herzegovina, Montenegro, Ukraine

* Membership could even rise to 37 countries, in the event that Kosovo gains full international recognition after declaring independence from Serbia in January 2008.

dimension of this accession. After seven years of Junta rule (1967–74), the European Council thought that a speedy integration of Greece would offer a much-needed buffer of popular support to a still tender democracy.

Political stabilization also played a role in the third enlargement in 1986. Both Spain and Portugal had only recently, in the mid 1970s, emerged from authoritarian rule.[2] A short-lived coup in Spain in 1982 highlighted the shaky foundations on which the two Iberian democracies were built. Until that year, accession negotiations were cumbersome, as Italy and France were concerned about the perceived competition in agricultural produce such as wine, olives, and tomatoes, while other member states worried about the prospect of cheap labor moving to northern Europe and the size of the Spanish fishing fleet. In the end, however, the coup of 1982 reaffirmed the notion that membership in the European club offered a crucial degree of democratic stability, especially since Spain and Portugal were also members of NATO.

In contrast to the often acrimonious negotiations with the Iberian countries, the fourth round of 1995 posed no major problems. With the end of the Cold War, the three formerly neutral countries, Finland, Sweden, and Austria, lost their political rationale as buffers between East and West. Instead, the economic benefits of gaining access to a highly integrated market now dominated the agenda. In contrast to previous rounds, the gross domestic product (GDP) of the three newcomers was well above the EU average. This naturally pleased poorer member states, as it posed no upcoming challenge to their status as main beneficiaries of the EU's cohesion funds. It was no surprise, therefore, that accession was speedily negotiated merely three years after the applications were submitted. Only minor difficulties arose over environmental damage in the Austrian Alps through increased truck traffic, and agricultural problems concerning Austrian hill farmers and North Scandinavian tundra farmers.[3]

With these four enlargement rounds the EU had turned into the world's largest market, with some 340 million consumers. Fifty years after the end of World War II, the Union was also the world's leading commercial power, attracting 20 percent of global imports and exports, excluding intra-EU trade. However, EU institutions were designed for a Union of six states, not fifteen; indeed, the nature of the EU had changed considerably. In particular, the Franco-German axis—long the driving force of European integration—had become less prominent over the years. Although calls for further European integration still often originated in Berlin and Paris, with many more members and divergent sets of interests, agreements were not always as straightforward as the two old partners would have liked.

The European Union did not stop at fifteen, however. With the end of communism, nearly all former Soviet satellite states decided that their economic and political futures were linked to a closer integration within the European Union. Between March 1994 (Hungary) and January 1996 (the Czech Republic), ten Central and Eastern European Countries (CEEC) submitted their applications to Brussels. The two noncommunist states of Cyprus and Malta had already done so in July 1990. Obviously integrating such a large number of countries imposed severe challenges. First, the number of EU citizens would increase by 32 percent to 485 million. Second, the level of economic development in the CEEC was sharply below that of Western Europe. In fact, upon accession in 2004, the absolute GDP of the EU grew by only 8 percent. Although per capita income in Slovenia (the most prosperous application country) was 74 percent of the EU average and in line with that of Portugal, incomes in Latvia were only 35 percent of the EU average.[4] In the run-up to accession, the developmental needs of all the candidate countries were therefore significant and covered every conceivable economic, political, and administrative sector. The EU tried to address this challenge with a series of programs, including support for the modernization of agriculture, environmental and infrastructural programs, and twinning schemes (the secondment of civil servants from the EU-15 to the accession states). The programs were designed to bring the candidates to an acceptable level of development that would make them ready for membership.[5]

The EU itself was also trying to get ready for enlargement. The objective of the summit meeting in Nice in December 2000 was to provide institutional and policy reforms preparatory to the upcoming wave of accession. Nice produced some results, most notably the reweighing of votes in the Council of Ministers. However, a number of crucial items were not addressed and were postponed for another intergovernmental round of negotiations. These items included, first of all, an agreement on the size of the budget. Integrating poorer countries necessarily required the potential expansion of the Common Agricultural Policy and the cohesion funds for a smooth extension of the Single Market and EMU. Yet Commission proposals to reform the budget were largely put on hold by the member states. The financial perspective covering the years 2000 to 2006 was left untouched, and the enlargement of 2004 was financed without additional budget contributions from the existing member states.

Second, a pressing problem demanding closer attention was agriculture, especially in countries with large rural populations such as Poland. The Commission's proposals were approved by the member states as late as December 2002.[6] Further, the EU's cohesion policy needed to be completely overhauled to cope with so many countries where economic development still lagged far behind that of Western Europe. But again the EU decided to stick to existing spending plans, with an overhaul of cohesion promised for the next financial perspective covering the years 2007 to 2013.

By the end of 2002 ten countries had successfully completed their negotiations, and the final seal of approval for integrating the new member states was given by the Copenhagen summit in December of that year. In May 2004 the union expanded to twenty-five states. All applicants were included except Romania and Bulgaria; the Commission deemed that the administrative capacities of the two Balkan countries was too weak, particularly their judicial systems, and the member states agreed on 2007 as a later date for accession.

Analyzing Enlargement: Key Principles

The EU follows four main principles in pursuing its objectives for enlargement and for imposing requirements on the candidate countries.[7] The first principle is that the EU insists on the full acceptance of the *acquis communautaire*. The acquis refers to the total set of rights and obligations attached to the European Union that emerged out of the EU's legislative processes. Hence the acquis consists of all treaties, EU legislation, and case law as developed by the European Court of Justice that was passed since the Treaty of Paris in 1951. It also includes every policy, including EMU, since opt-outs are not granted to new member states. This massive set of laws, rules, and regulations, totaling some one hundred thousand pages in the English version, must be integrated into a candidate's national law before membership is granted. Because future members have to satisfy this requirement to qualify for admission, negotiations to join the EU have become increasingly difficult, complex, and time-consuming—especially in view of the ever growing acquis—both for the countries holding the Presidency, which conducts the negotiations, and for the applicant countries.

The second principle is that the EU tends to address diversity by creating new policy instruments. Each round of enlargement showed that the economic structures of the new member states did not fit existing patterns within the EU of expenditures and incomes. The accession of the UK in 1973, for instance, was complicated by the country's large quantities of cheaper food imported from Commonwealth countries, which clashed with the Common Agricultural Policy (CAP). In return for Britain's acceptance of the CAP, the EU agreed to establish a Regional Development Fund (ERDF) to support regions with lower economic output and productivity. So, instead of making structural adjustments to key polices such as the CAP, the EU preferred to keep those policies relatively untouched and instead established new policies that offset detrimental consequences.

As a third principle, the EU integrates new member states with institutional adjustments that are subject to lengthy and often acrimonious treaty negotiations. The years have seen only slow progress in institutional adaptations as new members joined the Commission, the European Parliament, and the Council of Ministers. Hardly any institutional innovations have occurred in parallel with enlargement until the summit meeting in Nice in December 2000 offered a change in direction. Nice reached an agreement on far-reaching institutional reforms, since a union of twenty-five members by 2004 and twenty-seven members by 2007 would make effective governance under the old system very difficult. In the end, the EU set new limits to the size of the European Parliament (capped at 732) and the Commission (a maximum of 27 commissioners), and also changed the voting procedure in the Council of Ministers. Likewise, the Lisbon Treaty of 2007 aimed to make the union ready for future enlargements and here, in particular, the integration of Turkey which by the time of accession might be the EU's most populous country. Again, as with Nice, the number of MEPs was capped (now at 754) and a new voting system was designed for the Council of Ministers.[8] Still, these much needed institutional adjustments took nearly a decade to negotiate, while the new voting system in the Council of Ministers will only be used from 2014 on; a full ten years after the big-bang enlargement of 2004 that took EU membership to twenty-five.

The EU's fourth principle is its preference to negotiate with groups of states that already have close relations with one another. This principle is a coherent theme throughout all EU enlargement processes, with the notable exception of Greece in 1981 and Croatia in 2013. For example, in 1973, prior to joining the EU, the UK and Ireland, as well as the UK and Denmark, had already established strong trade links. Moreover, the EU did not attempt to decouple the relatively straightforward applications of Denmark and Ireland from the complicated British negotiations, where the terms for British entry (CAP and the budget) took years to be finalized.[9]

How Does the EU Enlarge?

At a summit meeting of the European Council in Copenhagen in 1993 the EU established a blueprint for how future accessions should be managed. The so-called Copenhagen criteria concentrated especially on a country's democratic institutions that ought to guarantee key liberal democratic principles promoted by the EU (see Table 2.2).[10] Every new member state also has to make the necessary

Table 2.2. The Copenhagen Criteria for Enlargement

1. Political criterion	Institutions guaranteeing democracy, human rights, rule of law, respect for and protection of minorities
2. Economic criteria	Existence of functioning market economy Capacity to cope with competitive pressure and market forces
3. Administrative criterion	Take on the obligations of membership (acquis communautaire)

economic adjustments in order to cope with the competitive pressures of the Single Market. A new administrative criterion was developed to ensure the presence of institutional capacities that guaranteed the continual implementation of EU law. This criterion focuses on the candidate's public administration, testing whether the bureaucracy, from ministries to law enforcement agencies and to courts, would be able to fulfill their functions against an ever increasing stream of legislation issuing from Brussels. In light of the Maastricht Treaty and its widespread reforms (which had entered into force a few months earlier), the Copenhagen criteria also required that the capacity to absorb new member states should not jeopardize the momentum of European integration.

When a country applies for membership, the Commission's responsibility is to assess the candidate's suitability for joining the union. The Commission therefore starts an intense dialogue that focuses initially on the political criteria. The entire acquis is then subdivided into negotiation chapters, which at the moment totals thirty-five. For instance, there are separate chapters on agriculture, the environment, and transport. The Commission screens the chapters individually and offers its opinion to the member states which, in return, have to agree unanimously on an EU position for each chapter. The EU country holding the Presidency chairs these negotiations. Chapters are opened and closed once again after a unanimous agreement among the member states who can also suspend negotiations (for instance, if a candidate no longer fulfills the political criteria) by a qualified majority vote. Hence the term "negotiation" does not refer to discussions held between the EU and the candidate on the terms of membership. Instead, it is the EU member states which negotiate among themselves on what to expect from the applicant.[11] Once negotiations reach a satisfactory conclusion, the Commission writes a report to the European Parliament and the European Council; both bodies must then agree to the applicant's membership, in Parliament with an absolute majority and in the Council by unanimity (see Table 2.3).

Who's Next? Future Enlargements

The European Union continues to be highly attractive for its neighbors and, beyond the 2004 and 2007 enlargement, additional countries are knocking on the door in Brussels. As of 2012, Croatia will become a full member in July 2013. Turkey,

Table 2.3. Working Mechanisms of Enlargement Negotiations

35 chapters
Commission screens chapters one after the other
Commission drafts EU's common position for each chapter
Member states negotiate on EU position for each chapter
Opening and closing of chapters agreed on by member states unanimously
Annual progress report by Commission on political criteria of candidate country
Suspension of negotiations possible with QMV

Macedonia, Montenegro, Serbia, and Iceland have the status of candidates, and Albania, as well as Bosnia and Herzegovina, have also expressed interest in joining. After the 2004 regime change in Ukraine, that country might also consider a future application. Hence the total membership of the EU could rise significantly (see Table 2.1). Enlargement does not come cheap, however, given the backward state of economic and political development in these countries. For the financial period of 2007–2013, the EU had earmarked a total of 11.5 billion Euros which is organized through the so-called Instrument for Pre-Accession Assistance (IPA).

Future members can be categorized into three groups:

- Candidate states: Countries that have been screened by the Commission as to their suitability for entering the thirty-five chapter negotiation process, and have been granted candidate status by the member states. Macedonia, Montenegro, Serbia, Iceland, and Turkey currently fall into this category.
- Potential Candidate States that have submitted an application: Countries that have submitted an application to join the EU, but either the screening process or the approval of the member states to elevate them to candidate level is still outstanding. This situation applies to Albania.
- Potential Candidate States that have not yet submitted an application: Countries that have a firm dialogue and EU funding in place and are working toward eventual membership, including Bosnia and Herzegovina and Kosovo.

In addition to these three categories, the Western Balkans—Albania, Bosnia and Herzegovina, Croatia, Kosovo, Macedonia, Montenegro, and Serbia—were at some point or are still included in the framework of the Stabilisation and Association Process (SAP),[12] a preparatory relationship between the EU and the accession states in the run-up to full candidate status. As with the states of the 2004 and 2007 enlargements, the Copenhagen criteria form the basis of any negotiations.[13] Given that the majority of these countries were involved in the acrimonious disintegration of the former Yugoslavia, one specific criteria of the SAP includes complete co-operation with the International Criminal Tribunal for the Former Yugoslavia (ICTY) over alleged war crimes. SAP countries also have to demonstrate a respect for minority rights, opportunities for displaced persons and refugees to return home, and a clear commitment to regional cooperation. Since September 2000 the EU has granted the countries of the region wide-ranging free access to the Union's market for almost all goods, with the aim of boosting economic development. Further, regarding regional cooperation, the Commission has reported positively on a number of agreements that were concluded on the return of refugees, border crossings, visa regimes, the fight against terrorism, and organized crime. In return for these considerable efforts, the EU lifted visa requirements for all countries but Kosovo.[14] In its frequent assessments, however, the Commission listed a number of political-structural problems that needed to be rectified in order for the thirty-five chapter negotiations to begin. The required improvements generally involve the functioning of government institutions; reform of the educational systems, public administration, and judicial systems; corruption; respect for human and minority rights; gender equality; the return of refugees; and media legislation. The objective of the EU with regard to the Western Balkans seems straightforward. Membership cannot be denied to these countries as long as they meet strict criteria—not only the enlargement criteria, as applied in 2004, but also the requirement for regional, cross-border cooperation as a vehicle for turning former enemies into partners.

Croatia. The country signed a Stabilisation and Association Agreement (SAA) with the EU in October 2001. In February 2003 Croatia applied for membership; this objective was endorsed by the European Commission, and in June 2004 candidate status was granted when the European Council decided that the accession process should be launched. The start of negotiations was scheduled for March 2005 but was delayed by the controversy surrounding the suspected war criminal Ante Gotovina, who, as an army general, gained the status of a national hero in the 1995 war between Croatia and Serbia. From the outset the EU expected that all suspected war criminals would be surrendered to the International Criminal Tribunal for the Former Yugoslavia (ICTY) in the Dutch capital of The Hague. The capture of Gotovina, in December 2005, therefore paved the way for accession negotiations to start in earnest. In December 2011, Croatia and the EU signed an accession treaty and the country was scheduled to become the twenty-eighth member state in July 2013. In case Croatia encounters difficulties in the implementation of the acquis communautaire, the EU imposed three safeguard clauses which could ultimately result in the suspension of specific rights. These clauses are in place until 2016 and apply to general economic conditions, the Single Market, and justice and home affairs.

Macedonia. As with Croatia, Macedonia signed an SAA with the EU in April 2001, and the application for membership followed in March 2004. The EU granted Macedonia candidate status in 2005 and completed the screening process a year later. Although the political situation remains relatively stable, paramount to the EU is a successful integration of the sizable ethnic minority of Albanians. In a 2009 report the Commission listed such challenges as transparency; professionalism and independence of the civil service, the media, and the judiciary; gender discrimination in the workplace; corruption; and the discrimination of the Roma. This assessment, however, represented a marked improvement from the controversial parliamentary elections of 2008, which were marred by voter intimidation and violence with an estimated 15 percent of votes deemed to be irregular by international observers. Given the multitude of challenges regarding the political and administrative criteria, by 2012 the member states had not started the thirty-five chapter negotiation process. There is also the continuing controversy over the official name of the country which, at the moment, is the rather awkward sounding Former Yugoslav Republic of Macedonia (FYROM). This issue is frequently brought to the fore by Greece, which has a province that is called Macedonia and does not want a term to be used that does not apply to its own territory. Until Greece and Macedonia (or FYROM, if you prefer) reach an agreement, the road to EU membership will remain rocky.

Turkey. Arguably Turkey represents the EU's biggest challenge. Much debate has already occurred over whether the Union should integrate a country with a predominantly Muslim population, especially as public opinion across the EU is fiercely divided over this issue. Moreover, Turkey's population of 70 million would make it the EU's second most populous member state with significant voting powers in the Council of Ministers. Given Turkey's low prosperity levels—around 50 percent of the average EU level and similar to that of Bulgaria and Romania—the possibility of considerable migratory movements to Northern and Western Europe was also causing concern in some member states. For these reasons, Turkey's application has repeatedly been put on hold, although it had applied for membership as early as 1987.

In November 2002, however, with the election of Prime Minister Recep Tayyip Erdogan, Turkey's application was reevaluated. Two years later the Commission issued a positive report confirming that the country met the political criteria and suggested that accession negotiations should commence in the fall of 2005. Nonetheless the Commission delivered a number of warning shots, stressing that "accession cannot take place before 2014, and that it must be thoroughly prepared to allow for smooth integration and to avoid endangering the achievements of over fifty years of European integration." More specifically, the Commission demanded an annual review of the progress of political reforms in Turkey and would recommend suspending negotiations if any principles of the political criteria were seriously and persistently breached.

Relations between the EU and Turkey were further strained by the continuous controversy over Cyprus. Ankara has refused to give diplomatic recognition to the Republic of Cyprus, though it is an EU member, and has closed off all its ports and airports to goods and people from that part of the island.[15] EU member states argued, however, that progress in Turkey's path toward Europe could only be achieved if the Turkish government reversed its position. In fact, the EU, led by the Finnish Presidency, even threatened to suspend negotiations should Ankara refuse to give in. In the end a last-minute compromise was reached at the EU summit in December 2006, with Turkey opening at least one port to the Greek-Cypriot–led Republic. Negotiations so far have been painfully slow. By 2011, only thirteen chapters have been opened with only one (the rather thin Science and Research) provisionally closed. In its annual report the Commission, in 2009, stated that "significant further efforts are needed in most areas related to the political criteria, in particular fundamental rights." Further points of criticism were corruption; the lack of a modernized, transparent, and merit-based civil service; gender equality; and women's rights. Turkish law also did not sufficiently guarantee freedom of expression in line with the European Convention of Human Rights (ECHR). Clearly the country has to undergo major social, economic, and political transformations before EU accession can even be considered. Therefore, in view of Turkey's size, relative economic backwardness, and the painstaking and time-consuming efforts to reform society and politics, an accession date of 2014, which has been suggested, seems hopelessly optimistic. And even if Turkey manages to complete the transformation processes, EU accession is not necessarily guaranteed, as France and Austria have frequently voiced concerns over the impact that a large Muslim country will have on the EU. Indeed, both countries have mentioned that they might hold referendums on whether Turkey should be allowed to join.

Iceland. Hit severely by the economic crisis that resulted in the collapse of its currency and banking system, the smallest of the Scandinavian countries applied for EU membership in July 2009. Iceland already has strong links with the EU. It belongs to the Schengen Area, which facilitates travel and work between signatory countries.[16] It is also a member of the European Economic Area (EEA),[17] which extends the EU's Single Market to Iceland as well as to Norway and Liechtenstein. From this perspective, integration into the EU would seem a relatively straightforward process, as the country has already implemented a significant part of the acquis communautaire. It therefore was a logical conclusion to grant the country candidate status in July 2010. Relations with the EU were undermined by the controversy over the repayment of loans issued by Landsbanki, one of Iceland's main banks, which had offered saving accounts to UK and Dutch customers but had collapsed during the credit crunch. With the Icelandic government unable to guarantee deposits, the British and Dutch governments were forced to step in to the tune of around four billion Euros. What followed was a farcical drama over the terms of repayment. The Icelandic parliament in 2009 passed a law to repay the debt but was defeated in a subsequent referendum. In the meantime though, Icelandic, Dutch, and British negotiators had agreed on a less punishing repayment schedule, which paved the way for entry negotiations to start.

Albania. Negotiations for an SAA started in February 2003. In a 2005 Progress Report the Commission noted improvements in a number of areas but called for better results in fighting organized crime and corruption, enhanced media freedom, further electoral reform, and swifter property restitution. Given the relatively short time since the communist regime was toppled in 1992, Albania surprised many with its speedy reform processes. In April 2009 the SAA entered into force and Albania submitted its application for EU membership. By the end of 2010, the Commission recommended that candidate status ought to be granted once key elements of the political aspect of the Copenhagen criteria were met, especially the establishment of institutions guaranteeing democracy and the rule of law. Albania has yet to complete this process.

Montenegro. In a referendum, in May 2006, Montenegro formed an independent country and left the state union with Serbia. In the run-up to the referendum, as well as after it, the government indicated that it regards the country as a future EU candidate state. Negotiations on a Stabilization and Association Agreement began shortly thereafter, which was signed in October 2007. A year later the country submitted its EU application. Between July and December 2009, the Commission implemented a screening process, and in December 2010, the European Council confirmed Montenegro's status as a candidate. The specific chapter negotiations started in June 2012.

Serbia. In April 2005 the Commission stated that progress on reform remained fragile, but it acknowledged that the country had significantly improved its economic and political capacities as well as its ability to negotiate and implement an SAA. On the other hand, Enlargement Commissioner Olli Rehn (2004–2009) continued to remind Belgrade that Serbia had little chance of formalizing closer links with the EU as long as two suspected war criminals—General Ratko Mladič and Radovan Karadžič—remain at large. It was no surprise, therefore, that the EU suspended negotiations with Serbia in May 2006 on the grounds that both men still had not been turned in to the War Crimes Tribunal in The Hague. Negotiations resumed in June 2007 after the election of a pro-EU government under Boris Tadič, and the SAA was signed in April 2008. Just months later Karadžič was arrested in Belgrade, where he had been working as a psychiatrist under a false identity. The arrest paved the way for the country's official EU application in December 2009. Upgrading to the level of candidate, however, seemed a remote possibility as long as Mladič was still on the run. With the General's capture in his Serbian hideout in 2011, and the subsequent appearance at the War Crimes Tribunal, that status was granted in May 2012.

Bosnia and Herzegovina. Discussions with the EU were based on the Commission's Feasibility Study of March 2003 in which Brussels listed sixteen priorities, including political dialogue and economic, police, judiciary, and other reforms, that should be addressed before the EU would agree to closer contractual relations. By 2005 progress was made on meeting these objectives, and the European

Council began SAA negotiations in November of that year, which concluded in June 2008. However, the country's accession process is complicated by the Dayton Agreement of 1995, which brought to an end the ethnic and political violence that emerged from the secession of Yugoslavia in 1991.[18] Dayton organized the country into three entities: the Republica Srpska (with a majority of Bosnian Serbs),[19] the Federation of Bosnia and Herzegovina (which is mainly inhabited by Muslims and Croats), and the Brčko district (a tiny entity with a mixed population). Each of these sub-entities was given substantial autonomous powers with the plan to pass responsibilities back to a federal government at a later stage. This process has been very slow and, despite the involvement of an EU High Representative, the entities have been reluctant to transfer powers (most notably authority over the police) back to a federal government in Sarajevo. In addition, the Commission, at several stages, has criticized shortcomings regarding cooperation with the International Criminal Tribunal for the Former Yugoslavia. Hence progress toward EU integration will continue to be slow, as long as the constitutional state of Bosnia and Herzegovina is not settled.

Kosovo. The province of Kosovo was under Serbian control until 1999, when a NATO-led intervention came to the rescue of a predominantly ethnic Albanian population. In the aftermath of this military confrontation, Kosovo came under the control of the United Nations with the establishment of the UN Mission in Kosovo (UNMIK). In 2007 the UN envoy Marti Ahtisaari proposed full independence with protective rights for the minority of ethnic Serbs. The Serbian government (as well as the majority of Serbian public opinion) rejected the proposal. The government of Kosovo nonetheless declared independence in February 2008. Within the European Union, France, the UK, and Germany were backing independence, while by 2012 Cyprus, Greece, Spain, and Slovakia still had not recognized the country. In October 2008 the UN General Assembly adopted a resolution asking the International Court of Justice (ICJ) for advice on the legality of Kosovo's declaration of independence. Two years later, the ICJ indeed stated that Kosovo had not broken international law, although it seems likely that Russia will use its veto in the Security Council to prevent Kosovo's admission into the United Nations. As to the EU, it has no contractual relations with Kosovo as such, although individual member states have formed closer bilateral relations. Nonetheless, in December 2008, the EU has taken over from the UN with the establishment of an administrative apparatus called EULEX (European Union Rule of Law Mission in Kosovo), which supports rule-of-law institutions (customs, police, and judiciary) with a staff of nineteen hundred internationals and eleven hundred locals.

****

After the long and controversial ratification process of the Lisbon Treaty, as well as the repercussions on Economic and Monetary Union and the Eurozone's sovereign debt crisis, enlargement is undoubtedly yet another monumental challenge that will shape the European Union for years to come. For the member states, an enlarged Europe would mean a bigger and more integrated market. It would also provide a buffer of stability and security on its southeastern border which would reduce migration levels. But apart from these positive effects, an enlarged EU of thirty-five or more member states would place EU institutions under considerable strain. It is doubtful whether agreements can easily be reached at the EU level given the dispersed state of economic and social development between the existing EU and its future partners. From a policy perspective, some EU programs, most notably agriculture and cohesion, would have to be completely revamped. While the current modus operandi might still be feasible to integrate the Western Balkans, major adjustments would be required once Turkey joins the EU.[20] It therefore comes as little surprise that skeptics of the current enlargement process warn of an institutional deadlock and a policy breakdown.

From the perspective of EU applicants, the Union provides a much-needed boost for economic development. Since the time of the 2004 enlargement, Poland, Slovakia, Slovenia, and Cyprus have significantly improved their standards of living, and there is no reason to doubt that the current applicants might also be in a position to turn their economic fortunes around. Likewise, from a political point of view, the EU has throughout its history represented a vehicle that fostered democracy among previously undemocratic regimes (Portugal, Spain, Italy, Germany, and most applicants of the 2004/2007 round), while also facilitating cooperation and understanding among former enemies (such as France and Germany). But the fault line of European politics is no longer at the river Rhine. The violent breakup of Yugoslavia in the 1990s shocked Europe, but in those dark hours the EU often stood by helplessly. What the EU failed to achieve in the 1990s—establishing peace within a highly antagonistic area—it could now help to promote some twenty years later: enabling former enemies to be integrated within an organizational vehicle whose founding rationale of the 1950s was that of creating peace through dialogue and multilateral cooperation. Hence, what was offered to the original Six cannot under any moral imperatives be denied to the current applicants. And if the EU indeed brings stability to the region, then it will have greatly enhanced its own raison d'être.

But the EU's role as economic and political missionary might find its limits in Turkey. Any aspirations of a union of Christian nations would have to be abandoned with the integration of such a large Muslim country. Still, and despite the considerable institutional and policy changes that a Turkish accession would impose on the EU, it would not be the member states that would be burdened with the most massive transformations. That job would fall to Turkey, which would have to modernize not only its economy but its political mechanisms—and, above all, its society—in order to meet membership requirements. If Turkey is able to make that transition, and indeed prove that its economic, political, and social structures are in line with those of established member states, the EU will find it morally difficult to deny Turkey accession. This would undoubtedly be the end of an integrated, federal United States of Europe, but it would mean that the benefits of EU membership are open to those who seek it and to those who are willing to undergo the necessary transformation processes.

PART TWO

INSTITUTIONS

Institutional relations within the EU represent a carefully struck balance between intergovernmental forces and supranational institutions. This chapter analyzes the EU's five main institutions—the European Commission, the European Council, the Council of Ministers, the European Parliament, and the European Court of Justice—along with the system of institutional checks and balance. The analysis of the EU's institutional setup focuses on five key issues:

1. *The legislative, executive, and judiciary powers of the institutions*
2. *The reasons why member states have delegated powers in certain areas to supranational institutions but maintained sovereignty in other intergovernmental institutions*
3. *The criticisms that some institutions are facing in relation to a perceived democratic deficit and lack of transparency*
4. *The balance of power between the institutions*
5. *The ways in which member states can control and influence policy-making processes in Brussels*

3

The European Commission

Organization

The European Commission is led by the Commission President who is joined by twenty-six commissioners, the equivalent of "ministers" at the national level, bringing the total to twenty-seven, or one from each member state (see Table 3.1).[1] Just as with any national administration, these politicians have staffs made up of many civil servants, the so-called Eurocrats, to assist them in fulfilling their duties. Whereas the commissioners usually come and go at five-year intervals, the Eurocrats have longer-term appointments, with many staff members of the Commission's civil service spending a large portion of their professional lives in Brussels. The organization of the Commission differs from national governments in a number of ways, reflecting the dual nature of the EU as both an intergovernmental union of states and a supranational union of European citizens.

First, the election of the Commission President is less straightforward than national elections of presidents or prime ministers, who receive their political legitimacy simply through elections. In the EU, all heads of government must agree on one candidate.[2]

Table 3.1. The European Commission, 2010–2014

Jose Manuel Barroso, Portugal	Commission President
Catherine Ashton, UK	Foreign Affairs and Security Policy
Viviane Reding, Luxembourg	Justice, Fundamental Rights, and Citizenship
Neelie Kroes, Netherlands Digital Agenda	Competition
Joaquin Almunia, Spain	Transport
Siim Kallas, Estonia	Industry and Entrepreneurship
Antonio Tajani, Italy	Inter-Institutional Relations and Administration
Maroš Šefčovič, Slovakia	Environment
Janez Potočnik, Slovenia	Economic and Monetary Affairs
Olli Rehn, Finland	Development
Andris Piebalgs, Latvia	Internal Market and Services
Michel Barnier, France	Education, Culture, Multilinguism and Youth
Androulla Vassiliou, Cyprus	Taxation and Customs Union, Audit and Anti-Fraud
Algirdas Šemeta, Luthuania	Trade
Karel de Gucht, Belgium	Health and Consumer Policy
John Dalli, Malta	Research, Innovation, and Science
Máire Geoghegan-Quinn, Ireland	Financial Programming and Budget
Janusz Lewandowski, Poland	Maritime Affairs and Fisheries
Guenther Oettinger, Germany	Energy
Johannes Hahn, Austria	Regional Policy
Connie Hedegaard, Denmark	Climate Action
Štefan Fűle, Czech Republic	Enlargement and European Neighborhood Policy
Laszlo Andor, Hungary	Employment, Social Affairs, and Inclusion
Cecilia Malmstroem, Sweden	Home Affairs
Kristalina Georgiewa , Bulgaria	International Cooperation, Humanitarian Aid, and Crisis Response
Dacian Cioloș, Romania	Agriculture and Rural Development

Second, whereas presidents and prime ministers appoint their team of ministers and assign them particular responsibilities such as foreign affairs, defense, or finance, the individual commissioners are appointed by the national governments, and the governments negotiate with one another over which ministerial responsibilities their candidates will have. Although this should be done in collaboration with the Commission President, some member states often insist on certain portfolios and the Commission President has little say in the matter.[3] Not surprisingly, the larger countries often secure more attractive and influential portfolios, and the Commission President then has to balance and juggle portfolios and candidates to form a coherent administration.

The choice of commissioners, therefore, is crucial for the course of European integration. Knowledgeable and motivated commissioners obviously contribute more to the European cause than candidates who might be past their political prime.[4] Naturally the choice of candidates deeply impacts the Commission President's performance. Imagine the president of the United States having to work with secretaries of state that are appointed by the representatives of the fifty states, who then dictate to the president which secretary of state will manage which portfolio. Despite these restrictions imposed on the Commission President, the fact is that the political influence of this post depends largely on the president's personal characteristics and policy ideals.[5] All commissioners (the College of Commissioners) usually meet once a week to discuss legislative proposals. When voting on whether to proceed with a legislative initiative, a simple majority decides the issue, with the Commission President exercising the deciding vote in case of a tie.

Despite the prominent scapegoating that goes on in Western Europe about a Brussels bureaucracy of vast proportions, only some thirty-eight thousand civil servants work for the Commission. The EU bureaucracy is composed of twenty-three so-called Directorate Generals (DGs) and sixteen services (see Table 3.2),[6] which are the organizational equivalents of government ministries in national administrations, and they fulfill many of the same functions as ministerial departments: policy development, preparation of legislation, monitoring of legislative implementation, and advice and support for the political executive.

Neither the number nor the responsibilities of the DGs correspond exactly to the number of commissioner portfolios, and, indeed, commissioners may have more than one DG at their disposal. Alternatively, a DG may be responsible for the portfolios of more than one commissioner. Conversely, a commissioner might not have a DG at all, which is somewhat similar to the position of a minister without a portfolio in parliamentary governments.

Every commissioner has a supporting cabinet, reflecting a strong French tradition in the organization of the EU's administration. Most cabinets have seven members, career Eurocrats or political appointees, whom the commissioner brings to Brussels. Their job is to facilitate the work of the commissioner, such as acting as liaison with other commissioners and between different DGs, or organizing and sometimes chairing committee meetings. A good cabinet undoubtedly can boost a commissioner's standing, whereas a bad cabinet can impair a commissioner's influence. It is no coincidence that the most effective commissioners have the best-staffed and best-organized cabinets.

The Commission recruits its personnel through an extremely competitive, EU-wide selection process that includes aptitude and language-proficiency tests, written examinations, and interviews. From the beginning of their careers, the Commission civil servants enter a world of unofficial but nonetheless finely balanced national quotas. The EU administration needs to reflect the population size and distribution of each member state. Hence promotions through the ranks are subject to an unofficial allocation of positions to each member state at every step

Table 3.2. Directorates General and Services of the European Commission, 2010–2014

Policies	External Relations
Agriculture and Rural Development	Development
Competition	Enlargement
Economic and Financial Affairs	EuropeAid—Cooperation Office
Education and Culture	External Relations
Employment, Social Affairs, and Equal Opportunities	Humanitarian Aid
Energy and Transport	Trade
Enterprise and Industry	
Environment	**General Services**
Maritime Affairs and Fisheries	Communication
Health and Consumers	European Anti-Fraud Office
Information Society and Media	Eurostat
Internal Market and Services	Joint Research Centre
Justice, Freedom, and Security	Publications Office
Regional Policy	Secretariat General
Research	
Taxation and Customs Union	**Internal Services**
	Budget
	Bureau of European Policy Advisers
	European Commission Data Protection Officer
	Human Resources and Security
	Informatics
	Infrastructures and Logistics, Brussels
	Infrastructures and Logistics, Luxembourg
	Internal Audit Service
	Interpretation
	Legal Service
	Office for Administration and Payment of Individual Entitlements
	Translation

of a civil servant's career ladder. Promotions to senior positions are highly political, not only because there are fewer jobs available compared to the number of lower positions, but also because national civil servants who are brought in from outside, such as cabinet members, further reduce the availability of senior jobs. The difficulty of progressing to senior jobs causes much frustration and resentment, especially as the obsession with national quotas means that a Eurocrat's professional competence and merit is not necessarily reflected in the level of his or her post.[7]

Powers and Responsibilities

The Commission plays six key roles: proposing legislation, implementing EU policies, managing the budget, conducting external relations, policing EU laws, and pointing the way forward.[8]

1. *Proposing legislation.* Typically, in democratic systems, a number of political actors can propose legislation. In the EU, however, only the Commission can both propose legislation and initiate the process of determining whether the proposal will become law. Other institutions, such as the European Council or the European Parliament, may ask the Commission to initiate legislation, but proposals predominately originate within the Commission. Most of the Commission's proposals have a clear legal base in the treaties. The Single European Act, for instance, elevated the subject of the environment to the European level, and from then on the Commission could propose legislation in this field. Other legislative proposals can flow from legislation already adopted—a legislative spillover to complete a particular policy or program—and others could originate in a particular court ruling by the European Court of Justice.

Within the Commission, proposals can follow different paths. The Commission President, an individual commissioner, the head of a DG, or even a section director can ask staff to prepare proposals. Even ambitious junior Eurocrats may bombard their superiors with ideas. On the other hand, proposals can also come about in response to a suggestion by a member state or an interest group. Annual legislative consultations also occur with other EU institutions, such as the European Parliament and the Council of Ministers, where the general agenda and priorities for the upcoming year are debated. Whatever the origin of a legislative proposal, it has to work its way through the Commission's internal committees that coordinate various parts of the Commission, as well as external committees where outside experts or national civil servants are consulted (see Table 3.3).

2. *Implementing EU policies.* More prominent than its role in legislation is the Commission's position as the executive authority of the EU. Whereas national governments have vast human resources to implement or enforce legislation, for example, police forces, customs officials, and tax authorities, the Commission has no such services but must rely on national authorities to assist in this area. National veterinary services, for instance, monitor EU regulations governing the health of livestock, and national customs officials check baggage at airports when travelers enter the geographical space of the European common market. Because the Commission depends entirely on this kind of support, it concentrates its executive powers on passing concrete rules and regulations that turn legislation into practice. The Commission issues around five thousand pieces of legislation annually, mainly on technical aspects of EU policies. Based on this authority, the Commission does have a great impact on the daily lives of Europeans by specifying such matters as product guidelines, environmental standards, and health and safety features.[9] The

Table 3.3. Powers of the European Commission

Legislative Side
Proposing legislation
Executive Side
Implementing EU policies
Managing the budget
Conducting external relations
Policing EU law
Pointing the way forward

Commission's implementation power is also illustrated by its role in enlargement. Based on legal criteria that candidate countries must satisfy in order to qualify, the Commission monitors the progress of each accession state until the candidate has reached the required EU norms. The Commission then issues a final report that the member states and the European Parliament use to decide whether to approve an application.

3. *Managing the budget.* The EU budget is relatively small, comprising only 1 percent of the EU's GNP,[10] and each year the Commission submits a draft budget to the member states and the European Parliament. The draft serves as a material basis for the EU's political, economic, and social objectives, one of which is to distribute financial support to members in need of help, such as farmers or economically backward regions. Technically the Commission manages the budget, yet the member states and the EP make the political decisions on how it should be spent.

4. *Conducting external relations.* The Commission maintains more than 130 offices and delegations across the globe. Although the heads of these delegations have the diplomatic status of ambassadors, this does not mean that the EU is comparable to a foreign service. The Common Foreign and Security Policy is under the authority of member states. Still, in the area of international trade, the Commission has proven to be a highly capable player. At the World Trade Organization (WTO), it is the Commission that negotiates on behalf of all EU member states.[11] Although association and accession agreements are negotiated by the country holding the Presidency of the EU and approved by the member states and the European Parliament, the Commission is heavily involved because it assesses the progress of an accession country and suggests to the member states how to proceed with a particular candidate.

The external dimension of the Commission was given a considerable boost with the Lisbon Treaty of 2007. The treaty establishes the new position of "High Representative for Foreign Affairs and Security Policy," who has the authority to propose security and defense measures. The first incumbent of this post, the UK Commissioner Catherine Ashton, was also asked to set up a diplomatic network to support her in achieving these new functions. The post of High Representative

merges two existing portfolios: High-Representative for Common Foreign and Security Policy (which ever since its inception in 1998 was held by Javier Solana from
Spain) as well as the commissioner for external relations. This reorganization was
deemed necessary because Solana's capacity to engage in world affairs was severely
curtailed: he was forced to operate outside the Commission and therefore with only
limited staff at his disposal, and under the direct supervision of the member states.
Moreover, previous commissions were often confronted with an awkward overlap
of responsibilities whenever an EU portfolio developed an external dimension, as,
for instance, with agriculture and WTO negotiations. The new post therefore also
aimed to create a new hierarchy within the Commission, in that all policies with
an external remit now fall under the authority of the High Representative.

5. *Policing EU laws.* The Commission is sometimes referred to as the "guardian
of the treaties," a rather grand description of its powers in this field. Still, under
Article 169 of the Treaty of Rome, the Commission has the authority to bring
member states before the Court of Justice for alleged non-fulfillment of a treaty
obligation. Usually, however, member states fulfill their treaty commitments; otherwise, the EU would simply collapse. When countries do fail to comply, which
occurs particularly frequently in the area of the Single Market, it is often the result
of a genuine misunderstanding or misinterpretation of Commission rules, or of
delays in translating EU legislation into national law. If the Commission takes a
member state to the European Court of Justice in Luxembourg, the case results
in a highly publicized and potentially embarrassing political affair. The member
states and the Commission, therefore, are generally reluctant to pursue cases all
the way to the ECJ, as the negative publicity it generates is detrimental to both the
Commission and the member state involved. Parties try to resolve most disputes
at an early stage.

6. *Pointing the way forward.* This considerable power is best exemplified by the
former Commission president Jacques Delors, who declared, in 1987, that the Commission has a unique obligation to point the way to the goal ahead. He explained
that the Commission alone cannot achieve much, but it can generate ideas. Its
main weapon is conviction. There are numerous examples, the most prominent,
perhaps, is the Single Market. Based on the prospect of falling behind the U.S. and
Japan, the member states undoubtedly were eager to complete the common market
by the early 1990s, but it was the Commission that put the package together after
mapping out a strategy on how to succeed. In contrast, the EU stagnates when the
Commission and its president are unable to lead. The tenures of Jacques Santer
(1994–99) and Romano Prodi (1999–2004) fall into this category.

4

The European Council

Organization

The European Council, commonly termed the "Summit," is made up of the political leaders of the member states, such as prime ministers, as well as the president of the European Commission. Foreign ministers also attend, but they are not considered members. The Summit meets at least four times a year but more frequently should grave problems such as the sovereign debt crisis in the Eurozone arise.[1]

The European Council was not mentioned in the Treaty of Rome and therefore was not part of the original institutional setup. But at the Paris summit in 1974, French President Valerie Giscard d'Estaing convinced his fellow heads of government that the Union needed a regular and high-profile organization that would allow national leaders to more aggressively shape the direction and speed of European integration. The institutional framework of the European Community was ill-equipped for increased cooperation at the highest level, and it could not offer the kind of distinct authority and leadership that Giscard believed only heads of government could provide. Nearly two decades later the Maastricht Treaty acknowledged the Summit's function as "providing the Union with the necessary

Table 4.1. The European Council

- Meeting of national heads of government, as well as President and Vice President of the European Commission
- Meets at least four times a year, more if deemed necessary
- Main function is to provide overall direction to the EU
- Chaired by the President of the European Council

impetus for its development and shall define the general guidelines thereof." Hence the primary function of the European Council can be described as that of a central political leadership which sets objectives, particularly for the long-term development of the EU (see Table 4.1).

Today, more than ever, the primary function of the European Council is to give strategic direction to the EU by going beyond the boundaries of national interests and viewing the Union as an organic whole. The Summit also has the distinct advantage of acquainting political leaders with one another and introducing new heads of government into this exclusive, but often rather informal, European club. Because media coverage of the EU has soared over recent years, clever politicians have frequently used this publicity for public-relations exercises that often serve domestic political purposes. This has often undermined Giscard's initial intention of providing an informal forum where national leaders could debate and exchange ideas freely without intense media scrutiny.

Working Mechanisms

1. *Preparing meetings.* With the Lisbon Treaty, the task of preparing Summit meetings is now the responsibility of the newly created President of the European Council. During the ratification process of the Lisbon Treaty, several high-profile candidates were mentioned, including the former prime ministers Tony Blair (UK) and Felipe González (Spain), as well as Luxembourg's current head of government Jean-Claude Juncker. In the end the member states agreed on the little-known Belgian prime minister Herman van Rompuy, who started his new assignment in December 2009.[2] This was a good decision, as the position is largely administrative with little scope for enhancing one's reputation, something the above-mentioned politicians were keenly aware of. It is too early to say to what extent the president will be able to exert influence on the Summit. One must keep in mind that the post does not come with much personnel or many resources, as the president does not have the administrative backup enjoyed, for instance, by the commissioners. Another uncertainty the Lisbon Treaty failed to clarify is the potential overlap of responsibilities between the President of the European Council, the Commission President, and even the country holding the rotating Presidency of the Council of Ministers (see chapter 5). On the foreign stage, in particular, all three posts can

make valid claims to represent the EU abroad. Over the next couple of years a clearer demarcation of authority will undoubtedly emerge, but, until then, the EU is set to see the occasional eruption of institutional rivalries.

2. *Issues discussed.* Some items are so important that they are always on the agenda. These usually include discussion of the general economic situation, enlargement, and, more recently, EMU and the sovereign debt crisis. The Commission also might focus on an issue in which it is particularly interested, such as debating the reorganization of the budget or institutional reforms. The President of the European Council also might want to pursue a particular agenda.[3] Discussions may sometimes resume on items not successfully concluded within the Council of Ministers or on business remaining from previous summits. Finally, special attention may be given to international circumstances such as the war in Iraq or the war on terrorism in the aftermath of the bombings in Madrid and London.[4]

3. *How the Summit actually works.* On the first day of the Summit, heads of governments, their ministers, and Commission officials meet for extensive talks. Lunch is usually a lengthy affair (as it allows for informal debates in a relaxed atmosphere) and is followed by more rounds of discussion. What happens after dinner depends on the progress that was made over the course of the day. Sometimes heads of government retire to fireside chats, conducive for informal consultations. At other times prime ministers have to forfeit brandy and a log fire to hammer out the final wording of agreements. Once these agreements are concluded, national officials and staff of the European President work feverishly throughout the night to prepare the draft conclusions that will be discussed by the heads of government on the morning of the second day. The summit often ends on the afternoon of the second day with a final statement and press conference.[5] The statement is usually agreed upon unanimously.[6]

Functions

1. *Setting the pace of integration.* The European Council informs the Commission of member states' preferences for the future direction of the European project, including new policies and institutional reforms. This is a high-profile event that the Commission cannot ignore, for it is the Commission's responsibility to turn the Summit's objectives into concrete legislative proposals. The Summit, therefore, might be referred to as an individual legislator.

2. *Initiating major policies.* An example of this function is the summit in Maastricht in 1991, which centered on the transition from the European Community to the EU with a Common Foreign and Security Policy (CFSP) and a single currency, as well as developments in Justice and Home Affairs (JHA). These extremely sensitive issues were hotly debated at this summit, and diverging opinions over the scope and practical consequences of these policies continue to determine the debate over the precise nature of the EU.

Table 4.2. Functions of the European Council

1. Setting the pace of integration
2. Initiating major policies
3. Resolving problems
4. Acting as decision maker
5. Being an international player

3. *Resolving problems.* Attempts are made to resolve potential disagreements in person-to-person discussions that offer the opportunity to broker deals and reach compromises. The European Council does not deal exclusively in one policy area, as does the Council of Ministers. It is therefore a useful venue for deal making between member states where different policy areas are affected. The European Council has proven to be a superb vehicle for resolving problems efficiently.

4. *Decision making.* The Summit also functions as a decision maker. Treaty amendments, new policies, and reforms are agreed upon in a unanimous fashion, and these decisions then have to be taken further by the European Commission (for economic matters), and the Council of Ministers (for foreign and security matters as well as justice and home affairs).

5. *Being an international player.* Exercising its responsibilities in the sphere of external relations, the Summit has, for example, imposed trade sanctions against apartheid South Africa, a weapons embargo against China, and, more recently, trade sanctions against Robert Mugabe's Zimbabwe (see Table 4.2).[7]

Institutional Relations

In retrospect, without these top-level meetings, the EU would not have been able to survive the Eurosclerosis of the 1970s, and certainly would not have launched the Single Market program in the 1980s. The Summit, therefore, is far more than a glorified, high-profile public-relations exercise and, arguably, has been the most influential institution in the processes of European integration. At the same time it is the epitome of intergovernmentalism in the Union; it is a thorn in the eye of passionate European federalists, since it upholds the national sovereignty of member states by sidelining supranational European institutions such as the Parliament (which is not involved in the Summit's agenda-setting or decision-making processes) or the Commission (whose president is only invited to attend Summit proceedings).

The responsibility of the Commission to initiate policies is undoubtedly curtailed to some extent by the Summit, which decides on the direction of policies that have far-reaching effects. But depending on the status of its president, the Commission might achieve some balance by playing an active role. Although some decisions are now reached by the Summit and not in the meetings of the Council of

Ministers, the hierarchies of these two institutions are not necessarily competitive, as both represent national interests. Indeed, there should be coherence between the policies pursued by heads of state at the Summit and their ministers in the Council of Ministers.

More important, in any case, is the position of the European Parliament, which is completely excluded from the Summit, apart from the opening address, which is delivered by the Parliament's president. This, of course, is a big blow to federalists and, some might argue, to the democratic legitimacy of the EU.

5

The Council of Ministers

Organization

The Council of Ministers epitomizes the special nature of the European Union as an international organization that balances supranational tendencies but also has to safeguard and represent national interests.[1] Its main objective is to set the EU's medium-term policy goals. It also approves the budget and legislation proposed by the European Commission (a function it shares with the European Parliament). Finally, the Council of Ministers holds certain executive powers for foreign and security policies and for justice and home affairs.

The Council carries out its operations through ten sub-councils with different responsibilities (see Table 5.1). Examples are the Environment Council, where all national environment ministers meet, or the Foreign Affairs Council, which brings together the national foreign ministers. The number of Council meetings depends on the scope and intensity of the particular legislative program. Some sub-councils meet monthly—the Economic and Financial Affairs Council (ECOFIN), the Agriculture Council, and the General Affairs Council—whereas others, such as the Transport Council, meet less frequently.

Table 5.1. Configuration of the Council of Ministers

- General affairs
- Foreign affairs
- Economic and financial affairs
- Justice and home affairs
- Employment, social policy, health, and consumer affairs
- Competitiveness
- Transport, telecommunications, and energy
- Agriculture and fisheries
- Environment
- Education, youth, and culture

These sporadic meetings are insufficient for effective politics, and so as early as 1958 the Committee of Permanent Representatives, or COREPER,[2] was created to meet at least once weekly to provide support. The COREPER staff consists of junior and senior civil servants, usually the member states' ambassadors and deputy ambassadors to the EU, who prepare the agenda of the Council of Ministers and decide which sub-councils should consider a given issue. COREPER also arranges some two hundred working groups of national officials. These groups discuss technical aspects of legislative proposals coming from the Commission and requiring special knowledge and expertise. The Council's political machine, then, operates on three levels: proposals from the Commission are scrutinized in the working groups; the evaluations are examined by COREPER; and COREPER then prepares the material for final decisions in the sub-councils.

The Process of Decision Making

How decisions are made depends on provisions elaborated in the treaties outlining whether legislative proposals are agreed upon by unanimity or by qualified majority voting (QMV). Roughly issues involving vital national interests require unanimous support, whereas the others require only a QMV. Issues such as taxation and defense are still decided by unanimity.

In QMV, every member state has a certain number of votes proportional to its population. The bigger states such as France, Germany, the UK, and Italy have twenty-nine votes, and smaller countries like Malta have only three. Legislation is then approved by the Council of Ministers under three conditions:[3]

1. A majority of states must approve the legislation.
2. The majority is defined as representing at least 62 percent of the EU Population.

Table 5.2. Qualified Majority Voting in the Council of Ministers

Conditions for passing legislation

- Approval by majority of member states
- Must represent at least 62 per cent of EU population
- Must represent at least 72.3 per cent of votes (250 out of 345 votes)

EU-15		Accession Countries Post-2004	
Country	Votes	Country	Votes
France	29	Poland	27
Germany	29	Romania*	14
Italy	29	Czech Republic	12
UK	29	Hungary	12
Spain	27	Bulgaria*	10
Netherlands	13	Lithuania	7
Belgium	12	Slovakia	7
Greece	12	Cyprus	4
Portugal	12	Estonia	4
Austria	10	Latvia	4
Sweden	10	Slovenia	4
Denmark	7	Malta	3
Ireland	7		
Finland	7		
Luxembourg	4		

3. The majority must have at least 72.3 percent of votes in the Council of Ministers, which, from 2007 on, is 250 out of 345 total votes.

The system is complex and, perhaps, difficult for outsiders to comprehend, and it certainly runs counter to such vital democratic principles as transparency and equity. Hence the failed constitution of 2005 proposed a much easier version. Every country simply gets one vote. Legislation would then be passed if approved by 55 percent of the member states representing 65 percent of the EU population. The Lisbon Treaty that was negotiated in June 2007 reiterated this double majority principle, while adding a further qualifying point: at least four countries are now needed to block a particular legislative proposal. At the end of all this wrangling over percentages and numbers, the cumbersome Nice formula will finally be confined to the dustbin of history, but not until 2014 (see Table 5.2).

Powers

The Council has legislative and executive powers. Regarding legislation, at the start of the European Community the Council of Ministers enjoyed sole decision-making power. Since then, in an attempt to strengthen the democratic legitimacy

Table 5.3. Powers of the Council of Ministers

- Approving legislation emanating from the Commission (together with the European Parliament)
- Budget approval (together with the European Parliament) on a proposal from the Commission
- Sole executive power in the fields of Common Foreign and Security Policy, as well as Justice and Home Affairs

of the integration process, member states have increasingly shared some of its legislative powers with the European Parliament. Shared power is seen, in particular, with association and accession treaties but also with standard EU legislation that is now enacted within the triangle of the Commission, Parliament, and the Council of Ministers (see Table 5.3).

One of the Council's executive powers is the approval of the EU budget. Although this responsibility is shared with the European Parliament, it is still fundamentally important, as the Council can influence spending priorities that directly affect the lives of EU citizens.

A number of executive powers have been delegated to the Commission. Because of its large bureaucracy and specialized departments, that institution is better equipped than the Council to tackle a variety of executive functions, especially in implementing economic polices in agriculture, the internal market, and the environment, as well as monitoring their implementation by member states. The Commission also has the advantage that, unlike the member states' ministers on the Council, it does not have to cope with domestic pressures.

Meanwhile, the Council exercises executive powers completely on its own in the fields of Common Foreign and Security Policy and partly in the field of Justice and Home Affairs, because, in these areas, the right to initiate policies remains with the member states. Politically sensitive executive powers and the vital issues of member states, such as foreign policy, security, immigration, and police cooperation, remain within the intergovernmental framework of the Council of Ministers, safe from supranational ambitions.[4]

The Presidency

The Presidency is not an EU institution but a distinctive organizational feature that has a bearing on the workings of the Council of Ministers and therefore profoundly influences the outcome, shape, and direction of EU politics. The term "Presidency" is a rather unfortunate choice, given that ever since the Lisbon Treaty we now have a President (of the European Commission), another President (of the European Council), as well as the Presidency (of the Council of Ministers). A more instructive term for it would therefore be chairperson, and every six months a different member state takes its turn in assuming this function. The order in which this occurs used to be alphabetical, but with the

Table 5.4. The Rotation of the Presidency

First Half (January to June)	Second Half (July to December)
2007 Germany	2007 Portugal
2008 Slovenia	2008 France
2009 Czech Republic	2009 Sweden
2010 Spain	2010 Belgium
2011 Hungary	2011 Poland
2012 Denmark	2012 Cyprus
2013 Ireland	2013 Lithuania
2014 Greece	2014 Italy
2015 Latvia	2015 Luxembourg
2016 Netherlands	2016 Slovakia
2017 Malta	2017 United Kingdom
2018 Estonia	2018 Bulgaria
2019 Austria	2019 Romania
2020 Finland	

enlargement of 1995 a new system was adopted to balance and reflect the different political and economic characteristics of EU member states. An effort is made, therefore, to rotate the Presidency so that a smaller country is followed by a larger one, and a richer country is preceded by a poorer one, although this formula can only serve as a rough guideline (see Table 5.4).

The Lisbon Treaty of 2007 severely limited the responsibilities of the Presidency. Prior to Lisbon, the member state chairing the EU had to prepare and chair summit meetings.[5] The Presidency also used to act as an EU spokesperson and represented the union internationally. These functions are now assumed by the President of the European Council. In addition, the High Representative for Foreign Affairs and Security Policy, who is a member of the European Commission, now chairs the powerful Trade Policy Committee which is instrumental in negotiations at the World Trade Organization (see chapter 15) as well as the Foreign Affairs Council within the Council of Ministers.

Still, despite these much-reduced responsibilities, the Presidency is still crucial to the functioning of the EU. It still has to prepare and chair meetings of the other nine sub-councils, as well as special committees, such as the Committee on Budgetary Control. It also still has to broker deals within the Council of Ministers should member states fail to reach an agreement. And it still has the chance to launch strategic policy initiatives[6] which, if approved by other member states, can result in an ambitious legislative program.

The Presidency is also responsible for maintaining good relations between EU institutions. Relations between the Council of Ministers and the Commission can be awkward at times, as the latter is a supranational organization designed to promote European integration, whereas the former represents the member states and is designed to safeguard national interests. Yet harmonious relations between the two are crucial for effective policy making, since the Commission proposes legislation that the Council of Ministers (and the European Parliament) subsequently votes on. The Presidency's job, therefore, is to mediate between these two institutions and, if necessary, broker compromises.

The Presidency also plays a role as liaison between the Council of Ministers and the European Parliament. The EP tends to see the Council as the jealous guardian of national sovereignty, and the Council regards the Parliament as the supranational newcomer to the EU's political power game, whose main intention is to increase its legislative and supervising powers. The Presidency has the task of meeting with parliamentary committees and filtering the committees' views back into the decision-making processes within the Council of Ministers.

These responsibilities can place an enormous strain on the country that holds the Presidency. Large member states have an obvious advantage here, as their sizable bureaucracies offer solid infrastructural support, not to mention the number of civil servants that are required to fulfill such a function. In contrast, smaller countries sometimes have difficulty finding enough qualified people to chair all the meetings. Some member states radically reorganize their bureaucracies in order to absorb the shock of the Presidency, often at the cost of diminished attention to domestic politics. Despite the organizational and administrative burden, small countries relish the chance to be at the helm of EU politics and, understandably, enjoy basking in the European limelight for this period. Regardless of the greater bureaucratic resources of larger states, by no means do they necessarily have more successful presidencies. Another feature of the Presidency is that it can be turned to the advantage of domestic politics either by distracting from pressing problems or by enhancing the government's prestige and popularity.

Although the Lisbon Treaty greatly reduced the impact an individual country can have on the EU, one had to admit that the previous system was hopelessly inefficient, as a term of six months was too short to pursue a coherent program. The frequent rotation of the summitry undermined political continuity and encouraged short-term views and policies.[7] It therefore came as no surprise that, prior to the 2004 enlargement, calls for reform were widespread. After all, with twenty-seven members, any given country would hold the Presidency only once every thirteen and a half years, hardly conducive for continuity or political effectiveness. One can assume that the Lisbon system, which divides responsibility between a permanent President of the European Council and a rotating Presidency of the Council of Ministers, may result in more coherence and more long-term strategic thinking and planning.

6

The European Parliament

Organization

The European Parliament stands out as the only directly elected political body in the EU. It has seen its powers increased significantly over the last fifty years, although organizational problems persist, which prompt many analysts to criticize the EU's democratic deficit: the gap in power between appointed institutions such as the Council of Ministers and the Commission, on the one hand, and elected institutions such as the European Parliament, on the other.

With the accession of Romania and Bulgaria in 2007, the EP had 736 members, elected every five years, with each member state having a specific allocation of representatives (see Table 6.1). The number of members allotted to each country does not perfectly reflect the size of its population. For example, an MEP from Luxembourg represents sixty thousand fellow citizens, whereas his or her colleague from Germany represents a constituency of around eight hundred thousand. One vital institutional feature of the EP is its party groupings. EP elections consist of parallel elections held in all member states, with different sets of national parties

Table 6.1. Allocation of Seats in the European Parliament

Country	Number of Seats
Germany	99
France	74
UK, Italy	73
Spain	54
Poland	51
Romania	33
Netherlands	26
Portugal, Czech Republic, Hungary, Belgium, Greece	22
Sweden	20
Austria	19
Bulgaria	18
Finland, Denmark, Slovakia	13
Ireland, Lithuania	12
Latvia	9
Slovenia	8
Estonia, Cyprus, Luxembourg, Malta	6
Total	754

campaigning for seats. In the UK, for example, competing for seats are British Labourites, British Conservatives, British Greens, and British Liberal Democrats; competing in Germany are German Social Democrats, German Christian Democrats, German Liberals, and German Greens; and so on. Party groupings therefore try to channel political activity within the EP along sometimes rough political-ideological lines. Table 6.2 shows the respective party groupings for the legislative period from 2009 to 2014.

The party groups are the organizational vehicles through which the EP functions. They appoint the leaders of the EP and assign speaking times or chair the committees. More important, if a party belongs to a party group, it receives secretarial support, research staff, and financial resources. Parties therefore tend to cobble together, as it is extremely difficult to secure any office or policy goals outside the party groupings. But although party groupings dominate the EP's daily operations, their importance is severely curtailed, for national parties still largely organize their own electoral campaigns. A Europe-wide party simply does not exist. Also, MEPs come from the national party system, and quite often still think along national lines with their domestic political agenda in mind; some also intend, eventually, to return to their national political scene. Although MEPs are the legislators of European politics, they are still influenced by domestic concerns.

The EP's leadership is comprised of a president and fourteen vice presidents, the latter responsible for chairing meetings and representing the Parliament

Table 6.2. Party Groupings in the European Parliament, 2009–2014

Name of Party Group	Ideology	Number of Seats
European People's Party European Democrats (EPP)	Center right	271
Progressive Alliance of Socialists and Democrats (S&D)	Center left	190
Alliance of Liberals and Democrats for Europe (ALDE)	Liberal centrist	85
The Greens European Free Alliance (Greens—EFA)	Environmentalist, regionalist	58
European Conservatives and Reformists (ECR)	Center right, anti-federal	53
European United Left—Nordic Green Left (GUE-NGL)	Left wing	34
Europe of Freedom and Democracy (EFD)	Nationalist—conservative, anti-EU	33
Non-Attached	11 national parties	30
Total		754

Note: Twenty-five MEPs from seven different member states are needed to form a party group.

vis-à-vis other EU institutions. The EP also has a secretariat similar to the Council secretariat and the Commission civil service, offering support services that include research, public relations, and translation. The Parliament also has a committee system that has evolved dramatically over the years, reflecting the EU's increasing impact on the daily lives of Europeans. For 2009–14 there are twenty permanent committees of varying size and importance,[1] with the job of discussing the legislative proposals that Parliament may vote on during plenary sessions. Two weeks each month are reserved for committee meetings in Brussels that may be attended by Council and Commission officials, and even, occasionally, by other MEPs. Apart from the standing committees, the EP occasionally also has committees of inquiry and temporary committees. This loose structure allows the EP to quickly respond to recent developments that have legislative implications for the EU.

Plenary sessions are the most visible but sometimes the least flattering aspect of the Parliament's work. For a week each month all MEPs meet in Strasbourg, France. These sessions include debates; speeches by commissioners, by the President of the European Council, and by members of the Council Presidency; a question period; and, most important, votes on legislation.[2]

The Powers of the European Parliament

As with any national parliament, besides its legislative functions, the EP plays a vital role in the supervision of the executive, the budget, and, to a limited extent, foreign and security policies. With respect to making laws, the history of the EP is one of relentless attempts to increase its institutional power. Until the Treaty of Lisbon came into effect at the end of 2009, the EU had four different paths for approving legislation, each giving the EP varying degrees of power, which could be as minimal as a right to simple consultation.[3] The weakened authority of the EP prior to Lisbon was testimony to the well-protected sovereignty of member states, which feared that a powerful supranational parliament might undermine the influence of the Council of Ministers and the European Council.

The Lisbon Treaty, however, greatly advanced the legislative power of the EP. Instead of four cumbersome procedures, most legislation in the EU is now passed by applying the so-called ordinary legislative procedure.[4] Under this process both the EP and the Council of Ministers have to work jointly on approving legislation that emanates from the Commission. If no agreement is reached, a conciliation committee is formed of members from both institutions to mediate a compromise. If the conciliation committee does not reach an agreement, the proposed legislation is abandoned, giving the EP an unconditional veto power.

For a small range of policy areas, the "special legislative procedure" is used. Although all policy areas and their respective procedures are listed in the treaties, one has to look deep into the Lisbon Treaty to find the relevant sections on the special legislative procedure which is now limited to some matters relating to justice and home affairs, budgets, taxation, as well as highly specific issues, such as the fiscal aspects of the environmental policy. For this procedure, either the Council of Ministers or the EP (but not both) determine a legislative outcome, although the other respective institution still needs to be consulted.[5]

The increase in the powers of the EP has been well received by most commentators. Likewise, abandoning the cumbersome four previous paths to legislation and replacing them with two relatively straightforward processes has also been much appreciated. In addition, the Lisbon Treaty increased the power of the EP with regards to the World Trade Organization (WTO). Before, the EP was merely informed about the progress of trade negotiations. Now, it decides jointly with the Council of Ministers on the framework of the EU's trade policy through the ordinary legislative procedure. Nonetheless, the EP still only has a consultative role in foreign and security policies. One might argue that this consultative function does not amount to much, but the main achievement for the Parliament is its involvement in a field considered to be high politics and of the utmost importance to the member states. This greatly enhances its political stature and impact, as sensitive issues are now given an additional public airing, not only at the national level in national parliaments but, after Maastricht, on the supranational level as well. Still, the power of the EP in these matters cannot be described as comprehensive.

Arguably the EP's most important power is its budgetary authority which is also agreed upon under the ordinary legislative procedure. The Parliament has exclusive authority to grant a discharge of the general budget by verifying the accuracy of the Commission's budgetary management and determining precise revenue and expenditure. The Parliament regards the discharge option as a potential weapon for censoring the Commission, which it did in 1982 by refusing to accept the budget of Commission President Gaston Thorn. A political crisis was only avoided by the premature departure of Thorn and the inauguration of the Delors administration.

Still, the EP's budgetary power ought to be viewed in perspective. The EU budget is small (recall, it is only around 1 percent of the joint GNP of all member states), and the most politically sensitive expenditure items of a budget—welfare spending, defense, and education—tend to fall outside the scope of the EU and are covered mostly by national budgets. The EP may have acquired budgetary authority, but as long as the budget remains insignificant, and as long as the EU cannot raise any revenue (for instance, by introducing taxes), its powers in this field will remain rather weak.

The Elections of 2009

In a time of economic crises, people tend to vote for center right parties, and the EP election in 2009 was no exception. The election represented a damning verdict to political groupings on the center left. Social democratic parties across the continent fared poorly, regardless of whether they were part of a government or in opposition at the national level (Germany, 20.8 %; France, 16.5%; the UK, 15.8%). The center left struggled to think of alternative ideas to center right policies; France and Germany, for instance, advocated tighter regulation, government spending, job creation, and continued support for welfare state policies that aimed to soften the negative impact of the economic downturn.

As seen in Table 6.2, the EPP party grouping gained 271 seats. Together with votes from the Liberal Group (85 seats) and the anti-federal European Conservatives and Reformists (54 seats), center-right parties were comfortably above the absolute majority of 369. Therefore many analysts believe that for now we have seen the end of consensual politics between the EPP and the Socialist group in favor of a more free-market approach. On the other hand, the support of the European Conservatives and Reformists cannot always be assumed. Formed by the British Conservative Party (which, incidentally, left the EPP grouping) and integrating hard-liners from the Polish Law and Justice Party, as well as from the Czech Civic Democratic Party, this group vehemently opposes any moves toward a more federal Europe that could in any way undermine national sovereignty.

Though only marginally below 2004 levels, the ever lower turnouts at EP elections are nonetheless a worrying trend (see Figure 6.3). It truly reflects European citizens' indifference toward the role of the EP, if not toward the importance of the entire European integration project. Even worse, some political parties simply could not be bothered to spend money on a campaign that is held in such low esteem by their supporters, and instead chose to save money in favor of upcoming

Table 6.3. Turnout in EP Elections

Year of Election	Turnout (%)
1979	63.0
1984	61.0
1989	58.5
1994	56.8
1999	49.8
2004	45.7
2009	42.9

national elections. As in the past, during the election campaigns, European issues or indeed the EU itself were hardly mentioned. Instead, national politics and their responses to the economic crises determined the agenda in all member states. A notable exception, however, was that Green parties did address transnational issues (most importantly climate change and the EU's response to it) and were able to increase their share of votes by attracting left-leaning, middle-class sections of society that had previously turned out for social-democratic parties. Oddly enough, with the rise of extremist parties, the EP may well increase media attention—something it has been wishing for decades. But extremists do not engage in consensus, and so the usual complacency in Strasbourg and Brussels may be replaced by controversy and headline-grabbing antics (see Table 6.4).

The rise of right-wing extremist parties can partially be explained by the low voter turnout. In fact, in some countries (most notably the UK) although the absolute number of votes for these parties did not increase by much, their percentage did. Extremist votes were also a reflection of the economic crisis. In the past, EP elections had often functioned as a ready-made safety valve for voters, who sent warning shots against the ruling elite. Such electoral behavior was encouraged by the perception that their electoral choices at the EU level had little impact on their lives, a notion fostered by the poor reputation the EP has garnered over the years. Apart from the fact that this perception is wrong (the EU and the EP, for instance, are now responsible for approximately 85 percent of economic legislation), the economic downturn might have prompted even more voters than usual to deliver a message of dissatisfaction with the status quo.

The Democratic Deficit and Other Shortcomings

Just as the Commission has no real equivalent in national politics, the EP is often misperceived as the EU's equivalent to a national legislature. Most MEPs and passionate European federalists argue that the role of the EP should be expanded to the status of a proper democratic parliament, with far-reaching legislative authorities.

Table 6.4. Rise of the Far-Right Vote, 2009

Country	Name of Party	Votes (%)	Number of Seats
Netherlands	Freedom Party	17.0	4
Hungary	Jobbik	14.8	3
Denmark	Danish People's Party	14.8	2
Austria	Freedom Party	13.1	2
Bulgaria	Attack	12.0	2
Belgium	Flemish Interest	10.7	2
Italy	Northern League	10.2	8
Finland	True Finns	9.8	1
Romania	Greater Romania Party	8.7	3
UK	British National Party	6.5	2
France	National Front	6.5	3

MEPs argue that the current sharing of legislative power within the triangle of the Council of Ministers, the Commission, and the EP limits the democratic legitimacy of the EU.

In a narrow sense, the democratic deficit is the gap between the power of non-elected institutions—the Commission and the Council of Ministers—and that of national parliaments and the European Parliament. The gap results, in part, from the transfer of powers from member states to the EU. Before the transfer, national parliaments held the exclusive power to pass laws. At the EU level, however, the EP shares these powers with other institutions. As the EU acquired greater competence, national parliaments relinquished some of their influence, not just to the European Parliament but also to the Council of Ministers, the Commission, and the European Council.

Nor does it help that the public and the media are quite indifferent to the fact that the only elected body, the EP, has no power to propose legislation. Although MEPs have consistently argued for more power to the EP, the introduction of the ordinary legislative procedure at the Treaty of Lisbon did not go far enough to meet their demands. Although Lisbon did increase the powers of the Parliament, it did not grant the power to propose legislation. At Maastricht, in 1991, the member states agreed on several provisions to promote an EU that is closer to European citizens, including voting rights for European citizens in local and European elections, even when living in another EU country, and the public's right to petition the EP on matters of EU competence. But despite the attempts in Maastricht and Lisbon, these provisions still do not set the EP on a par with the powers held by national parliaments.

Despite the calls for increasing the EP's powers, some doubt whether a more powerful EP will solve the problem of the democratic deficit. The introduction of various decision-making procedures, after all, did not bring the EU closer to the people but actually distanced it even more. This, of course, has something to do with the unique nature of the EU, specifically that it is not a state with a clearly defined executive and legislative wing. Moreover, the precise course of the EU's institutional future is not yet properly set, as supranationalism clashes with intergovernmentalism. Until this debate is settled, improvements in the direction of a proper Europe of citizens will constantly vacillate between the jealously guarded powers of national governments on one side and increased transparency of the political process and power to democratically elected institutions on the other.[6]

Unfortunately the performance of the EP is often questioned, and the Parliament can appear to shoot itself in the foot when arguing for greater political power. The work of the EP takes place in three different cities. The secretariat sits in Luxembourg, but general plenary sessions take place in Strasbourg and committee meetings are held in Brussels, with endless numbers of boxes, files, and documents having to be shipped around Europe. This wastes time and money—indeed, according to estimates, some 200 million Euro per year. Although this is more the fault of the patriotic vanities of France and Luxembourg, who are unwilling to agree to a permanent and complete move to Brussels, the performances of some MEPs also leave something to be desired. Generous travel allowances and occasionally lavish spending patterns by individual parliamentarians have brought much criticism. In trying to solve the problem of the democratic deficit, one needs to recognize that a popular perception about the EP is that the Parliament is not the solution but actually part of the problem.

In addition to the democratic deficit, a number of organizational shortcomings in the EP are not flattering to a presumably democratic polity. First, the EP would be more powerful and more like a national parliament if it had more effective ways of holding to account the executive of the European Union, and particularly the Commission. As a start, since 2004 the Commission President must be approved by a majority of MEPs, although the Commission President is first proposed by the member states. The EP's other controlling powers are the rather extreme mechanisms of dismissing the College of Commissioners or discharging the budget, but neither is designed to have a fine-tuning influence over the executive nor are they conducive to debates and agenda sharing. One solution would be for the EP to directly elect the Commission President, or an electoral college similar to that of the United States could be organized, with national parliamentarians as well as MEPs casting their votes. Some critics argue, however, that such a move would greatly advance the power of the EP over the Commission, and thus severely curtail the Commission's role as an impartial broker in the EU's political processes. The EU would gain democratic legitimacy for the EP but at the expense of the Commission.

Another problem is that the European elections are what political scientists term "second-order national contests"; European voters perceive them as having lesser importance than national elections, resulting in low voter turnout (see Table 6.3) Voters in EP elections also direct their dissatisfaction with domestic politics against the ruling party; the result is that in EU elections governing parties most often lose votes, whereas opposition and smaller parties do better than in national electoral contests. Analysis has shown that around 20 percent of voters depart from their usual electoral behavior during EU elections. We have seen in the 2009 elections that this can produce a rather distorted result. The 2009 elections also reminded us that European elections are not necessarily about Europe but more about domestic affairs.

A third weakness is that the style of EU elections is closely related to the European party system, in which transnational party federations coordinate the party groupings through loose arrangements with no coherent program, no party hierarchy, and no annual party conference. Indeed, MEPs are not only elected on a national basis but quite often also act out their national identities. European politics is seen through national spectacles with politicians often addressing national instead of European issues, which are dutifully absorbed by the nationally focused media and public. This phenomenon of an often prevailing national mind-set is counterproductive to the EP's development toward a truly European institution with a truly European agenda. A solution would be to establish genuine European political parties competing over European issues. Only then would competitive party democracy emerge. European voters would decide on the winning coalition, and the coalition's political program would be translated into legislative and executive action. At the moment, however, national parties largely commandeer European elections and treat them as quasi-referendums on national politics, which makes for an incoherent European tapestry and a patchwork of different designs.

7

The European Court of Justice

Organization

Although not explicitly mentioned in the Treaty of Rome, the ECJ consists of one judge from each member state who are all appointed by their national governments for a six-year term (see Table 7.1). The treaty only mentions that judges must act independently, and past records show that decisions have been reached without national biases. The judges are assisted by eight advocates general who consider cases and give opinions for the Court's guidance. Judges are free to accept or reject these opinions, but only rarely do they go against them. The positions of judge and advocate general attract the top individuals in their respective fields, usually from the upper echelon of a national judicial hierarchy or from academia. Despite the recent criticism of the EU and its institutions, being a judge at the ECJ in Luxembourg is still regarded as a highly prestigious job.

The duty of the Court is to interpret and apply EU law. To speed up the process, cases need not be decided in plenary sessions (i.e., with all judges present) but can be decided in chambers, with three or five presiding judges. Full plenary sessions are required when a member state or an EU institution is a party in the case and

Table 7.1. The European Court of Justice

- One judge per member state
- Renewable term of six years
- Eight advocates general who analyze cases in greater depth
- Single verdict (no dissenting opinions)

requests a full hearing. In contrast to the judgments rendered by the U.S. Supreme Court, only a single verdict is issued, with no dissenting or concurring opinions. As a result, judgments are sometimes awkward and diplomatically worded to reflect the different views that may arise.

Sources of EU Law

In reaching a verdict, the ECJ can base its judgment on a number of sources of law that are not necessarily restricted to the EU but apply outside the Union's confines. The sources of EU law include treaties such as the Single European Act, the Maastricht Treaty, the treaties of Amsterdam, Nice, and Lisbon, and the three founding treaties of the European Community; European legislation produced within the triangle of the European Commission (which proposes legislation) and the European Parliament and the Council of Ministers (both of which vote on the Commission's proposals); international law; and general principles of law, which are defined somewhat vaguely but typically include the constitutional traditions of member states as well as traditional principles of human rights such as nondiscrimination, proportionality, and legality.

How Do Cases Reach the ECJ?

Individual citizens cannot bring their cases to the ECJ but must first exhaust their national judicial systems. The Treaty of Rome allows lower national courts to seek authoritative guidance from the ECJ; the highest courts of a member state must seek this guidance. National courts, therefore, do not interpret EC law but ask Luxembourg for guidance on any aspects of Community law raised by domestic issues. Based on the advice given, the national court considers the case and decides whether the national rule is compatible with EC law. The entire process, called the "preliminary reference procedure," is intended to ensure uniform interpretation and application of Community law in each member state.

With the preliminary reference procedure, the Treaty of Rome established a useful tool for the ECJ to strengthen both Community law and the Court's own role within the political system of the European Community. It also became a way for European citizens to force their national courts to clarify national laws in relation to European laws. In particular, the lower court judges, not the national

Table 7.2. How Do Cases Reach the ECJ?

- References from national courts
- Actions brought by the Commission or member states against other member states
- Actions brought against EU institutions by other institutions or member states
- Appeals from the Court of First Instance

High Court judges, contact Luxembourg. Some less successful judges conclude that calling for an opinion from the ECJ is a good way to raise their own profile within their national judicial system. Most judges, in any case, are attracted to the concept of the European Union governed not by economics or politics but by law. Whatever the reasons, over the past five decades national and European judges have developed a symbiotic relationship, with national judges becoming the upholders of Community law in their own states.

Legal actions that are brought by the Commission or member states against other member states and go to ECJ judges are mainly for failing to fulfill treaty obligations. Actions are also brought against EU institutions by other EU institutions or member states. Two classes of action occur: cases concerning the legality of EU legislation and cases brought against EU institutions for failure to act. A third class of cases has the ECJ deciding on appeals from the Court of First Instance (see Table 7.2).

The Court of First Instance

By the mid-1980s the ECJ was seriously overworked. As the caseload increased, the time it took to hear a matter and reach a verdict grew to unacceptable proportions.[1] To relieve the burden of cases, in 1989 a new court was introduced—the Court of First Instance—which hears mainly litigation brought by individuals and companies, as well as competition disputes arising from the ECSC and cases involving employees of EU institutions. Like the ECJ, twenty-seven judges, one per member state, are appointed to the Court of First Instance for a renewable term of six years. As with the ECJ, judges must be independent of national governments and, again like the ECJ, work is usually done in chambers and occasionally in plenary sessions for important cases. But unlike the ECJ, the Court has no advocates general to call upon for assistance and advice, and its decisions can be appealed to the ECJ.

Advancing the Case Law of the EU

For much of its existence, the ECJ was the EU's least-known institution. The major decisions of public interest were taken in the Council of Ministers and the Commission, and so the Court enjoyed a rather quiet existence in the sedate Grand Duchy of Luxembourg. Only gradually did the ECJ manage to make an impact on

Table 7.3. The Case of *Van Gend en Loos*, 1963

Dutch company imported chemicals from Germany

Dutch customs added import tax

Response of ECJ:

- Breach against Art. 12, which prohibits member states from introducing new duties or increasing existing duties in the common market

- *Direct effect* of Community law

- Any treaty provision that was "self-sufficient and complete" does not require intervention from national legislators

- Treaty provisions apply directly to individuals

- Community constitutes a new legal order

---

the non-legal world. Despite the Empty Chair Crisis of the 1960s and the Eurosclerosis of the 1970s, the Court persevered and produced groundbreaking rulings that permanently changed the nature of the Community and paved the path toward greater European integration. A number of landmark cases shaped the legal, and hence the political, essence of the EC.[2]

The first landmark case was in 1963, when the Dutch transport firm Van Gend en Loos brought a complaint against Dutch customs for increasing the duty on a chemical product imported from Germany. The firm argued that the Dutch authorities had breached Article 12 of the EEC Treaty prohibiting member states from introducing new duties or from increasing existing duties in the common market. The company claimed protection, citing the direct effect of Community law on national law. The ECJ agreed and ruled that Article 12 had a direct effect, because it contained a "clear and unconditional prohibition." The Court also ruled that any treaty provision that was "self-sufficient and complete" does not require intervention from national legislators and therefore applied directly to individuals. Even brasher was the ECJ's statement that the EU constituted a new legal order whose subjects were not only member states but also their nationals, who then also enjoyed a set of rights (see Table 7.3).

Van Gend en Loos and the principle of direct effect would have had little impact if Community law did not supersede national law. Otherwise the member states would simply ignore the ruling and go about their business as in the past. Although the Treaty of Rome is vague about this, the ECJ did not hesitate to assert its supremacy. The first chance to do so came in 1964, one year after the *Van Gend en Loos* case, with the case of *Costa v. ENEL*. Costa, a shareholder in an electricity company that was nationalized by the Italian government, refused to pay his electricity bill and was taken to court by ENEL, Italy's largest power company; Costa's claim was that the nationalization had infringed upon Community law. The ECJ in its verdict did not question the legality of nationalization, which meant that Costa lost his case, but the Court also pointed to the supremacy of EC law over national

Table 7.4. The Case of *Costa v. ENEL*, 1964

Italian government nationalized electricity company.

In protest, Costa refuses to pay electricity bill.

Verdict of ECJ:

- Nationalization was a legal act: Costa has to pay
- *Supremacy* of EC over national law

law. By signing the Treaty of Rome, the member states had transferred sovereign rights to the Community, and so Community law could not be overridden by domestic legal provisions. Otherwise the legal basis of the Community itself would have been called into question (see Table 7.4).

This, of course, did not sit well with some member states. Here one needs to evaluate the significance of *Costa* and *Van Gend en Loos*. Direct effect and supremacy had established a completely new configuration for the national judiciary and, indeed, for national politics. In certain circumstances a member state was no longer completely sovereign, and laws and political programs had to be checked against the principles of a supranational legal order. Obviously some national courts reacted quite strongly against this kind of encroachment. The biggest threats came in the late 1960s from the supreme courts of Italy and West Germany. In several verdicts they hinted that, because Community law apparently guaranteed a lower standard of fundamental rights[3] than did national law, the validity of Community law was called into question.

So the match between national courts and the ECJ continued. In 1974 the Luxembourg Court responded strongly in *Nold v. the Commission*. Nold was a coal wholesaler seeking the annulment of a decision by the Commission authorizing the publicly owned Ruhr coal-selling agency to adopt certain restrictive criteria for its supply of coal. This meant that Nold could only purchase coal under the burdensome condition that he suffer a financial loss because he no longer could buy directly from his supplier. Nold claimed that the Commission's decision was discriminating and breached his fundamental rights. The case was dismissed on the grounds that the disadvantages claimed by Nold were not related to the Commission's decision but resulted, instead, from economic change and the recession in coal production. But Nold also claimed that the Commission had violated both his proprietary right and his right to the free pursuit of business activity as protected by the German constitution. The ECJ responded to this by stating that fundamental rights form an integral part of the general principles of EC law, and, in order to safeguard these rights, the Court is bound to draw inspiration from the constitutional traditions of the member states as well as from international law (see Table 7.5).

In the matchup against national courts the ECJ had won the battle. Since then, national courts have generally and relatively easily accepted Community law, and

Table 7.5. The Case of *Nold v. the Commission,* 1974

Coal wholesaler Nold argued for breach of his fundamental rights.

Nold sought annulment of Commission decision authorizing the Ruhr coal-selling agency to adopt restrictive criteria for its supply of coal.

Verdict of ECJ:

- Disadvantage for Nold was the result of economic change, not Commission decision
- EC legal order incorporates fundamental rights
- EC law draws inspiration from international law and constitutional traditions of member states

indeed have become an integral part of the new European legal order by applying EC law to their own domestic cases. Still, sometimes the public and politicians are astonished by the extent to which the Court has established its supreme position. An example of the Court's reach is the *Factortame* case of 1991, where, for the first time, the ECJ overruled a British act of parliament. The British Merchant Shipping Act of 1988 had banned Spanish trawlers from fishing in UK waters, and the act blatantly stated that 75 percent of directors and shareholders of vessels operating in UK waters must be British. This was an attempt to stop the so-called quota hopping by Spanish vessels simply by taking a British registration. The Court stated that the Shipping Act contravened Community law. The Treaty of Rome already mentioned the freedom of establishment and the freedom to provide services, and the ECJ expanded this to argue that the UK could not demand strict residence and nationality requirements from owners and crew. This outraged British fishermen, and, indeed, also the British tabloid press and the wider public. But in this case Luxembourg proved to be more powerful than the UK Parliament and, in the process, deeply rocked the British political establishment and its understanding of democracy and sovereignty.

The Impact of Community Case Law

With the two principles of direct effect and supremacy, the ECJ was able to significantly advance the objectives of the Treaty of Rome. The free movement of people, for example, was established in *Van Duyn v. Home Office* in 1974.[4] The famous *Cassis de Dijon* case, in 1979, cemented the free movement of goods.[5] In that case, the ECJ established the principle of mutual recognition, which stated that member states must respect the trade rules of other states and cannot seek to impose their own rules on goods that represented a vital cornerstone in the subsequent development of the Single Market. Regarding social policy, the Court made special inroads on women's rights with the case of *Defrenne v. Sabena* in 1976.[6]

In the wake of these victories by the ECJ, significant shortcomings remain in the development of EC law, notably in the area of human rights. The original Treaty of Rome did not mention fundamental rights, although these are an essential ingredient of any constitutional democracy. In 1986 the preamble of the Single European Act acknowledged the Court's repeated emphasis on fundamental rights by referring to the "member states' determination to work together to promote democracy on the basis of fundamental rights recognized in the member state constitutions, in the Convention for the Protection of Human Rights and Fundamental Freedoms, and the European Social Charter." But there was never an explicit charter of fundamental rights. Despite vigorous attempts by the EP, even the Maastricht Treaty did not include a human rights charter but merely an article that the Union shall respect fundamental rights, as guaranteed by the 1950 European Convention for the Protection of Human Rights and Fundamental Freedoms. In the prelude to the Nice summit in December 2000, a panel of appointed experts developed an EU human rights charter, but Britain refused to allow this document to be enforceable under EC law. The Lisbon Treaty of 2007 finally established a more coherent human rights agenda. The treaty incorporates the Charter of Fundamental Rights into EU law, which lays down the rights that EU citizens already possess (for instance, through the Council of Europe's European Convention on Human Rights or through existing EU law). A further aim of the Charter is to ensure that EU institutions abide by these principles. Alas, Poland and the UK insisted on adding a protocol which clarifies that the Charter does not create any new, legally enforceable rights other than those that are already provided in these two countries and that no European court can strike down Polish or British legislation in human rights matters.

Although such cases as *Van Gend en Loos* enunciated an unwritten bill of rights, this process can only be described as, in effect, a constitutionalization of bits and pieces. Despite the undeniable fact that the ECJ took significant steps in the creation of a more complete legal system covering increasingly more aspects of the lives of European citizens, much remains to be done. First, there is still disagreement over the precise nature of the EU: Is it an economic union or a political one, and, in either case, to what extent? As a consequence of this debate and despite changes in the Lisbon Treaty, the ECJ is still largely excluded from foreign and security matters, and does not have full jurisdiction over justice and home affairs.[7] Second, experts are still divided over the existence of a European demos, that is, a unified European political people. Some argue that the absence of this demos means that the ECJ can never fully develop a proper citizenship agenda—a complete set of rights and responsibilities of the individual versus the EU. Others argue that the EU ought to establish a citizenship agenda as a precondition for establishing a European demos. As a result, the ECJ is forced to interpret many cases under the principles of the Treaty of Rome, particularly the four freedoms of movement regarding goods, services, people, and capital.

The dilemma is illustrated by *The Society for the Protection of Unborn Children (SPUC) v. Grogan* in 1991. The union of students in Ireland, under their president, Stephen Grogan, had produced a leaflet containing information on abortion clinics

Table 7.6. The Case of *SPUC v. Grogan*, 1991

Irish student organization produced a leaflet containing information on abortion clinics in Britain.
The Irish High Court asked ECJ whether the provision of abortion is a service that falls under the Treaty of Rome and whether this restriction on information about this service is contrary to Art. 59 (free movement of services)
SPUC: abortion is not a service; it is immoral and forbidden by the Irish Constitution
Verdict of ECJ:
• Was abortion a service (Art 59,60)? Yes
• Was the information ban a restriction on services? Yes
• Was the restriction justified? Yes
• Should the ECJ review national law for its compatibility with fundamental rights? No

in Britain. Some years earlier the Irish organization Open Door Counseling had provided advice to pregnant women on abortion in Britain, and the Irish Supreme Court ordered it to stop this practice. In 1991, however, this concerned only information, not counseling. The Irish High Court, before passing it to its own Supreme Court, submitted the case to the ECJ asking for advice on whether the provision of abortion was a service that falls under Article 59 of the Treaty of Rome (free movement of services) and whether the restriction in one member state on information about this service was contrary to Article 59. The plaintiff in this case, the SPUC, argued that abortion could not be categorized as a service, since it is simply immoral and, after all, forbidden by the Irish Constitution (see Table 7.6).

The advocate general's view was that abortion constitutes a service, and although abortion was forbidden in Ireland, Irish people had a right to obtain information about lawful abortion in other member states, and thus this case was within the scope of EC law. But the advocate general concluded that an information ban was justified, as it was in the public interest of Ireland, meaning that it would be in accordance with the Irish constitution. The ECJ, however, had a very different view. Although it agreed with the advocate general that abortion is a service, the ECJ maintained that there was no "economic link" between British abortion clinics and the Irish students, and therefore the case does not fall within the scope of EC law. The verdict left the impression that it is very difficult to assess whether a national law falls within the scope of the EC, and that a clear definition of the Court's relationship to the Court of Human Rights in Strasbourg would have offered better guidelines. In *Grogan*, however, the ruling was based on the fact that no commercial link existed between the students and the providers of a medical service. In the end an economic fact was used to settle an issue of morality and social and human rights. This did not do the case proper justice.

8

Checks and Balances

Checks on the European Court of Justice

Once in place, a court should be able to rule and act as independently as possible in interpreting and applying law. Throughout the ECJ's existence its judges in Luxembourg operated quietly outside the political limelight of Brussels. Granted, legal wrangles have occurred with national supreme courts that often criticized the establishment of a superior European legal order by the ECJ's case law, but, from an institutional perspective, no political player in the EU has ever questioned the authority of the ECJ. Given that every member state has to appoint one judge, one could assume that rulings tend to be in line with the national backgrounds of the judges. But past experience yields the overwhelming impression that judges do not vote in line with any political objectives of their member state governments. The ECJ, therefore, can be described as a beacon of judicial independence and, as such, gives great credit to the European project.

Checks on the European Parliament

As in any democratic system, the parliament is controlled by the citizens who vote the parliamentarians into power. As mentioned earlier, elections to the EP tend to have a much lower turnout than national elections, often producing different majorities than, for instance, an election to a national parliament would. This inconsistency and unpredictability might not be welcomed by the political elite, but it represents a vital form of direct democracy in a European Union which evidently prefers that EU officials are appointed by national governments rather than by direct public elections. The office of the Commission President is a good illustration of this point. More worrisome, however, are the low voter turnouts; this obviously suggests that the public has little political interest in EU affairs, which certainly undermines the public's influence over the one organization designed to represent the values and standards of the European citizen. Another hindrance to the performance of the EP is the organizational problems, most notably France's insistence on keeping the EP, at least partially, in Strasbourg. A complete relocation to Brussels would certainly improve the political effectiveness of the EP, but such a move would require unanimous agreement within the European Council.

A further problem is that the EP is still largely excluded from some policy areas, most notably foreign and security policies. On such vital matters, the representative organ of the citizens ought to be integrated more fully in the legislative process. On the other hand, some analysts argue that citizens are indeed represented, although only indirectly, as it is the Council of Ministers that can put its mark on legislation in these areas. Individual national ministers, after all, assumed their positions through proper democratic elections. But, following this argument to its logical conclusion, the EP's entire raison d'être could come into question. What is the point of a European Parliament with insufficient powers? Would it not be better to abolish the EP completely, and let national parliaments assume supervisory and legislative functions? At any rate, the European Parliament can have its powers increased only through a treaty change, which happened, for instance, with the Lisbon Treaty when the ordinary legislative procedure was introduced. But the final wording and approval of all is undertaken by the European Council, and it rarely happens that twenty-seven heads of government increase the powers of the very organization that is supposed to keep them in check on behalf of European citizens.

Checks on the Commission

Over the years the EP has significantly increased its controlling powers over the Commission. Although the EP has no voice in determining the exact responsibilities of the individual portfolios, it does have the power to dismiss the entire Commission (by a two-thirds majority vote). Also, as the appointment of the Barroso

Table 8.1. The Comitology System

Type of Acts	Interaction between EU actors	Policy Field
Delegated Act	Commission free to act Council of Ministers and EP with veto power	Sensitive areas (financial services, restricted substances in the environment, body scanners at airports)
Implementing Act		Routine issues
A: Examination procedure	Committee of national officials approve/reject with QMV	Trade
B: Advisory procedure	Commission free to act	Competition, mergers, state aid

Commission in 2004 demonstrated, the threat of an embarrassing dismissal can hang powerfully in the air.[1] But the EP cannot dismiss individual commissioners. Once the Commission President starts his five-year term, the Parliament pretty much has to go along with his personnel decisions. As a small token, however, Commission President Romano Prodi (1999–2004) agreed that, at the start of every tenure, every commissioner had to appear before the EP's plenum in Strasbourg for probative questions.

When implementing legislation, the Commission has to respect the rather complicated Comitology system which was subject to a drastic reform in the Lisbon Treaty. In the past, Comitology represented a complex system of committees, chaired by Commission officials and composed of national representatives from member state governments. These committees scrutinized executive acts by the Commission and thus monitored the executive powers of the commission by involving the member states in the process of policy implementation. Before Lisbon, Comitology consisted of five different committees, and depending on the policy in question member state officials might only have had an advisory function (for instance on competition issues), while on policy matters including health and EMU, it was the member states themselves that held the executive power.

Lisbon, however, removed these five committees altogether and categorized the implementation of policies along two lines: delegated and implemented acts (see Table 8.1). Lisbon also attempted to clarify a gray area that often undermines democratic governance: On the one hand, executive acts should simply concentrate on policy implementation based on prior legislative approval. On the other, we quite often see executive acts that represent a rather broad and not necessarily intended interpretation of legislation. A good example of this confluence between executive and legislative powers was the controversy over genetically modified food. The Commission argued that legislation on the Common Agricultural Policy gave it the right to make executive decisions with regard to GM food. The member states, however, reasoned that this issue had an altogether different quality and that the Commission required prior legislative approval before it could embark on implementing GM policies.

Table 8.2. Who Controls the Commission?

- European Parliament (by approving the entire team of commissioners)
- Comitology system
- Member states (by appointing commissioners)

The new Comitology therefore aimed to establish a clearer delineation of power (see Table 8.1). "Delegated acts" are used for sensitive policy areas including financial service regulation or body scanners at airports. In these areas, the Commission does not have to face any committees at all and can amend or delete any non-essential elements of the underlying legislative acts. The control function over the executive is exercised by the Council of Ministers and the European Parliament, which have the right to veto any decisions made by the Commission. Committees still remain in place for "implementing acts," which are reserved for routine policy areas such as agriculture or the market authorization of products. Implementing acts are further categorized into two types of procedures. Under the examination procedure, member state officials can approve or reject executive acts by the Commission with a qualified majority. This procedure is used, for instance, for trade issues. The advisory procedure applies to such policy areas as competition, state aid, and mergers. Here the commission continues to exercise a free reign and only has to inform member states without facing the threat of its actions being overruled.

The new system to a certain extent covered new ground. For the first time the European Parliament is included in the monitoring of executive powers. What is normal in any democratic system, in that the legislative has a controlling function over the executive, took sixty years to be implemented at EU level. Secondly, delegated acts are an entirely new form of interaction between the Commission, the member states, and the EP. Previously, the Commission had to liaise closely with member states before implementing policy. Now, the Lisbon Treaty favored a "sledgehammer style" of interaction in which the Commission is free to act, but can be roped back should its actions displease the EP and the member states. What is worrisome is the power of the Commission to delete or amend any "non-essential elements" of legislative acts, which is extraordinary, given that the Lisbon Treaty failed to offer a clarification of essential and non-essential elements. Despite these legal uncertainties, however, the Commission tends to communicate with other political actors prior to implementing policies in order to avoid a potentially embarrassing row between EU institutions.

Apart from the Comitology system member states, because of practical necessities, exert a degree of control over the Commission. With a staff of only some twenty-eight thousand, the Commission does not have its own customs, immigration, or veterinary services, or indeed any other public service that would help give real effect to EU legislation. Instead, the Commission relies heavily on the member states' civil services. Without the existence of national officials, it

Table 8.3. Who Controls the European Council?

- The President of the European Council
- The President of the European Commission
- The public

---

would be impossible to make the CAP work. Where legislation matters most—in factories, on farms, or at airports—the Commission depends entirely on national officials. This is another indicator of the unique nature of the EU as a complex web of supranational bodies and authorities supported by, and dependent on, national executive powers.

National governments, as noted above, have complete discretion in choosing their commissioners and ought to choose them, as the Treaty of Rome puts it, "on the grounds of their general competence." In reality, however, personal and political considerations determine the appointments as much as ability and merit. Appointments are too sensitive politically and bear too much political influence to be left to such idealist virtues as ability or merit. Indeed, nominees rarely come from outside the governing party. Often candidates are appointed to Brussels as a convenient political solution, since the future commissioner might simply be out of political contention for a domestic post.[2] Should commissioners aspire to a high political office after their stint in Brussels, they ought to be sensitive to domestic political developments and carefully try to avoid antagonizing the national governments that are their future masters (see Table 8.2).

Without question, commissioners are subject to intense pressure from their national governments and their national electorate, especially if they intend to return to a domestic political career. A line must be drawn, however, between upholding national interests and taking instructions from national governments. Upholding national interests is not necessarily counterproductive to European integration. The European Union thrives on contributions from several traditions and ideologies, whether economic, social, or political. A commissioner, via his or her member state government, can act as a crucial mediator for policy options that could enrich the Union's agenda.

Checks on the European Council

The European Council was not mentioned in the founding treaties, and so, from a strictly legal standpoint, the Council is not an institution of the EU. Its precise functions have gradually developed over time, and the Maastricht Treaty of 1993 describes the Council as a body above the EU, and therefore not subject to the constitutional checks and balances of the other institutions. Still, three points should be mentioned here.

First, the heads of state have to follow an agenda devised by the President of the European Council, and so member states cannot advance items of their own

Table 8.4. Who Controls the Council of Ministers?

- The public, indirectly, by voting for their head of government, who then appoints the individual ministers
- The Committee of Permanent Representatives (COREPER)

particular interest but must adhere to the issues identified by this newly created post. In the run-up to these summits there are consultations, even intergovernmental conferences, that prepare and shape the agenda of meetings, but, undoubtedly, the President of the European Council has considerable powers to shape the outcome of any summit.

Second, the Commission presidents and their vice presidents are invited to the summit meetings and, depending on their persona, stamina, and political reputation, can influence negotiations. Jacques Santer (president in 1994–99), Romano Prodi (1999–2004), and Jose Manual Barroso (2004–14) found it difficult to make their marks on summits, but Jacques Delors (1984–94) was able to shape the agenda, at least to some extent. One might recall the now legendary clashes between Delors and UK Prime Minister Thatcher. The summit, then, can be used to great advantage by a talented Commission President to seek support for the Commission's policies among the top power holders in Europe, surely an opportunity that no driven Commission President can resist (see Table 8.3).

Third, in today's world of intensive media coverage, heads of government and their ministers must always keep an eye on domestic politics and the way potential decisions could be received by the public and electorates. An illustration is the performance of the former British prime minister John Major in the 1990s. Trapped by his own Euroskeptic party and at least a partially Euroskeptic public, Major was forced to walk a tightrope between slowing down European integration and promoting economic policies at the EU level. Promoting European integration would have meant antagonizing his party and large segments of the electorate, but resisting European integration would have meant a loss of jobs and, again, a negative reception by elements of the British public. In the end his tenure was a disaster of unconstructive vacillation without a clear vision of Britain's place in Europe.

Checks on the Council of Ministers

An indirect control of the Council is exercised by the public of the member states, which elects their heads of government, who, in turn, form their cabinets with ministers participating in the respective councils (see Table 8.4). This, of course, is only an indirect form of control that is exacerbated by the fact that European politics still does not enjoy the same public attention as domestic politics. Neither journalists nor citizens follow the political process in Brussels as closely as they do their national agenda. This gap of information and interest is aggravated when Council meetings are held in private, behind closed doors, without the public or journalists present or with no television coverage, thus hiding European politics from media scrutiny.[3]

One could also argue that COREPER—the Committee of Permanent Representatives—controls the Council, since it sets the agenda and prepares and streamlines proposals for the final decision-making round in the Council meetings. The existence and functions of COREPER are little known outside Brussels. Yet it is an extremely powerful group and even more secretive than the Council of Ministers.[4] COREPER's ability to shape the Council's agenda and to influence decision making by categorizing items as either A (ready for automatic approval) or B (needs more discussion) illustrates its importance. But this system clearly is not democratic, as COREPER is not accountable to the electorate and is inaccessible to the public.

PART THREE

POLICIES

9

The Single Market and Competition

The founding fathers of the European Union envisaged the establishment of a Single Market—the free movement of goods, services, capital, and labor—as a crucial guarantor of peace, stability, and economic progress for a region recovering from the catastrophe of World War II. In the early nineteenth century the German philosopher Immanuel Kant argued in his essay, "Perpetual Peace," that trading nations do not go to war with one another simply because war would have a detrimental effect on profits. More than a century later the EU's original six member states set out to make Kant's dictum a practical reality. Article 2 of the Treaty of Rome of 1957, which established the European Economic Community (EEC), stated that its purpose was "to promote throughout the Community a harmonious development of economic activities, a continuous and balanced expansion, an increase in stability, an accelerated raising of the standard of living, and closer relations between the states belonging to it." But not until 1993 did the European Union fully realize the objective of the treaty. This chapter analyzes the reasons for this delay, how the European Commission managed to convince the member states of the extraordinary benefits that a Single Market could bring, and whether, some twenty years on, the initiative lived up to its promises. Areas and sectors currently earmarked for further European integration are also discussed. Finally, one must address the EU's competition policy which is aimed at preventing the emergence of distortions to the market, either through the establishment of monopolies or oligopolies, or through mergers and state aid. The issue gained further prominence during the credit crunch of 2008/2009, when governments across the EU intervened on a grand scale to prevent their economies from sliding even further into recession. The key issues here include:

1. *How does market regulation differ from redistribution?*
2. *Is the EU competition policy free-market or interventionist?*
3. *How did the credit crunch affect state aid provisions?*
4. *Why has the Commission gained so much power in the regulation of the Single Market?*

The Development of the Single Market Program

A truly single market would give EU citizens a wide choice of products and services from both their home country and from every other member state. Capital would freely move from banks in one member state to banks in other member states. A completed single market would give EU citizens the right to work and live anywhere inside the EU. In envisioning a single or common market, the EU planned to create a European sphere of economic activity that would rise above national regulations. However, events did not go according to plan.

Although, by 1968, tariffs and custom duties were all abolished within the EEC, the establishment of the four freedoms long remained an unfulfilled promise. The oil crises of 1973 and 1979, and the subsequent recessions, prompted some member states to adopt protectionist measures to shield their national markets and industries from global and even European competition. In the end a multitude of different product standards spread across the EU, with different national regulations governing the service sector, restrictions on capital mobility, and different standards for professional qualifications. All these national restrictions made trading across borders, not to mention settling in another member state, a difficult and sometimes impossible exercise. Despite an emphasis on reducing direct barriers to trade, indirect or national actions kept markets highly fragmented.

By the mid-1980s a different global environment forced the EU into a major reevaluation of the potential benefits of a truly single market. In the United States President Ronald Reagan had just embarked on an ambitious defense program aiming to protect the U.S. against nuclear attack by using satellite technology. As a result, military innovation spilled over into the civilian economy, and the U.S. became a global leader in such fields as computer or robotics technology. On the other side of the Pacific, Japan continued to expand its position as the world's leading provider of consumer products, ranging from television and audio equipment to cars. With advancing globalization, however, Europe was seen to be falling behind. Instead of offering products and services across Europe (as the Treaty of Rome had envisioned) industries were often confined to their own national markets, which had detrimental effects on innovation, efficiency, and profitability. Against the backdrop of Europe's increasing inability to compete with Japan or the United States, the Commission, as well as several member states (most notably Britain under Prime Minister Thatcher) and large European companies advocated new initiatives.

A significant advance toward a truly single market was achieved with the Commission White Paper of 1985. The White Paper argued for the introduction of qualified majority voting in the Council of Ministers (except on tax issues) so that agreement on certain issues could be achieved more easily than under the previous system of unanimity voting. More important, however, the White Paper planned for the completion of the EU Single Market by 1 January 1993. The member states merely had to implement into law 270 measures that were distributed over three areas: physical barriers, technical barriers, and tax barriers.

Physical barriers, the Commission argued, should not only be reduced but should be eliminated. Goods and citizens should not to be held up at frontiers.[1] Technical barriers, too, should be removed; goods should be able to be sold anywhere in the EC as long as they were lawfully produced in one member state, and as long as the health and safety of the public were not compromised. An exchange of financial products, such as insurance policies, should be made possible, and transport and passenger services, still largely controlled by national governments, should be liberalized. Finally, currencies should move freely across borders, and professional qualifications should be uniform throughout the EU.

Regarding fiscal barriers, the Commission did not argue for uniformity in income or corporate taxes, as the tax system of any member state is also a moral value system that societies use to express their objectives. Societies with high taxes, such as the Scandinavian countries, have reached a consensus to finance public goods (education, transport, health care, and pensions) through the state budget, whereas societies with lower taxes, such as the UK under Margaret Thatcher, supported reduced state spending and greater individual responsibility. Thus making the tax structure uniform across the EU would mean unifying value systems and societal agreements that have developed over a long period. The Commission therefore concentrated mostly on indirect taxation in the form of a value-added tax (VAT) on goods that differed significantly from state to state. With VAT affecting prices, different VAT rates represented a trade distortion. To remedy this, the Commission proposed a narrow band of VAT across the EU of a 5 percent difference between the highest and the lowest rates.[2]

The Benefits of a Single Market

The Commission needed to convince all member states that eliminating national barriers to the four freedoms would ultimately be worthwhile. Indeed, the expected benefits for member states were too significant to resist, and in 1988 a steering group, headed by the senior Commission official Paolo Cecchini, issued a report predicting that the GDP across the EU would rise by 5 percent or more mainly because of lower costs for business transactions. Cecchini also emphasized that the Single Market would create 2 million more jobs. In that same year the consulting firm Price Waterhouse was even more optimistic, predicting a rise of 7 percent in the GDP, with 5 million more jobs created and a drop in prices of 4.5 percent. The Cecchini Report warned that the failure to implement would cause member states to lose money as a result of extra costs (which Cecchini termed the costs of non-Europe). These extra costs, the Commission bluntly stated, would amount to 200 billion Euros. Against these powerful arguments, national governments would indeed have been foolish if they did not implement the 270 measures and adhere to the seven-year deadline of 1993.

In 2003 the Commission took stock and analyzed whether the Single Market program had really delivered on its promises. In retrospect, the analysis showed fewer gains than the Cecchini Report had predicted, but the results still justified the massive regulatory program. The Commission estimated that, because of the Single Market, in 2002 the GDP was 1.8 percent higher, and around 2.5 million additional jobs had been created. These improvements are not necessarily a benefit of the Single Market, however. The first ten years of the Single Market coincided in part with a worldwide economic boom, and it is difficult to judge precisely whether the GDP rise was a result of increased global trade or increased intra-EU trade.

Nonetheless, the final verdict on the success of the Single Market must take into account a number of positive developments. First, the EU continues to witness a large increase in cross-border mergers, which testifies to the easing of national regulations regarding the movement of capital. Additional cross-border mergers also indicate that many businesses accept the whole of the EU as their sphere of economic activity. Second, the EU benefited from a massive fourfold increase in foreign direct investment (FDI), which may be regarded as an indicator of the attractiveness Europe now enjoys in the global business community. Third, member states prefer to trade with one another; only 36 percent of the overall EU trade volume is done with non-EU countries, whereas intra-EU trade accounts for 64 percent. Surely the removal of barriers had worked.[3] A fourth positive result was that national firms were clearly oriented toward a more competitive European and global climate. Through the Single Market, companies such as Deutsche Bank, Nokia, and Ciba-Geigy could use their European base as a springboard for entering the global market. Fifth, increased competition led to increased rationalization and economies of scale, resulting in more choice, higher quality, and, above all,

Table 9.1.Transposition Deficit of Single Market Legislation by
Member State's Number of Directives, as of November 2011

Member State	Number of Directives	Member State	Number of Directives
Belgium	30	Greece, Romania	17
Italy, Poland	29	Germany	15
Cyprus	28	France, Spain	14
Czech Republic	26	Bulgaria, Lithuania, Estonia	13
Portugal	23	Slovakia, Sweden	8
Austria	21	Denmark	7
Hungary, Luxembourg	20	Latvia	5
Slovenia	19	Ireland	4
UK , Finland, Netherlands	18	Malta	2

Source: European Commission, Directorate Internal Market, Internal Market scoreboard No. 22, November 2011.

significantly reduced prices.[4] And finally, in 2002, 15 million Europeans had taken advantage of the free movement of people and were living in another member state.[5]

A Work in Progress

Although the deadline for establishing the Single Market was at the end of 1992, the EU still produces new legislation aimed at either new product standards or services (such as harmonizing mobile-phone technology) or certain sectors that were not addressed previously. By 2011, for instance, the total number of directives related to the Single Market had risen to 1,388.[6] Outstanding European legislation still needing ratification into national law always remains. Here the Single Market scoreboard of the European Commission[7] is an effective way to monitor the progress and performance of individual member states by indicating their relative performance in implementing Single Market legislation (see Table 9.1). Applying pressure on the member states has worked well, as the EU average deficit has steadily fallen from 6.3 percent in 1997 to 1.2 percent in November 2011. The enlargement of 2004 resulted in a momentary rise to 7 percent, but this dropped to 0.7 percent in November 2009.

The Single Market has had a substantial impact on the liberalization of air transport, triggering the explosion in budget airline services as well as in telecommunications, and, to a lesser extent, in electricity, gas, and railways. The most notable program to close the gap was the so-called Lisbon Strategy, which was developed under the Presidency of Portugal in March 2000 to implement economic, social, and environmental renewal by 2010. According to Lisbon, the EU aspired to

Table 9.2. Aims of the Lisbon Strategy, 2000–2013

Liberalize telecommunication, gas, and electricity
Establish an EU-wide patent
Liberalize postal systems and rail transport
Rationalize the road tax system
Reduce red tape in the labor market
Aim for pension portability
Raise the employment rate
Harmonize corporation taxes
Promote the use of the internet and e-commerce
Complete the Single Market in financial services
Open up government procurement
Reduce state subsidies

become the "world's most competitive and dynamic knowledge-based economy." But in contrast to the U.S., Europe's emphasis is not only on growth but also on social and environmental cohesion. As targets, Lisbon set out an ambitious agenda, illustrated in Table 9.2. As the vehicle for Lisbon, the EU agreed on the so-called open method of coordination, which calls for a collaboration between the twenty-seven member states and the Commission.[8]

Until 2009, however, progress was slow, and some national governments blamed this on the overall economic downturn at the beginning of this decade, as well as on the credit crisis of 2008–2009. But one also has to look at the nature of the Lisbon Strategy. It was largely associated with the "Anglo-Saxon" model of achieving high levels of employment and growth through deregulation and trade liberalization without worrying much about potential income inequalities. In other words, Lisbon was very much about supply-side economic reforms, which contrast sharply with the continental model of economic governance that advocates higher minimum wages, generous welfare benefits, and extensive worker rights, but also suffers from growing unemployment levels. The problem for many national governments in the implementation of Lisbon was therefore straightforward. In the age of globalization, politicians are facing an increasingly skeptical public that seems reluctant to give up much of the welfare state. In the spring of 2005 French President Jacques Chirac had already described neoliberalism (i.e., the Anglo-Saxon model) as the new communism, and it was always unlikely that continental member states are willing to partially dismantle their own postwar models. Indeed, in 2009, Prime Minister Fredrik Reinfeldt of Sweden, whose country had the Presidency at the time, stated that with only a year remaining the Lisbon process had been a failure. A reevaluation of priorities and objectives seemed necessary, and the Commission argued that future priorities ought to include sustainable development (which it termed "'green growth'") innovation and education in a new agenda rebranded the "'EU 2020 strategy.'"

Apart from Lisbon, the Commission frequently sets further priorities when fine-tuning the Single Market to new developments. As such, in its Single Market strategy, in 2003–2006, the Commission concentrated on removing obstacles to trade in goods and services, and on cutting red tape, tackling tax barriers, and expanding procurement possibilities. These objectives emerged against the backdrop of the sluggish progress of Lisbon, the 2004 enlargement, and the economic malaise, as well as the demographic challenge of an ageing population. In light of the credit crisis, in 2008 the Commission advocated safer financial products as well as clearer information for citizens about their Single Market rights. This 2007–2008 Single Market review also focused on stronger contractual rights, the removal of unjustified obstacles to cross-border buying, as well as the introduction of simpler company rules, particularly for small and medium sized enterprises (SMEs).

The politically most controversial adjustment to Single Market rules has arguably been the establishment of an integrated services market. The so-called Boltkestein Directive[9] aimed at completely liberalizing services across the EU, which provided 75 percent of jobs and 66 percent of the GDP. The Commission argued that freeing this market from national regulations, such as labor laws, registration procedures, and professional standards, would lead to increased competition across borders, followed by better and cheaper services. In reality, this would have meant that a company based in, say, Poland and subject to the domestic labor laws of that country could have made a contract in Germany, for example, and sent its workforce there without being subject to the much more stringent German labor or workplace regulations. Thus some member governments feared that the Boltkestein Directive would result in a regulatory race to the bottom, with member states that have the least amount of social protection (and therefore the lowest costs for businesses) gaining a distinct competitive advantage. It therefore came as no surprise that the Commission's proposal was watered down by the member states and by the European Parliament in order to avoid "social dumping." As such, services of "general economic interest," such as mail, water, electricity, and waste, must be registered and taxed in the country where the service is delivered. On the other hand, national authorities continue to have the right to regulate social services, gambling, lotteries, health care, and other "non-economic services of general interest."[10]

The Commission also managed to close a much-abused regulatory vacuum in the field of mobile phone services. Before Commissioner Viviane Reding (2004–2009) took on the might of the telecommunications industry, mobile-phone users were the victims of often outrageous charges when using their mobile phones in another EU country. Although calls within one country were subject to national regulations, no regulation was in place governing mobile phone calls that were made to and from another EU country. These so-called roaming charges—a fee charged by a company for connecting someone's call to a mobile phone abroad—varied enormously. More striking, fees for downloading data across borders were also largely unregulated, a fact brought to the attention of the European media when a German businessman working in France downloaded a movie onto his mobile phone, for which the French operator charged some fifty thousand Euros. The mobile phone regulations of 2007 and 2008 put an end to this madness, and we now have unified price structures that govern incoming calls, receiving calls, and data downloading.[11]

Safeguarding the Single Market: Competition Policy

A coherent competition policy aims to create a system of undistorted competition between economic players by preventing monopolies and oligopolies. Competition policy refers to the establishment of fair rules of the economic game, and thus it places constraints on the behavior of economic actors. Exceptions are allowed so as to guarantee the reliable provision of vital goods and services (in the EU, for instance, in agriculture and transport) or to safeguard the public interest (for example, the restrictive selling of alcohol in Sweden). Monopolies and oligopolies can harm consumers, since a market dominated by only a few players may result in inflated prices and inferior quality. In its efforts to ensure fair competition, EU policy makers are constantly faced with the problem that every member state is responsible for implementing EU policy while at the same time protecting its own national business interests.

EU competition policy is based on a number of treaty and other legal provisions, with the key elements listed in Table 9.3. The Commission's paramount goal is to prevent individual actors or groups of actors from abusing a dominant market position (Articles 82 and 81, respectively), defined as a market share of at least 50 percent. Similar to the U.S. antitrust laws, the Commission is entitled to impose restrictions on economic actors. For example, the Commission imposed a fine of 75 million Euros on the Swedish company Tetra Pak, one of the world's market leaders in packaging liquid foods, with an EU market share of 95 percent, for unfair marketing, contract, and pricing policies.

The most notorious case of recent years, however, has been the Commission's pursuit of Microsoft. Competition Commissioner Mario Monti (1999–2004) launched an investigation into how the company controlled access to its Windows operating system (which is installed on 95 percent of the world's desktop computers and 80 percent of corporate servers). Monti's successor, Neelie Kroes (2004–9), concluded that Microsoft restricted access and held back information on Windows, which made it difficult for other software producers to come up with competitive products. Frustrated at delays in granting easier access, the Commission started to impose heavy fines, totaling 1.7 billion Euros, until Microsoft finally complied.[12]

Table 9.3. The Competition Policy

- Treaty Article 81: Agreements between undertakings (i.e., companies) which may affect trade between member states and which have as their object or effect the prevention, restriction, or distortion of competition . . . are prohibited.
- Treaty Article 82: Any abuse by one or more undertakings of a dominant position . . . shall be prohibited.
- Regulation 1/2003 (formerly known as 17/62): The Commission is responsible for ensuring Articles 81 and 82.
- Treaty Article 86: Extends Articles 81 and 82 to public enterprises.

EU Competition policy has correctly been defined as the "first supranational policy,"[13] as it grants member states limited advisory capacity in the Commission's executive decisions. By 2000 the European Commission's caseload had grown so heavy that Regulation 17 was reformed to include the application of European law by national authorities and a shift from a before-the-fact notification procedure to an after-the-fact control system. This meant that national competition authorities became highly "Europeanized" as agencies operating under European law, and that the European Commission would concentrate its resources on "hard-core" cases while monitoring the application of European law among national competition authorities.

Avoiding Market Dominance: Merger Policy

When the EU's merger policy was established in 1989, it was complicated by the fact that mergers at a national level were organized according to different national rules. The body ruling over mergers in Germany, for instance, is politically independent, and its decisions are rarely overruled by the government. Rulings in the UK, in contrast, are made by a quasi-governmental institution, the Office for Fair Trading. For a long time the Commission investigated only mergers that affected enterprises across borders, unless the merged company's annual turnover was 5 billion Euros (worldwide) or 2.5 billion (EU wide). In these cases, even if the companies were from the same member state, the Commission had to grant its approval. Nowadays a different procedure has emerged, which sees the Directorate General for Competition investigating cases even if the merging companies come from one member state, and even if the above-mentioned financial thresholds have not been reached. Member state authorities have therefore been reduced to executing the EU's competition law, and high-profile cases will always have to seek the ultimate approval of Brussels.

The Commission bases its rulings on whether effective competition is preserved (i.e., whether a dominant market position of 50 percent or more might be established as a consequence of the merger), while acknowledging other factors such as technological development and economic progress.

The fall of national barriers as a result of the Single Market program, along with the introduction of a single European currency, has caused a steady rise in the number of mergers. Between September 1990 and February 2010 the Commission issued verdicts on 4,317 applications, but it only blocked less than one per cent of mergers. In 133 cases, the applicants themselves abandoned the merger during the Commission's review. In 1994, for instance, the Commission blocked the merger of Deutsche Telecom, Bertelsmann (one of the world's biggest media providers), and Kirch (a German pay TV company) on the grounds that the new company, MSG Media Service, would gain a dominant market position for pay TV and cable networks. On the other hand, in 1992 the Commission approved the merger of Nestlé and Perrier, but only after Nestlé agreed to surrender control of 20 percent of the French mineral water market. Likewise, in 2010, the Commission approved the merger of the mobile network operators T-Mobile and Orange. The new company became the UK's biggest mobile-phone company, with more than 30 million customers (out of a UK population of 60 million). In return, it agreed to allow other companies to use its wireless spectrum which is used for fast broadband services.

Keeping a Level Playing Field: State Aid Provisions

As a general rule, state aid, or the financial support of private or public enterprises through public funds, usually distorts competition, since publicly funded economic players generally have a competitive advantage over those not receiving public assistance. Article 87 has provisions, however, allowing companies to receive financial support from the state or publicly owned organizations. These provisions allow public funding under the following circumstances:

- The state aid has a social character and is granted to an individual without discrimination against others.
- The state aid compensates for damage caused by natural disasters.
- In the case of eastern Germany, state aid is granted in order to overcome the economic and social disparities between the former communist East Germany and the former West Germany.

Other exceptions may be made where aid would promote the economic development of an area with a low standard of living, execute an important project of common European interest, or, as a final legislative loophole, promote certain economic activities.

State aid is widespread and, prior to the credit crunch of 2008, accounted for around 100 billion Euros annually. The Commission receives about six hundred notifications and investigates another one hundred unregistered cases but rarely voices objections. Reasons often cited for providing state aid are economic circumstances such as the preservation of jobs, or when the aid contributes to EU objectives such as environmental protection, and social and regional cohesion. The Commission was adamantly opposed, however, in the case of the French government and its financial support of 3.5 billion Euros for Air France in 1994. Because the airline was a prestigious symbol of French national pride, the Commission had to carefully avoid antagonizing one of its key allies in the drive for further European integration. However, DG Competition, which makes decisions on competition law cases including infringements, mergers, and state aid, ruled that this cash injection had to be the last of its kind and imposed the condition that the money could only be used for restructuring purposes, not for anticompetitive measures such as ticket price cuts. Despite the restrictions, the ruling outraged private airlines, most notably British Airways.

The credit crisis, however, saw widespread infringement on previously agreed-upon state aid provisions. Given the severity of the downturn, governments across the EU pumped unprecedented amounts of money into their economies to prevent an even deeper slide into recession. Germany, for instance, departed from its former model of *Ordnungspolitik* (where the state fine-tunes the market without controlling it), in favor of a more proactive handling of the crisis. The government orchestrated wage settlements and invested eighty billion Euros to stimulate demand. It also established the "Germany Economy Fund" worth 100 billion Euros. In France the former model of *Dirigisme*—an active state intervention in the economy—resurfaced with astonishing consequences. President Sarkozy secured 6 billion Euros to rescue the car makers Renault and Peugeot/Citroên, and never tired of assuring the public that saving jobs through government intervention was his prime motive. Ireland—formerly referred to as the Celtic Tiger—became one of the Eurozone's weakest links. By 2008 Ireland endured a severe banking crisis with government bailouts, nationalizations, tax increases, and budget cuts. Together with the U.S., Great Britain had been recognized as the country with the most proactive approach to crisis management. The government set up 500 billion pounds (around 600 billion Euros) of rescue packages and 37 billion pounds for bailouts of failing businesses, while taking responsibility for 260 billion pounds worth of risky assets. The country also followed a policy of quantitative easing (i.e., the central bank's purchase of government bonds) and 20 billion worth of stimulus packages.[14] One may well argue that these massive state interventions were justified. Given the enormous challenges that European economies had to face, the state aid certainly had a social character with its desperate attempt to safeguard jobs. It therefore came as little surprise that the Commission kept a rather low profile—a smart move given that calls for tighter spending would have antagonized a European public that was confronted with job losses, higher taxes, and reduced wages. A return to a level of state aid that was prevalent before 2008 is, in any case, a necessity, given that the budgets of the member states had been stretched to the breaking point.

Further Implications of the Single Market

A number of key debates that must be kept in mind when assessing information on the Single Market can be grouped under four general issues.

1. *Why was the Single Market program launched in the mid-1980s?* As noted above, the Single Market program, as well as the Single European Act that laid the institutional foundations for economic policy reform, emerged in the context of different interests demanding liberalization of trade between member states. For some, the Single Market initiative represents a major triumph for the European Commission in that it served as a "policy entrepreneur" in shaping the agenda and pushing it through. Others point to the considerable importance of big business, which demanded not only a single market but also the development of a merger policy regime designed to resolve previous legal uncertainties. In many ways the Single Market program especially targeted those sectors where trade flows across national borders were particularly high. And, finally, for some, the Single Market program represents little else than the convergence of national political preferences. These debates point to the different governmental approaches in Germany, the UK, and France, suggesting that the Single Market, in various ways, extends domestic economic policy agendas as well as responses to domestic business demands.

2. *The EU as a regulatory state.* Regulation is the key mode of governance in the European Union. Rules give member states and businesses a predictable foundation on which to base their transactions, while they are monitored by a "neutral referee" (i.e., the European Commission). Like any organization, however, the Commission has its own self-interest. Within the EU's institutional setup, the Commission has very little power to demand additional financial resources, and even where it has appropriate funds, these remain largely connected to highly fixed schemes, for instance, the support of farmers through the Common Agricultural Policy. Given this lack of financial muscle to shape policies, the Commission has used regulation in an attempt to maximize its power.

3. *Deregulation or re-regulation?* Many have feared the deregulatory consequences of a single market. The big question, then, is whether the Single Market advanced the cause of negative integration (the removal of national barriers) over positive integration (the creation of new policies at the European level). In many ways, this refers back to the old dualism of the supranational character of EU law, which emphasizes economic freedoms versus intergovernmental policy making that blocks attempts at "positive integration." At first sight, one should expect "negative integration" to be more predominant. What is widely known as the

Delaware effect predicts that member states will seek to attract industry by offering a low-cost base for production. Firms will therefore move to the place where they can produce in the cheapest possible manner. As all member states compete to attract investment, a spiral of deregulation emerges, resulting in a "race to the bottom." But such a race has hardly been in evidence. Instead, what has emerged are relatively high environmental standards, owing particularly to the political preferences of large and rich member states, as well as "product standards" that visibly alter the quality of the good being produced. Even the area of "process standards," such as labor regulation, has witnessed an emphasis on defining minimum standards rather than a race to the bottom. The picture that emerges from the different sectoral experiences is actually one of far higher diversity than a simple "negative" versus "positive" integration argument would suggest.

4. *What has been the impact at the national level?* The evidence from across policy domains and member states suggests that there has been considerable and persistent diversity rather than a "convergence" of different starting points toward a unified policy. As shown in Table 9.1, some member states, more than others, have proved resistant to the complete implementation of the Single Market program. Also, member states have sometimes applied substantial creativity in interpreting EU law. For example, EU law that was meant to liberalize road haulage across member states led Italy to take a far more restrictive approach to cross-border traffic. These experiences suggest the pivotal importance of national administrations in interpreting and implementing EU law in their own jurisdictions.

The Single Market, one of the key achievements of the European Union, has largely been a program of "re-regulation" and not "deregulation." Even measures that have supported the liberalization of economic activities, such as increased competition in telecommunications, require a substantial number of rules, in many ways even more rules than the previous age of protected national markets. In this regime of "re-regulation," the European Commission has played a key role as policy entrepreneur in shaping the policy agenda and seeking to maximize its influence over the substance of policy. Finally, the Single Market has not led to uniform economic policies across member states or policy domains. Far from it. Indeed, the economic landscape is characterized by a regulatory patchwork with different member states choosing different strategies to respond to the Single Market and with the European Commission choosing different strategies for different policy domains. In many ways the Single Market continues to be far from single.

10

Regional Policy and Cohesion

Cohesion intends to close the prosperity gap between rich and poor, or, more specifically, it is the process of reducing economic and social disparities between regions. The EU has 268 regions, 81 in the 12 new member states and 187 in the old EU-15. Some regions are simply synonymous with established historical entities, such as Catalonia in Spain, Tuscany in Italy, or Bavaria in Germany, but regions had to be created in countries without a federalist tradition, such as the UK. Thus Britain has the South West region, which has no historical precedent. A region ought to represent a coherent, geographical, administrative, and, above all, economic entity. The EU measures the wealth of a region based on its GDP per capita. Three questions surround the current picture of cohesion:

1. *Is EU cohesion simply a side payment to buy support for European integration?*
2. *Has EU cohesion reduced economic disparities in the EU?*
3. *Should the EU be concerned with cohesion at all?*
4. *Why were some countries (such as Ireland) able to use their cohesion money effectively to promote economic growth, whereas others (most notably Greece) were not?*

The Rationale behind Cohesion

Why does the EU's cohesion policy focus on the economic development of regions and not of individual member states? Cynics would argue that the former offers the European Commission an elevated position because it is able to bypass the authority of national governments by directly communicating with regional authorities. More realistically, however, the emphasis on regions as economic units is explained by the fact that some member states are simply too big to make one unified approach toward economic development a practical solution. For instance, countries such as Spain have a wide inner cohesion gap. On the one hand, Catalonia has considerable foreign direct investment and attracts high-tech businesses, whereas Andalusia suffers from high unemployment and a weak infrastructure. Both regions are in Spain, but each demands a completely different approach to foster further economic development. The emphasis on regions, therefore, is a practical necessity and not a supranational plot to undermine national sovereignty.

Cohesion represents a desirable goal for any given society for three reasons. First, from an economic perspective, in a liberal market economy market forces alone cannot solve long-standing regional problems; the market will always go where the most affluent consumers are and where the highest profit margins are to be expected. Across Europe, one often sees a core with a very active and successful economy surrounded by a periphery incapable of reaching comparable standards of living. Underutilized resources in the periphery, mainly human capital, could significantly contribute to growth and productivity if used more efficiently, which is the precise aim of cohesion. Second, from a social perspective, attempts to reduce the long-standing trend of people moving away from the periphery and into core urban areas could result in fewer urban problems such as overcrowding, traffic congestion, and crime. Moreover, efforts to preserve rural communities as well as cultural and social traditions seem worthwhile against the backdrop of the streamlining trends of globalization. And, third, from a political perspective, one might argue that every member of a society should have the possibility of sharing a country's wealth. Any political system able to distribute wealth in a just manner will enhance its democratic legitimacy.

Why should the European Union tackle such idealistic objectives? Cohesion and closing the gap between rich and poor would result in a more unified Europe, which is certainly in line with the ideals that brought the European project into existence some sixty years ago. Cohesion could also compensate for the negative effects of other EU policies, particularly the Common Agricultural Policy that mainly benefits large-scale producers, whereas the small-business farmers, so prevalent in Greece, Ireland, Spain, Southern Italy, and Portugal, find it hard to achieve acceptable standards of living. Another example is the Single Market initiative; ever since the Single European Act was signed in 1986, economic activity has tended to concentrate on the so-called blue banana,[1] with outlying regions missing out. On the other hand, growth and economic prosperity in disadvantaged

Table 10.1. Financial Breakdown of the Cohesion Policy, 2007–2013

Objective	Share	Amount (in billion Euros at 2004 prices)
1. Convergence	81.9%	252.349
2. Regional competitiveness and employment	15.7%	48.375
3. Territorial cooperation	2.4%	7.395
Total		308.119

Source: European Commission, Directorate Regional Policy

regions would lead to reduced unemployment and higher tax revenues for the state. And because the EU budget is the sum of national contributions in the region of around 1 percent of every member state's GDP, the EU has a vested interest in spreading prosperity. Most important, however, is that the EU is the only entity in the position to tackle cohesion. With bilateral aid the exception rather than the norm, poorer member states and their regions depend on support from Brussels.

How Does the EU Implement Cohesion?

Cohesion is organized around a number of funds and the process can get complicated, as often happens when money is at stake. Any investigation of how cohesion works will encounter a multitude of funds, some with confusing names and most with unique program objectives and their own bureaucratic jargon (see Table 10.1).

In making its financial projections for 2000–2006, the EU's cohesion policy did not properly address the integration of twelve new and largely poor countries. With the enlargement rounds of 2004 and 2007, the current multiannual budget for 2007–2013 had to consider the vastly changing circumstances of a Union that had never before witnessed such a wide gulf in prosperity and development. In July 2004 the Commission published its first proposal arguing for funding to be concentrated only on the neediest regions. Brussels argued for an increase to 336 billion Euros—about one-third of the EU's budget—which was still only the same share spent on cohesion in the previous financial projections for 2000–2006. Further, the Commission intended to simplify the program structure by dividing the entire pot of money into three distinct spending categories.[2]

The European Council meeting of December 2005 largely approved the Commission's proposal. After much negotiating, the member states agreed to set a financial ceiling for cohesion at 308.119 billion Euros, somewhat less than the Commission wanted. Cohesion in the EU is now allocated to three areas:

• Objective 1: 81.9 percent is for *Convergence* projects in the poorest regions to reduce the gap between the poorer and richer regions[3]

- Objective 2: 15.7 percent is for *Regional Competitiveness and Employment* projects related to innovation, sustainable development, greater accessibility, and job-training projects[4]
- Objective 3: The remaining 2.4 percent goes to *European Territorial Cooperation* projects to achieve broader cooperation between frontier regions, including regions bordering non-EU territory[5]

A further simplification was to reduce the number of financial vehicles to three: the European Regional Development Fund (ERDF), the European Social Fund (ESF), and the Cohesion Fund.[6] The ERDF is used to reduce regional disparities by supporting research, innovation, environmental protection, and risk prevention, with the strongest emphasis on infrastructure. The ESF focuses on human resources by promoting skills, access to and participation in the labor market, and social inclusion. The Cohesion Fund is exclusively for poorer member states with a GDP of less than 90 percent of the EU average;[7] together with the ERDF, the fund contributes to multiannual investment programs in transport infrastructure and environmental protection (see Table 10.2).

How Is Money Distributed?

Cohesion in the EU requires that all projects adhere to three principles, regardless of the fund they relate to. These include:

1. *Concentration.* Funds must be spent primarily on areas that fulfill one of the three objectives of the structural funds, namely, to concentrate resources on regions with the greatest needs.
2. *Connection.* Funds should improve the connection of peripheral regions with growth centers through infrastructure and access to services.
3. *Cooperation.* Projects should be implemented within the triangle of the Commission, regions, and national governments, thereby bringing together different actors working together across administrative boundaries.

Arguably the most crucial player in the distribution of financial support is the European Council, or Summit, which determines the allocation of funds and the policy objectives. It also sets the financial limits and decides, in often acrimonious debates, the amount of money each member state will receive.[8] It is then up to each member state to divide the funds between its own regions. Countries might use cohesion money to finance thematic programs covering the whole country (such as environment or transport), or they might concentrate on individual regions to which they channel a majority of their allocation. The Commission, however, cannot influence a member state's decision on how and where to spend cohesion money.

Table 10.2. The EU's Budget, 2007–2013 (in billion Euro)

Budget Heading	Purpose	Total
1A: Competitiveness for Growth and Employment	Lisbon Strategy, research and technology, education and training, and nuclear de-commissioning	72.010
1B: Cohesion for Growth and Employment	Cohesion Policy	308.119
2: Preservation and Management of Natural Resources	Agriculture, rural development, fisheries, and environment	252.460
3A: Freedom, Security, and Justice	Asylum, immigration, border control, cross-border problems, terrorism, organized crime, and judicial cooperation	6.630
3B: Other Internal Policies	Culture, youth, audiovisual matters, and health and consumer protection	3.640
4: The EU as a Global Partner	Global security, pre-accession stability, and development and economic cooperation, European neighborhood, humanitarian aid, and macro financial assistance	50.010
5: Administration		50.300
Others		122.194
Total		865.363

Each region shoulders the responsibility for getting projects started, but first each must design the project, identify partner organizations, develop an implementation plan, draft a budget, and then lobby its national government to approve the project. The project is then passed to the European Commission, which starts a close dialogue with the regional authorities over funding, organization, and planning.[9]

It is important to realize that the EU does not entirely fund projects but only offers to make up the needed difference. A considerable share of the costs must be met by local, regional, or national sources, and most projects receive a contribution from Brussels of around 50 percent. Also, funding must be delivered through multiannual development programs. One-off funding for projects does not exist. Instead, specific projects must fit into a wider strategy. When assessing the projects, the Commission checks on a number of criteria that can make or break a proposed project. A project ought to create long-term, sustainable jobs. It also should improve the overall infrastructure of a region, not necessarily just through roads, harbors, airports, and rail links but also by improving communication. All this, of course, must be done in a manner that does not harm the environment but might even improve it. Projects offering economic diversity by integrating elements of business, civil society, and academia will also improve their prospects for funding. Finally, the criteria of competitiveness and enterprise are applied to cutting-edge projects using novel ideas and new approaches that will have long-term commercial viability.

The Challenge of Enlargement

With the accession of twelve new member states in 2004 and 2007 the EU population grew by 128 million people, or around 32 percent, to 485 million. Most of these new EU citizens live in regions with a GDP of less than 75 percent of the EU average, thus falling under Objective One status. But even among the new member states, a widespread gap exists. For instance, in 2011, Cyprus had reached 92 percent of the EU's average prosperity levels, while Bulgaria and Romania lingered at the bottom of the table with 45 percent and 49 percent, respectively (see Table 10.3). With the integration of Bulgaria and Romania, the EU's GDP per capita in 2007 had actually dropped by around 18 percent relative to the EU's original fifteen-member states.

Given this widened cohesion gap, it seemed astonishing that the EU made no special arrangements when the financial perspective of 2000–2006 was agreed upon at a summit in Berlin in March 1999. Back then, enlargement was still deemed a distant possibility. In fact, the EU-15 still believed that, were any countries to be added, perhaps only five candidate countries (Poland, Hungary, the Czech Republic, Estonia, and Slovenia) would make the grade in the medium-term future. In Berlin, therefore, the member states agreed to offer relatively modest financial assistance, delivered through various programs, amounting to 21.8 billion Euros for the years 2000–2006, or around 3 billion Euros per year.[10] Already prior to Berlin, Europe Agreements had been signed with all candidate countries to gradually establish free trade and monitor the implementation of the acquis communautaire. The candidate countries were also invited to participate in existing EU programs for education, training, the environment, transport, and research. Brussels also established the Technical Assistance Information Exchange Instrument (TAIEX), which delivers information on all aspects of the acquis communautaire through seminars and conferences. Finally, a twinning program was launched, in which member states offered the secondment of their civil servants and advisers to the accession countries.

By 2002, however, it became clear that the surprisingly speedy progress of the candidate countries would permit ten states to join in 2004. The EU therefore was forced to somehow find the resources in its current seven-year budget to establish further financial programs. At the Copenhagen summit in December 2002, the member states agreed on a new financial formula and increased the total volume of funds available to the candidate countries to 9.9 billion Euros in 2004, which rose to 14.9 billion in 2006.

Does the Cohesion Policy Work?

Cohesion in the EU is torn between politics and policies. In policy terms, funding should be focused on backward areas requiring support. But politics dictates that cohesion must be supported by a majority of member states. Thus we find a wide

Table 10.3. GDP per Inhabitant (in Purchasing Power Standards)

	2006	2011
EU 27	100	100
Euro Area	109	108
Luxembourg	272	274
Netherlands	131	131
Austria	124	129
Ireland	145	127
Sweden	121	126
Denmark	124	125
Germany	116	120
Finland	115	116
Belgium	118	115
United Kingdom	120	108
France	109	107
Italy	104	101
Spain	105	99
Cyprus	91	92
Slovenia	88	84
Malta	77	83
Greece	93	82
Czech Republic	77	80
Portugal	76	77
Slovakia	63	73
Estonia	65	67
Hungary	63	66
Poland	52	65
Lithuania	55	62
Latvia	52	58
Romania	38	49
Bulgaria	36	45

Note: Purchasing Power Standards (PPS) is an artificial currency unit that interprets statistical data in line with the differing costs of living in the various member states.
Source: Eurostat, 2012009

Table 10.4. Regions with the Highest and Lowest GDP per Inhabitant, 2009 (in PPS)

Highest GDP		Lowest GDP	
Inner London (UK)	332	Sud-Vest Oltenia (Romania)	36
Luxembourg	266	Yuzhen tzentralen (Bulgaria)	31
Brussels Belgium)	223	Severen tzentralen (Bulgaria)	29
Hamburg (Germany)	188	Nord-Est (Romania)	29
Bratislava (Slovakia)	178	Severozapaden (Bulgaria)	27

Note: EU 27 = 100.
Source: Eurostat, 2012.

range of funds that also caters to the supposedly richer regions in the "old" EU of fifteen member states, which prompts observers to remark that the Cohesion Policy gives "something for everyone." The policy problem, however, is substantial. Before the enlargement of 2004, 22 percent of EU citizens (some 80 million people) lived in regions with a GDP of less than 75 percent of the EU average, but, with enlargement to Central and Eastern Europe, economic disparities increased even more to the point where over 30 percent of EU citizens now live in areas with Objective One status. As Table 10.4 shows, the gap between the five richest and the five poorest regions is also quite considerable. Furthermore, regarding employment, the extreme difference between regions is illustrated by the mere 2.7 percent unemployment rate in the prosperous Dutch region of Zeeland compared to more than 28 percent in the Spanish region of Andalucia (both 2010 figures).

But cohesion in the post-enlargement era is not merely a distant objective. When looking at Table 10.3 we can see that some new member states—most notably Cyprus, Slovenia, and the Czech Republic—have significantly narrowed the gap to the EU-15. Furthermore, some regions (particularly those with Prague, Bratislava, and Budapest at their core) are now above the threshold of 75 percent of the EU's average GDP,[11] which means that they no longer are eligible for Objective One funding. Evidence suggests that, undeniably, cohesion is increasing in the EU. Completion of the Single Market has led to, and will continue to spur, increased specialization. Poorer regions in this respect will benefit from the competitive advantage of having lower wages and production costs. Before the credit crunch of 2007, Ireland was often cited as an example where the cohesion policy is widely seen as a major reason for the country's astonishing economic success. When Ireland joined the EU in 1973, its GDP languished at 64 percent of the EU's average. By 2006 its GDP had reached 145 percent of the EU average, the second-highest in the Union.

The remarkable case of Ireland, however, might not be enough to convince the critics of cohesion,[12] who argue that cohesion remains only wishful thinking given both the increasing North-South divide within the old EU-15 and the persistent West-East divide between old and new member states. Even apart from these divisions, today Germany, Denmark, and France, in particular, have less inner co-hesion—the prosperity gap within a member state—than in the past, and the years have seen increasing gaps between richer and poorer regions in Britain, Greece, and Italy. Whereas the pro-cohesion camp cites Ireland, cohesion skeptics present the case of Greece, which in 1983 had a GDP of 62 percent of the EU average and by 2003 the figure had improved only marginally to 65 percent. Even after enlarge-ment, when the EU average GDP had dropped significantly, Greece still only man-aged 93 percent in 2006. Unemployment, too, remains a widespread problem, not only in some regions of the 2004 and 2007 accession states but also in Greece and Spain. After all, how can funds that only amount to 30 billion Euros combat such widespread social malaise in the face of globalization and the sovereign debt crisis?

It remains difficult, then, to determine the success of cohesion, since economic progress is influenced significantly by non-EU factors. Again, the case of Ireland offers insight into some of these factors. As noted, Ireland is often portrayed as the champion of cohesion: a country that was propelled from the economic back-wardness of the seventies to become the Celtic tiger of the nineties. But Ireland is an English-speaking country with strong links to the U.S., and so even before EU money began pouring in, Ireland had low wage levels, a highly educated work-force, and relatively harmonious industrial relations; these factors, in the age of globalization and the European Single Market, were highly conducive to business regardless of any EU cohesion policy. Greece, on the other hand, was unable to attract the same level of foreign direct investment as Ireland did. Frequent strikes, corruption, but also an awkward geographical location, far removed from the rich markets of the blue banana, meant that a Greek miracle never happened. Clearly, then, cohesion and economic success not only depend on a well-managed and coherent allocation of funds from Brussels but also on efficient coordination between the EU and national and regional authorities, as well as on sensible macro-economic policies, a favorable international economic climate, and a fortuitous geographical location.

Even enthusiasts of the EU's cohesion policy cannot ignore the challenge posed by the core versus periphery problem. Economic activity in the EU remains centered on the blue banana, the area marked by low assembly costs, an afflu-ent consumer base, good market access and transport links, and the presence of multinational companies, all of which allows for brisk intra-industrial trade. In contrast, the EU's periphery is characterized by a lack of competition, with det-rimental effects on labor skills and infrastructure. Also, labor migration in the EU will never reach U.S. levels, which means that any competitive advantage in the periphery (lower wages, lower taxes) might not lead to economic gains. The periphery might always be engaged in a permanent game of catch-up. Projects to improve the infrastructure of the periphery will undoubtedly move it closer to the richer European markets of the center, and indeed this has been the EU's focus in the post enlargement era. Furthermore, the new member states also offer an attractive option for EU-15 industries: instead of relocating or outsourcing production to India or China, businesses might prefer the political stability and closer geographical proximity of the peripheral regions of Central and Eastern Europe. In any case, regardless of when, and to what extent, the new members will close the gap, the EU's cohesion policy continues to remain one of the crucial cornerstones of the European integration project. Few other EU policies can match the positive impact that the building of roads and railways, or the retraining of formerly unemployed people, has on the lives of European citizens. Through cohesion the EU can for once demonstrate tangible results. Still, in a union of twenty-seven members stretched across the map of Europe, and with the existing sizable gap between rich and poor, the cohesion policy in the EU still has a long way to go before it can fulfill its laudable objective.

11

The Common Agricultural Policy

From its beginnings in the 1950s the Common Agricultural Policy was a cornerstone of European integration, yet it has always been severely criticized. At first glance it seems odd that a program providing for only 2 percent of the EU's GDP and employing only 5 percent of its workforce should swallow up nearly half its budget. Ever since 1967, when for the first time there was free trade in practically all agricultural products across the European Community, the CAP has been censured for being a uniquely wasteful bureaucratic way of supporting agriculture, and for being managed based on endless negotiations between national ministers who themselves are subject to fierce lobbying. Critics point out that this system, which gives direct subsidies to farmers and sets artificially high prices, shields farmers from market discipline and prevents products from selling more cheaply at world-market prices. Euroskeptics have a great deal of ammunition here in depicting the EU as an overly bureaucratic and inefficient exercise; indeed, the CAP even appears unnecessary in view of the economic insignificance of European agriculture in the twenty-first century. Yet every EU citizen supports it, either directly or indirectly—directly through EU payments to farmers and indirectly by paying food prices that in the past were up to 40 percent above the world-market level. So a fundamental question is why the EU's founding fathers decided to support what appears to be institutionalized madness. The key issues in this controversy revolve around the following questions:

1. *What are the CAP's key structural design faults?*
2. *Who are the CAP's losers and beneficiaries?*
3. *Why has the progress of CAP reform been so slow?*
4. *What challenges did the 2004/2007 enlargements pose for the CAP?*
5. *Should the organization of agriculture be left to the member states and not to the EU?*

Reasons for Organizing Agriculture

There are profound reasons why agriculture requires the support of governmental intervention and governmental authorities—whether at the national or EU level. First, without any financial support, many farmers might be forced to sell their farms and ultimately move to towns and cities, leaving their land to either remain idle or be taken over by bigger farms. Europe would then witness the transformation of its countryside along American lines, with acre upon acre of identical crops farmed by big agro-businesses stretching toward the horizon. The diverse European landscape would become a distant memory.

Second, agricultural production predominantly takes places in rural areas, where it is quite often one of the few employment opportunities. Without local jobs available, people would either have to commute, considerably impacting the environment, or move altogether to more urban areas, seriously undermining the economic and social livelihood of smaller communities. Schools and shops would then have to close, and a village might turn into a dormitory for the retired or for second-home owners.

Third, farmers are also land managers. As part of their daily business, they keep pests and animal populations under control. Without farmers, governments would have to employ park rangers to keep the land in a manageable condition.

Fourth, in contrast to any industrial sector, the production of many agricultural commodities is subject to forces beyond human control such as droughts, earthquakes, floods, and pests. Obviously agricultural production is difficult to plan or predict under these randomly occurring natural circumstances. In 1952 the Dutch Minister of Agriculture Sicco Mansholt stated that the principle of economic liberalism (by which he meant the forces of supply and demand) may be suitable for industrial sectors of the economy but it cannot be applied to farming.

Fifth, agricultural products have low income elasticity of demand. A company such as Apple, for instance, can constantly reinvent its product line: in consumer electronics, for example, the iPod was followed by the iPhone and the iPad. Farmers have limited opportunity to expand their product line. Simply put, a consumer

Table 11.1. Objectives of the CAP

- To increase agricultural productivity
- To ensure a fair standard of living for farmers
- To stabilize markets
- To assure food supplies
- To provide consumers with food at reasonable prices

Source: Article 39, Treaty of Rome, 1957.

can buy a TV set for the living room, and another for the bedroom, but one is not inclined to eat two meals instead of one at dinnertime. As general prosperity levels rise, consumers spend smaller proportions of their income on agricultural products, and so farm incomes tend to lag behind the incomes of those working in the industrial sector.

Prior to the signing of the Treaty of Rome in 1957, a number of EU-specific political conditions favored the adoption of an agricultural policy. First, in the early 1950s some 25 percent of the total workforce of the original six member states was employed in agriculture. In Italy the figure was close to 40 percent, and in France 26 percent. Although in West Germany it was only around 20 percent, farmers represented a major constituency of the ruling Christian Democrats. An agricultural policy therefore had a much larger impact on the lives of Europeans than it has today.

Second, except for Luxembourg, the original member states already had a system of farm-price support. Especially in France, West Germany, and Italy, most farmers were small holders and required subsidized prices to maintain an acceptable level of income. But against the backdrop of the establishment of a European Single Market in 1957, a unified and streamlined agricultural market simply became a necessity.

The third reason for adopting an agricultural policy was the insistence of the French government, which was prepared to help get the European project off the ground only if a strong and durable system of support for prices and farm incomes was developed. France regarded the CAP as a powerful counterweight to West Germany's perceived industrial dominance within the Community. If Germany, with its strong, export-oriented manufacturing industry was to benefit from the free movement of goods, the French farmers ought to benefit from a European agricultural policy.

The Objectives of the CAP

Based on these political, structural, and welfare ideological points, the original six member states spelled out the objectives for the CAP in Article 39 of the Treaty of Rome; the goal was to increase agricultural productivity, ensure a fair standard of living for farmers, stabilize markets, assure food supplies, and provide consumers with food at reasonable prices (see Table 11.1). On close inspection, two of these goals contradict each other. A fair standard of living for farmers clashes with the objective of providing reasonable prices for consumers. Because farmers receive a substantial portion of their income through food prices, the higher the prices, the higher their standard of living.

How Does the CAP Work?

As a system of indirect income support for farmers, the CAP functions by separating the European Union's internal market from the world market through three distinct measures:

1. *A unified market:* the free movement of agricultural products across all borders within the EU
2. *Community preference:* EU products are preferred over imports from non-EU countries
3. *Financial solidarity:* the CAP is exclusively funded from the EU budget, and national governments are not allowed to subsidize farmers' incomes

Even better for European agriculture, every product is guaranteed a price higher than the world-market price that is set annually by the Council of Agriculture Ministers through unanimous voting.[1] The EU also buys any crop surpluses from European farmers, and it imposes a duty on non-EU producers to bring the prices of their products from the (lower) world-market level to the (higher) EU level. In return, EU producers receive an export subsidy that brings the cost of their products down from their (higher) EU standard to the (lower) world-market standard. This organizational structure requires the member states to set up agencies that pay farmers for their products, and also to buy food surpluses. Member states forward the amount of their CAP expenses every month to the Commission for reimbursement (see Table 11.2).

The Structural Shortcomings of the CAP System

The most obvious problem here is that guaranteed prices bear no relation to demand, and they encourage overproduction. The more the farmers produce, the more the EC will buy from them.[2] Indeed, between 1973 and 1988 the price guarantees stimulated agricultural production at a rate beyond what the European market could absorb.[3] This led to the problem of having to store the surpluses, some of which are perishable and need refrigeration, thus adding another burden to the taxpayer. A further unwanted effect of the CAP is that in attempting to support small, often family-owned farms, the system does exactly the opposite: because the CAP rewards are based on quantity, the greatest beneficiaries are big farmers who

Table 11.2. The Pricing System of the CAP

- *Target price:* Guarantees EU farmers a minimum price for every product
- *Intervention price:* The price at which CAP agencies buy off surplus products (the same as the target price)
- *Entry price:* The price that EU importers have to pay (higher than the target price)
- *Levy:* The duty on EU imports, which raises them to the level of the target price
- *Refund:* Given to EU exporters in order to bridge the gap between high EU prices and lower world-market prices.

have the finances to invest in new technology and equipment.[4] The environment, too, suffered, since farmers, in order to produce more, have an incentive to use pesticides and artificial fertilizers. Finally, Community preference imposes protectionist measures—import taxes and quotas on non-EU farmers—that conflict with the trend toward global free trade, competition, and market liberalization, while export price supports distort world prices, undercut non-EU farmers, and lead to trade disputes and serious disadvantages for developing economies. Admittedly the EU gives much of its food surplus to the underdeveloped world, accounting for over 70 percent of the world's food aid; but although this may be laudable, the CAP still denies producers from developing countries access to rich European markets. Even worse, the dumping of overproduction on Third World markets robs local farmers of the incentive to be self-sufficient and to find their market niche. Picking up an EU food parcel from the aid agency seems much easier than carving out a meager existence by working one's land.

In the 1970s the increasing financial burden of the CAP left the EU facing the prospect of bankruptcy. With unlimited market guarantees and increased productivity, and prompted by technical progress, expenses grew as high as around 70 percent of the EU's budget by 1984. Overproduction reached obscene proportions. In the early 1990s, for example, the EU of twelve member states produced 20 percent more food than it could consume, resulting in the infamous wine lakes and the butter and sugar mountains.[5] Clearly something had to be done (see Table 11.3).

Attempts to Reform the CAP

Given the fundamental problems with the CAP, politicians had a limited number of options for remedying the growing concerns. These included:

1. Reduce food prices for consumers
2. Establish production ceilings to lessen overproduction
3. Create land set-aside programs to reduce production
4. Direct payments to poorer farmers to satisfy welfare considerations
5. Set a maximum ceiling of financial support for richer farms

Table 11.3. The Shortcomings of the CAP

- Overproduction
- Storage
- Big farms benefit more than small farms
- Environmental damage
- Trade protectionism
- Disincentive for farmers from the developing world to become self-sustainable

6. Establish environmental standards
7. Allow non-EU farmers access to EU markets and limit export subsidies for EU farmers

Every reform idea used a combination of these solutions to different effect. As a first serious attempt, the European Community introduced the so-called Stabiliser Reform Package of 1988. Initial negotiations were complicated by two opposing fundamental conceptions on how agriculture should be managed. On one side, Britain and Denmark argued for budgetary adjustments, production ceilings, and a producer's tax to help defray the cost of storage and export subsidies. On the other side, Belgium, France, Germany, and the Mediterranean countries emphasized the socio-cultural necessity of supporting agriculture to maintain the livelihood of rural communities, and argued for continued price support at current levels, with producers suffering only marginal penalties for exceeding their production ceilings (see Table 11.4).

A number of reforms were finally adopted, but none addressed the basic flaws in the CAP. Germany funded a compromise by paying an extra 5 billion ECU[6] to the EC budget over the next five years. Production ceilings were set for all major crops, and price penalties were imposed on producers who exceeded the ceilings. Unfortunately the ceilings were established at relatively high levels, and the fines were low. Member states were also asked to introduce a land set-aside program, as well as early retirement schemes. However, the major problems remained: developments on the world market still did not necessarily influence EC farmers' decisions; the reforms completely ignored the problem of overproductivity; the introduction of environmental standards was not achieved; and the income gap between the highly productive minority of large agricultural producers and the economically less efficient but socially important majority of small-business farmers continued to widen.

More radical steps were needed, and these came with the 1992 MacSharry Reform Package, named after the Irish Agricultural Commissioner Ray MacSharry. By the 1990s, with the proposal of a single currency and the development of the Single Market taking center stage in European politics, the CAP, to some degree,

Table 11.4. Problems and Solutions for the CAP

Problems	Solutions
High prices	Lower prices
Overproduction	Production ceilings
Storage	Land set-aside programs
Environmental damage	Direct payments to poorer farmers
Distortions of world trade	Subsidy ceiling for richer farmers
Disincentive for Third World Farmers	Environmental standards
	Open up to world trade (and, specifically, reduce export subsidies)

had lost its meaning as one of the vital cornerstones of European integration. Market intervention as practiced in the CAP was an anachronism for a community that advocated the free movement of goods, services, capital, and labor. By the 1990s, moreover, the contribution of the agricultural sector to the GDP and to overall employment had dropped significantly since the 1950s.[7]

MacSharry was appalled by the levels of overproduction still afflicting European agriculture.[8] He attempted to solve this problem by implementing a widespread reduction in prices,[9] land set-aside programs,[10] environmental measures,[11] and direct payments to all producers, large and small, at an average of 207 ECU per hectare.[12] The result was a massive increase in the cost of the CAP, a consequence of the direct payments and the land set-aside subsidies. MacSharry argued, however, that in the long run the reduced use of agricultural land would lead to significant savings. More important, the new CAP represented a major shift from a policy of nontransparent consumer subsidies (through higher prices in supermarkets) to one of transparent taxpayer subsidies (through direct payments to farmers). Thus the CAP was now more open to regular public scrutiny and evaluation. MacSharry's reforms also enabled the EU to come to an agreement in the General Agreement on Tariffs and Trade (GATT) rounds. After an agricultural cold war between the U.S. and the EU that stalled negotiations for seven years, the Uruguay Round finally came to an end in December 1993. The new GATT covered all farm products and further reduced the EU's subsidies to its farmers.[13] Although the GATT certainly did not force the EU to open its agricultural markets to the world, and particularly to developing countries, it nonetheless represented a much-needed step in the right direction (see Table 11.5).

The reforms of the early 1990s, however, could not guarantee a stable CAP in the face of continued technical progress and rising productivity. EU members were well aware that drastic reforms were needed to avoid a further budget crisis and to maintain Europe's political legitimacy before increasingly dissatisfied taxpayers. More important, with the countries of Central and Eastern Europe applying for EU membership, a radical overhaul of the CAP seemed appropriate. The Commission

Table 11.5. Key Attempts to Reform the CAP

- Stabilizer Reform Package (1988)
- MacSharry Reform Package (1992)
- Agenda 2000 (1997)
- 2003 Reform of the CAP (enlargement, WTO, and cross-compliance)

argued that the entry of the candidate countries would at least double the agricultural land and the number of people working in agriculture, and would also cost the CAP an additional 15 billion Euros, an increase of 40 percent.

Responding to this challenge, in 1997 the Commission published its Agenda 2000, proposing reforms that continued down the path taken by MacSharry with a further reduction in prices[14] along with higher standards for food safety and the environment. The Commission intended to establish a program that would create alternative sources of income for farmers, with the clear aim of reducing the number of CAP recipients. In any case, the Commission estimated that the total costs for the CAP would rise by 6 billion Euros per year. Not surprisingly, the Agenda 2000 was therefore hotly debated at the Berlin summit in March 1999. French President Jacques Chirac, who had always been responsive to his own domestic agricultural lobby, managed to convince the fourteen other heads of government that enlargement to Central and Eastern Europe remained a remote prospect and so immediate action was not required. Hence reform of the CAP, specifically a more widespread cut in prices, was delayed until negotiations with the candidate countries had reached a more mature state—a decision many commentators judged to be short-sighted. As a minor concession, the new CAP included long overdue standards for food safety and the environment.[15] The summit also agreed to increase direct aid payments, either per hectare or per head of cattle. This meant that at least the annual budget stayed at approximately the same level of 42.3 billion Euros. The package also meant that further drastic reforms were needed to prepare the CAP for enlargement. The summit acknowledged this by asking the Commission to return with another proposal in 2002. Government leaders found it difficult to confront their agricultural constituencies with the bitter truth that they ought to get used to a future of reduced subsidies and lower guaranteed prices. In the end the Berlin summit reached a compromise that failed in its attempt to please both taxpayers and finance ministers, on one side, and the powerful agricultural lobby, on the other.

A further point of controversy was the reform of the World Trade Organization (WTO). The Seattle meeting in 1999 dramatically displayed the ideological differences between countries concerning the global market. Many EU trading partners—particularly the U.S. and Australia—demanded the complete elimination of export subsidies. In return, the EU pointed to other less transparent forms of subsidies such as tax breaks, which the U.S. delegation tried not to mention.

The EU also wanted full recognition of the multifunctional role of agriculture, with such objectives as environmental preservation, landscape conservation, and food safety.

In Seattle the Agriculture Commissioner Franz Fischler and the Trade Commissioner Pascal Lamy at least offered special trade concessions, such as tariff-free access for the least-developed states. Nonetheless, negotiations stalled at the follow-up meetings in Doha (2001) and in Cancun (2002). Fischler managed to reignite the debate in December 2002, with a detailed proposal for the next WTO round.[16] The centerpiece of his plan was to allow goods from the poorest countries to enter the industrialized world duty-free. However, Fischler continued to insist on the socio-cultural and environmental objectives of the European agricultural model, arguing that measures supporting such standards ought to be exempt from the reduction commitments. He also took a parting shot at the United States by pointing out the need to address export credit systems and shipping food aid merely to dump surpluses in order to keep up prices. The proposal undoubtedly was a step in the right direction, but the establishment of these unquestionably more favorable conditions for developing countries depended largely on the ability of First World competitors to settle their differences.

Regarding enlargement to the countries of Central and Eastern Europe, the Commission dutifully presented two key proposals on how to rejuvenate the CAP. In January 2002 DG Agriculture outlined its plans on how to integrate twelve new member states, which would increase the number of farmers in the EU by 70 percent. The key was the gradual introduction of direct payments, but, in reality, this meant that, in 2004, farmers in the accession countries would receive only 25 percent of the financial aid given to their counterparts in Western Europe, with the amount gradually rising to 100 percent by 2013.[17] Fischler argued that a full introduction of EU payments would reduce the incentive for badly needed structural reforms in the farming sectors of Central and Eastern Europe. Clearly the EU did not want to create a dependency culture, but it had to face the criticism that it was trying to establish a two-tier system, with accession farmers treated as second-class citizens.

To the Commission's delight, the European summit in Copenhagen in December 2002 fully accepted Fischler's ideas, which then became the legal basis for organizing agriculture in the post-accession era. The summit also determined the exact amount of money the new member states could expect, rising from 9.9 billion Euros in 2004 to 14.9 billion Euros in 2006. This meant that Poland—the largest of the accession countries—would secure a transfer of 1 billion Euros from the EU's Structural Funds; for all new entrants the financial package increased by 408 million Euros. In the end the costs related to enlargement rose to a total of around 37 billion Euros between 2004 and 2006. The existing member states therefore avoided an increase in their contributions to the EU budget, which currently runs at a maximum of 1.045 percent of their GNP. Instead, enlargement was financed from existing funds.[18]

Table 11.6. Share of the Agricultural Sector's Workforce, 2010 (in percent)

EU-27	5.2		
Old Member States		**New Member States**	
Greece	12.5	Romania	30.1
Portugal	10.9	Poland	12.9
Austria	5.2	Lithuania	9.0
Ireland	4.6	Latvia	8.8
Finland	4.4	Slovenia	8.8
Spain	4.3	Bulgaria	6.8
Italy	3.8	Hungary	4.5
Netherlands	3.1	Estonia	4.2
France	2.9	Cyprus	3.8
Denmark	2.4	Slovakia	3.2
Sweden	2.1	Czech Republic	3.1
Germany	1.6	Malta*	1.3
Belgium	1.4		
United Kingdom	1.2		
Luxembourg*	1.1		

*estimates
Source: Eurostat, Labour Force Survey, 2006.

Fischler's intention to shake up the CAP did not stop with enlargement or the WTO. In July 2002 he proposed further radical steps for the internal reform of the CAP, with a plan that de-coupled subsidies from the amount that farmers produced. The Commission also proposed a new system, "cross-compliance," which set conditions for the granting of subsidies: farmers had to follow highly specific guidelines for upholding environmental, animal welfare, and hygienic standards, and for preserving the countryside. Hence Fischler's objective was to address, once and for all, the embarrassing anachronism of the traditional price support scheme that allowed 20 percent of EU farmers to receive 80 percent of CAP money.[19] The member states approved the Commission's idea and this new regime was implemented by mid-2003, with a more detailed list of compliance factors agreed upon at the European Council meeting in June 2005.[20]

As the next step in the EU's long attempt to change its most costly budget item, the so-called revision clause called upon the Commission to outline reform ideas before the new financial perspective of 2014–2020 enters the negotiation phase. As such, the EU agriculture ministers, in 2008, agreed on a "health check" with the aim of simplifying the CAP in order to push further environmental and bio diversity standards while also allocating an additional 90 million Euros to farmers in Central and Eastern Europe.[21] But the real challenge is to reduce the overall costs of the CAP before the 2014 deadline. France, in particular, will be expected to give up some of its current level of subsidies, which runs at over 9 billion Euros per year. It remains to be seen whether President Nicolas Sarkozy (or his successor) will be willing and able to convince the influential French agricultural lobby to accept such a move.

Why Is the CAP So Difficult to Reform?

Given the costs of supporting agriculture in the EU, as well as the high level of bureaucracy and the limited economic contribution that agriculture makes to the Union's prosperity, were all the reforms radical enough? Some analysts believe that the CAP should be abolished,[22] but politics can never be as straightforward as this. The political reality is that a number of factors continue to guarantee the existence of some form of supranational support for agriculture. First, it is difficult to turn proposals into political action because of the requirement of unanimity voting in the Council of Agricultural Ministers. Most often political compromises result in watered-down versions of the original proposals. Second, the agricultural sector, although small, continues to have disproportionately powerful influence on domestic politics. Despite the decreasing workforce and agricultural share of the overall GDP, almost no member state government can ignore agricultural welfare. Third, the clash of interests, as set out in the objectives of the CAP in the Treaty of Rome, has never been properly addressed. What is at stake—agricultural welfare or low consumer prices? So far the EU has tried to maintain an acceptable standard of living for an ever decreasing number of farmers, with consumers and taxpayers footing the bill. A proper equilibrium satisfactory to both sides is almost impossible to obtain. Fourth, the agricultural sector is very well organized both at the national and European levels, and the umbrella pressure group COPA (Committee of Professional Agricultural Organisations)[23] is a particularly powerful and determined player in EU politics. Finally, the reality is that the CAP has now been in existence for more than fifty years, and at least two generations of farmers have become accustomed to subsidies. To break this dependency is indeed a formidable task.

One fundamental question remains: Despite the recent reform efforts, has the EU done enough to make the CAP fit for the twenty-first century? Back in the 1950s, when the CAP was first conceived, member states were just emerging from a decade of food shortages as a result of World War II. But assuring food supplies and increasing agricultural productivity among EU farms are much less pressing issues now as evidenced by the fact that the EU has gradually become the world's largest food importer. Hence the objectives of the CAP as outlined in the Treaty of Rome are outdated. But the EU tried to adjust to new challenges and developments by developing an increasingly complex agri-environmental agenda and by opening up to global food trade. On the other hand, despite cuts, the CAP still accounts for a significant chunk of the EU budget that continues to be an anachronism given the low GDP and employment shares of the sector (see Table 11.6). In some areas in northwestern Europe, agriculture has virtually lost its economic relevance. Instead, in parts of England, France, and Italy, we have seen the emergence of life-style farmers who quit their stressful office jobs and retired to the countryside to look after the odd sheep or olive tree. But agriculture continues to be much more relevant for newer member states (such as Romania, Bulgaria, and Poland) and indeed for some of the candidate countries (Turkey and Macedonia). Hence the CAP still has an important role to fulfill in the ambitious plan to reunite a once divided continent and to spread acceptable standards of living across the whole of Europe. Agriculture still matters, and as long as this is the case, calls for a re-nationalization of financial support and regulations seem premature.

12

Economic and Monetary Union

The introduction of a single European currency and the coordination of economic and monetary policies are perhaps the most ambitious aspects of European integration. Without historical precedent, the launch of the Euro in 1999 was awaited with much euphoria but also with skepticism. This chapter establishes the reasons for launching EMU and points out the criteria that member states must now meet in managing their national economies. The discussion then turns to an analysis of the advantages and shortcomings of having a supranational EMU while also focusing on the EU's responses to the economic crisis in Central and Eastern Europe in the aftermath of the credit crunch of 2008 and 2009. The sovereign debt crisis which engulfed a number of states of the Eurozone, and the subsequent repercussions on the financial and policy mechanisms of Economic and Monetary Union will be discussed in a separate chapter (see chapter 17). The key issues are the following:

1. *What are the economic and political benefits and costs of EMU?*
2. *Why did the member states embark on EMU?*

3. *How and to what extent were member states affected by the credit crunch of 2008 and 2009?*
4. *How did the European Union respond to the credit crunch?*

Political-Economic Challenges

Economic and Monetary Union is a classic example of political economy and how public authorities manage a state's economic and social well-being through political, economic, and fiscal policies. Of the many approaches to political economy, the theories of John Maynard Keynes have long been the most influential in driving Western governments to adopt proactive economic policies moderating the societal effects of alternating recessions and economic booms. Keynesianism was adopted successfully in the United States by President Franklin D. Roosevelt in the 1930s, at the height of the Great Depression. During this world economic crisis the Roosevelt administration undertook massive public works projects to create jobs.[1] Roosevelt calculated that a growth in employment could boost the economy, since people simply would have more money to buy products. According to Keynes, the money required for such massive public projects would eventually be recuperated by increased tax revenues arising from the subsequent economic upturn. He referred to this investment by the state as deficit spending and argued that governments should adopt a so-called anti-cyclical policy, meaning that in a time of recession state authorities should act as if the overall economic climate was positive.[2]

Keynesian principles were questioned in the 1970s as a result of a steep increase in oil prices, a devalued U.S. dollar, and widespread recession across many Western countries. One of Keynes's chief critics, Milton Friedman of the University of Chicago, argued the opposite: instead of being proactive, the state should not interfere with the economy but should retreat and concentrate only on providing a stable monetary framework within which market forces could freely interact. This so-called monetarist theory is based on the principle that governments should never act to moderate business cycles but should concentrate on stabilizing the value and supply of money.[3]

Governments have various instruments with which to fine-tune and manage their economies. To name just two, central banks can regulate interest rates[4] and apply a policy of quantitative easing.[5] Apart from these monetary instruments, a government's tax policy—directly through income taxes or indirectly through sales taxes and on duties imposed on tobacco, petrol, or alcohol—can also be effective, as it directly affects consumers' disposable income. Every government is also an employer, and so setting wages naturally has an impact on the amount of money that can be spent on cinema tickets, restaurants, and holidays.

The key economic objectives that governments must attempt to meet are growth, high employment levels, price stability, and trade surplus. However, governments often find it difficult to keep all four objectives in balance. For example, if a positive investment climate increases employment and therefore economic growth, inflation may result as prices often rise when businesses attempt to profit from higher disposable income. Inflationary tendencies (and thus higher prices), in turn, may lead to a negative trade balance, as a country's exports become more expensive on the international market. The end result may be reduced employment as companies lay off staff, which then would lead to a decline in economic growth.

Clearly, therefore, societies that attempt to reform their monetary and economic systems face potentially monumental changes. This chapter describes how EU member states approached this delicate balancing act by focusing on the instruments, provisions, and institutions that now determine monetary and economic matters in the EU. The process was quite daunting: to merge different national policies for managing their economies into a unified and coherent European standard.

What Is an Economic and Monetary Union?

EMU refers, above all, to the establishment of a single European currency—the Euro—which eliminates exchange-rate controls for financial transactions, and allows businesses and consumers to freely trade across borders without paying to convert money from one currency to another. EMU also includes a common pool of foreign exchange reserves and a single standard group of monetary instruments, such as a single interest rate set by a European Central Bank (ECB).

Some analysts believed that only a single currency would truly complete the EU's Single Market; otherwise different interest rates would result in different prices across Europe. Price differences would undermine the free movement of capital, as money would end up in the countries offering the best rates and the free movement of goods, and these would be bought in countries where prices were lowest. Moreover, federalists saw in EMU a way to accelerate the move toward political integration, as Europe's economic challenges could only be met by a single decision maker with state-like authority. In the run-up to the Maastricht negotiations in 1991, EMU was also regarded as a means for integrating an ever more economically powerful and unified Germany.[6]

The Road to EMU

Article 2 of the Treaty of Rome (1957) had already promulgated the "progressive approximation of the economic policies of member states." The treaty had no provisions for creating a regional currency bloc. This was not regarded as necessary since the Bretton Woods system of 1945 established fixed exchange rates using the U.S.

dollar as the undisputed global monetary standard. Hence monetary integration was not on the agenda in the 1950s, at which time European countries were more concerned with trade, particularly trade in goods. The Werner Report of 1970, however, changed this perspective. U.S. President Richard Nixon was about to abandon Bretton Woods, which had set exchange rates at a fixed level, a move that led to a much cheaper dollar. The Hague Summit of 1969 therefore decided to explore the possibility of monetary integration and handed this task to a committee chaired by Luxembourg Prime Minister Pierre Werner and comprised of bankers from several central banks across Europe as well as leading officials from the European Commission. The committee produced a three-stage plan to achieve EMU: complete the free circulation of goods, services, capital, and persons; centralize monetary policies; and fix exchange rates. The report also recommended the creation of a community system of central banks and a new organization for deciding economic policies. The report caused severe disagreement over the strategy of how EMU might be achieved, a detail Werner had not specified. Belgium and France argued for the implementation of a single currency to generate economic convergence, whereas Germany and the Netherlands advocated the opposite—first convergence and then a single currency. In the end EMU was buried by the oil shock of 1973 and the subsequent recession across Western Europe.

Another idea emerged in 1972, termed the "Snake," that allowed European currencies to fluctuate in a narrow band of plus or minus 2.25 percent of the U.S. dollar. But the international exchange-rate market was so volatile that the British pound, the Irish punt, the Italian lira, the Danish crown, and the French franc were forced to abandon the Snake soon after. The problem was straightforward: the economies of Europe at that stage were simply too divergent. On one side was the Deutschmark with low interest and inflation rates, and on the other were countries like Italy, France, and the UK with high interest and inflation rates, which subjected their currencies to speculation and overvaluation.

Not until 1979 was a more coherent system established. The brainchild of German Chancellor Helmut Schmidt and French President Valerie Giscard d'Estaing, the European Monetary System (EMS) created a zone of relative monetary stability and was promptly supported by Denmark, the Netherlands, Belgium, and Luxembourg, with Ireland, the UK, and Italy adopting a wait-and-see approach. Similar to the Snake, it proposed a 2.25 percent margin,[7] but this time it was not pinned to the U.S. dollar but to bilateral relationships between the currencies involved. Also in contrast to the Snake, national central banks were required to intervene when a currency approached the upper or lower limit of 2.25 percent. Of overall importance, the EMS established the European Currency Unit (ECU), a basket of all European currencies used as a means of settlement between European central banks (see Table 12.1).[8]

By the early 1990s, however, the EMS came under intense pressure. The immense costs of German unification raised the country's public debt to new heights.

Table 12.1. The European Monetary System (EMS) and the European Currency Unit (ECU)

Member State Currency	Percentage of ECU Value 1979	Percentage of ECU Value 1989
Germany	33.0	30.53
France	19.8	20.79
Netherlands	10.5	10.21
Belgium/Luxembourg	9.5	8.91
Italy	9.5	7.21
Denmark	3.0	2.71
Ireland	1.1	1.08
United Kingdom	13.6	11.17
Greece	—	0.49
Spain	—	4.24
Portugal	—	0.71

The Bundesbank responded to subsequent inflationary pressure by keeping interest rates at high levels which prompted a rise in the value of the Deutschmark. As a consequence, speculation began to accelerate with currencies that were seen as candidates for devaluation such as the lira, the French franc, and the British pound. Fueled by massive speculation by, for instance, the financier George Soros, the UK was forced to abandon the EMS on 16 September 1992.[9] Later the currency-fluctuation margins were increased to plus or minus 15 percent, which was merely a verbal token to monetary convergence.

The Final Steps toward EMU

The EMS crisis of 1992 could not stop EMU. Already in 1988 the Delors Report[10] had described in detail a three-stage plan which was remarkably similar to Werner's ideas. It would be used as a blueprint for establishing EMU.

- *Stage 1.* Completion of the Single Market, particularly free capital movement and macroeconomic coordination, by July 1990
- *Stage 2.* Coordination between national central banks within a system comprised of European central banks
- *Stage 3.* Fixed exchange rates, resulting in a single monetary policy and currency, and the establishment of a European Central Bank

EMU, and with it the merging of national currencies, required new tools for developing, coordinating, and managing economic and monetary policies. To accomplish this, the European Council created two institutions to ensure a smooth implementation of EMU: the European Central Bank (ECB),[11] which acts independently

Table 12.2. EMU's Convergence Criteria

In order to join EMU, member states have to streamline their economies to meet certain criteria:

1. Price stability (inflation rate of no more than 1.5% above the three best-performing states)

2. Limited public debt (no more than 3% of GDP annually and a total of no more than 60% of GDP)

3. Limited exchange rate fluctuation (remain within EMS for two years)

4. Reasonably low interest rates (no more than 2% above the three best performers)

of political authorities and is authorized to issue money solely to maintain price stability; and a European System of Central Banks (ESCB), comprised of national central bank officials and the ECB, and responsible for conducting foreign-exchange operations. Finally, a more central role was given to ECOFIN (the meeting of national economies and finance ministers within the Council of Ministers), so that it could produce broad guidelines for economic policies within the EU.

Delors also learned from the Werner Commission's mistake of not providing guidelines for implementing its recommendations. The Stability and Growth Pact, adopted in 1997, issued clear guidelines on how convergence could be achieved: member states wishing to participate in EMU agreed to satisfy convergence criteria that shaped national economic and monetary policies, not only in the run-up to EMU but also as long as the Stability and Growth Pact remained in place (Table 12.2).

Although Delors had provided the EU with a clear timetable from which there was no turning back, EMU was a typical European compromise: Germany achieved its objective of having the ECB organized along the lines of its own national central bank and functioning as a watchdog on inflation, but France managed to push the other member states into a clear commitment toward an ever closer union.

Not every member state was enthusiastic about Delors's plan. During previous negotiations over the Maastricht Treaty, the UK and Denmark had secured an opt-out and decided to stay outside EMU.[12] Sweden, which joined the EU after the Maastricht Treaty in 1995, also decided against the Euro in a referendum in 2004. In the end eleven countries embarked on the project in 1999, with Greece joining in 2001 despite having debt levels that exceeded the targets set by the Stability and Growth Pact. As for countries that joined the EU in 2004 and 2007, their eventual participation in EMU was one of the vital entry criteria. Or, put differently, the EU was no longer willing to grant an opt-out of EMU to current or future member states. From now on, joining the EU also meant adopting the Euro. But every accession state had a different timetable that was set by the European Commission in line with the country's economic performance and structure. Slovenia, as the first new member, introduced the Euro in 2007, followed by Malta and Cyprus in 2008, Slovakia in 2009, and Estonia in 2011 (see Table 12.3), bringing the total number of Europeans that lived inside the Eurozone to 330 million.

Table 12.3. Membership in the EMU

Year	Membership Count	Countries
1999	11	Austria, Belgium, Finland, France, Germany, Ireland, Italy, Luxembourg. Netherlands, Portugal, Spain
2001	12	Greece
2007	13	Slovenia
2008	15	Cyprus, Malta
2009	16	Slovakia
2011	17	Estonia

The Credit Crunch and the
Crisis in Central and Eastern Europe

During 2008 and 2009 Central and East European countries (CEEC) experienced the worst economic crisis since the region's transition to liberal market democracies in the 1990s. The downturn was so severe (see Tables 12.4 and 12.6) that some commentators feared for the European integration project in general, and for the stability of the Euro in particular. Ever since the region's accession to the EU in 2004–2007, the CEEC had been on a spending binge fueled by foreign investment and the prospect of the Euro's pending membership, resulting in an unprecedented building and consumer boom. In many countries, businesses and private citizens took out loans and mortgages in Euro because of better interest rates and administrative ease. After all, why take out a mortgage in a national currency, which was about to be abandoned within the next years. Initially it seemed that the CEEC was immune to the credit crunch, as banks operating in the region were not linked to U.S. subprime mortgages. However, with collapsing global demand, exports stagnated, investors pulled their money out, and some national currencies started to collapse. Job cuts, spiraling debts, and shrinking output were the consequences. The crises in the East then started to hit the Eurozone, since many lenders in the CEEC were owned by EU-15 banks (and, in particular, banks from Sweden, Austria, and Italy) and losses in the East entered Western balance sheets.

Given the severity of the crisis,[13] the international community and, above all, the EU had to act. Between October 2008 and February 2009 international institutions including the World Bank, the European Bank for Reconstruction and Development (EBRD), and the European Investment Bank contributed 24.5 billion Euros. Even more substantial support started to arrive with the conclusion of the G-20 Summit in London in April 2009, which agreed to a major expansion of the funds of the International Monetary Fund (IMF) and the World Bank to one trillion U.S. dollars. The IMF, in particular, came to the rescue, and packages were agreed to with Latvia, Hungary, and Romania.[14] At the summit in March 2009, EU

Table 12.4. GDP Growth in Central and Eastern Europe, 2009–2011

	2009	2010	2011
EU average	−4.2	2.0	1.5
Eurozone	−4.3	1.9	1.5
Bulgaria	−5.0	0.4	1.7
Czech Republic	−4.8	2.7	1.7
Estonia	−14.1	2.3	7.6
Hungary	−6.3	1.3	1.7
Latvia	−18.0	−0.3	5.5
Lithuania	−15.0	1.4	5.9
Poland	1.7	3.9	4.3
Romania	−7.1	−1.6	2.5
Slovakia	−4.7	4.2	3.3
Slovenia	−7.8	1.4	−0.2

Source: Eurostat, May 2012

leaders also agreed to double the balance of payment assistance to the region to 50 billion Euro, while also frontloading 30 billion Euro of cohesion money. Previously, in January 2009, the European Central Bank (ECB) had managed to galvanize the banking sector through its so-called Vienna initiative. The declaration committed parent groups of banks to stay in the region and to recapitalize their subsidiaries in Central and Eastern Europe. The initiative gathered momentum with the continuing bailouts by western European governments of western European banks (see chapter 17), which in turn kept their central and eastern European offices afloat.

In some cases, the prospects for recovery were grim.[15] Some countries (Latvia, Lithuania, Estonia, and Bulgaria) had pegged their currencies to the Euro. This has been the centerpiece of their economic policy ever since the Euro came into existence. Abandoning this principle could have bankrupted large sectors of the economy (particularly those areas with loans in Euro). Hence, un-pegging their currencies was not an option, which left these countries with the inability to devalue their currencies and regain a degree of competitiveness. The other countries of the region had floating exchange rate currencies. They all also had widespread loans in Euro. And all of them responded to the crises with cuts in interest rates and quantitative easing. Hence there was a pronounced risk of draining any remaining currency reserves. On the other hand, an increase in public spending to boost the economy was also only a limited option, given the convergence criteria (an annual maximum deficit of 3% of the GDP) in order to qualify for Euro membership.

By the time of the crises Eastern and Western Europe had closely linked economies resulting in an almost symbiotic relationship. Western Europe discovered new markets, and the East offered low wage levels and high skills with many factories moving from the EU-15 to the EU-12. But the CEEC wasted borrowed money on construction and consumption without much concern about balance sheets and repayment schedules. Still, the EU had no choice but to meet the expense, since a financial and economic collapse of the CEEC would have posed severe moral questions to the EU integration project and to further enlargements. After all, is not an ever more united Europe a raison d'être of the EU project?

Many countries in the region justifiably stood accused of reckless approach to economic governance. A return to some degree of normalcy, however, could not be achieved without major adjustments—whether in the East or the West. In particular, large public debt can be crippling to an economic resurgence as debt and interest payments severely limit any government's options. As a consequence of the crises, the previous road maps and timetables for EMU membership were rendered obsolete and needed to be redrawn. One can only hope that the establishment of the European Systems Risk Board will, in the future, prevent the reckless approach to economic governance of which so many countries in the region justifiably stand accused.[16]

By 2011, however, GDP levels had recovered to a remarkable extent (see Table 12.4) with all but one of the CEEC states (Slovenia) enjoying higher growth than both the Eurozone and the EU average. The region also experienced an expansion in exports. Fiscal consolidation and balanced budgets returned. This turnaround was impressive in light of the global economic slowdown and the widespread ramifications of the sovereign debt crisis in some countries of the Eurozone (see chapter 17). Growth projections by the World Bank for 2012 offered an even more promising picture, with predictions of a GDP rise of 2.1 percent for the region. In addition, production in some countries returned to pre-crisis levels.[17]

The rapid responses by the EU and the IMF certainly helped to turn the crisis around. But the CEEC economies also made drastic adjustments by raising taxes and imposing painful budget cuts that prompted surprisingly little social unrest (with Hungary, Lithuania, and the Czech Republic as notable exceptions). In addition, from 2010 onwards the region received a massive boost from the speedy economic recovery of Germany. Europe's economic powerhouse is the key player in the northern part of the CEEC, and, not surprisingly, it was this area that recovered most quickly, especially Poland and Slovakia, both of which continued to benefit greatly from German foreign investment. The German boost was set to continue as the country extended the free movement of people to most central and eastern European EU citizens in May 2011. (Romania and Bulgaria are the last to be granted this privilege in 2014.) This meant that workers from the region were now free to enter the German job market, and the German government estimated that on average 100.000–150.000 people annually would join its workforce, giving in return a welcome support to the German labor market which has a projected shortfall of five million workers by 2025.

Table 12.5. Currency Performances: National Currencies against the Euro

	2007	2009	2011	Change 2007–2011
Hungarian forint	251.35	280.33	304.00	−21%
Polish zloti	3.7838	4.3276	4.4533	−18%
Romanian lei	33.353	42.399	43.077	−29%

Note: Annual figures represent average currency value during that year.
Source: www.oanda.com, accessed on July 2, 2012.

Although the economic recovery in the CEEC was impressive, a number of underlying structural deficiencies continued to undermine the region's economic potential. First, corruption was endemic and widespread. Government contracts, also those involving EU projects, were often the subject of favoritism and crony-ism, with "tax demands" being placed on potential project implementers just to be allowed to enter the bidding process. Second, unemployment continued to be at worrying heights. The case of Slovakia showed that an economic recovery (plus 4% in 2010) went hand in hand with a staggeringly high unemployment rate of 14.4%. Against the backdrop of such an economic recovery without job creation, social unrest and strikes as witnessed in Spain and Greece during 2011 and 2012 cannot be ruled out in the future. Third, EMU and the subsequent Euro mortgages issued by CEEC banks at least partially caused the economic downturn and as long as the sovereign debt crises in Greece, Ireland, Spain, Portugal and Italy are not under control, the whole of the European Union—not just Central and Eastern Europe will be plagued by a heightened degree of uncertainty (see chapter 17) and as a consequence, the region will continue to fall short in its attempt to realize its significant economic potential.

The Pros and Cons of EMU

A number of factors undoubtedly make a convincing case for the introduction of the Euro and EMU (see Table 12.6). Without the need to exchange money from one currency to another, businesses and consumers save approximately 2 percent on transaction costs, and importers and exporters within the EMU no longer face the risk of currency fluctuations.[18] Another factor is that the transnational coordination offered by the ESCB makes it unlikely that Europe will see a repetition of the 1992 crisis that forced the British pound out of the European Monetary System. Although the EU has often been criticized as distant, bureaucratic, and faceless, with no distinct tangible identity, the Euro now gives Europeans a concrete reminder of their existence within a community of European states. On a daily basis, when at home, or when traveling to other countries of the Eurozone, simply by paying with notes and coins, Europeans become aware that they form part of an entity that extends beyond their national boundaries.

But despite these positive experiences, a number of shortcomings still offer plenty of ammunition to critics of the Euro. The most notable problem has been the rise in prices across the Eurozone, which surprised both economists and consumers. The increases were sometimes so steep that even German Chancellor Gerhard Schröder and Italian Prime Minister Silvio Berlusconi publicly pleaded with businesses to stop their profiteering practices. Ironically many businesses, mostly restaurants, were able to get away with hefty price rises, because their customers found it difficult to manage the mental conversion from their national currency into Euros.[19]

The single European currency also has split the instruments for managing an economy between the supranational level (where the ECB sets an interest rate engaged in quantitative easing) for the whole Eurozone and the national level (where governments still control fiscal policies and are involved in some wage-bargaining processes). This arrangement could result in a scenario where a national government, having lost control over interest rates, is forced to counterbalance the effects of the ECB's interest rate increase by raising taxes and lowering wages.[20]

Also coming under severe criticism was the Stability Pact of the Maastricht Treaty, which is the basis of EMU. Romano Prodi, Commission President from 1999 to 2004, described the Pact as the "Stupidity Pact," given the rigid criteria with which member states had to comply. Particularly disquieting was the requirement to have a maximum annual deficit of 3 percent of the GDP.[21] Underlying this criterion was the straightforward idea that countries wishing to adopt the single currency should have a balanced budget, thus sheltering the Euro against inflationary pressures. But critics of the Pact argue that this criterion is too inflexible and curtails a country's ability to proactively shape its economy and provide investment boosts in times of economic slowdown. Indeed, during the credit crunch most Eurozone countries embarked on a public spending spree that violated the Stability and Growth Pact momentarily but also kept their economies afloat. A solution would be to adhere to the deficit level of 3 percent but increase the time span during which it is applied. A country could then go into debt, for instance, 6 percent in one year, as long as the average deficit over five years does not exceed the level agreed upon. But the Stability Pact is part of the Maastricht Treaty, and any treaty revision requires the consent of all member states. However, with the credit crises, the ratification of the Lisbon Treaty and its institutional reforms, as well as the envisaged integration of Turkey, the EU had to deal with a number of pressing issues that moved any amendment to EMU mechanisms to the bottom of the political agenda.

Euroskeptics often question whether a single currency is truly required for a single market. Yes, when buying a car, consumers can use the internet to easily identify the country offering the cheapest deal. For bigger and more expensive items, transnational price comparisons are indeed done on an increasingly regular basis. But would consumers fly to Vienna only because the Austrian McDonald's

Table 12.6. Unemployment in Central and Eastern Europe, 2009–2011

	2009	2010	2011
EU average	9.3	10.1	10.2
Eurozone	9.6	10.1	10.9
Bulgaria	7.2	10.1	12.6
Czech Republic	7.5	7.3	6.7
Estonia	15.2	17.9	11.7
Hungary	10.7	11.1	11.2
Latvia	19.9	19.3	14.6
Lithuania	14.6	18.3	14.3
Poland	8.5	9.6	10.1
Romania	7.2	7.1	7.5
Slovakia	13.0	14.4	13.9
Slovenia	6.5	7.3	8.5

Source: Eurostat, May 2012

offers the cheapest Big Mac in Europe? We have already seen an approximation of prices in the Eurozone, especially in big metropolitan areas, and price differences probably will remain largely as a result of the still significant variations in national tax rates.

Some analysts also point to the danger of a single currency for a region with such highly dissimilar economic structures. When comparing the highly developed economies of northern Europe with those of the south, particularly Spain, Portugal, and Greece, one has reason to believe that a single currency and a common monetary approach might not be the best solution to guarantee growth and prosperity for all. This challenge is set to continue once all of the enlargement countries of 2004–2007 have adopted the Euro. The stringent convergence criteria of the Stability Pact also mean that large-scale public investment to help economically backward countries improve their competitiveness is difficult without violating the Stability and Growth Pact.[22] Even before the sovereign debt crisis, when every Eurozone member exceeded the deficit targets of EMU, we had already witnessed a dilemma, where a single interest rate is not suitable for the entire Eurozone: Ireland, for instance, needed a higher rate to cool off inflationary pressures, but Portugal, and at some stage also France and Germany, needed a lower rate to revitalize their economies. The argument thus put forward is that the EU is not an Optimum Currency Area (OCA).

A further point of concern about the single currency is the coordination of policies between the ECB and ECOFIN. The objective of the former is simply to maintain price stability. Unlike the U.S. Federal Reserve, which sets interest rates by analyzing the country's overall economic performance, the ECB's sole mandate is to keep inflation under control. ECOFIN, however, analyzes the larger economic

Table 12.7. The Pro's and Con's of EMU

Pro:

    1. Lower transaction costs

    2. Does away with exchange rate uncertainty, leading to a more predictable investment climate

    3. Transnational coordination makes repetition of the 1992 crisis unlikely

    4. Concrete symbol for a European identity

Contra:

    1. Divides the instruments for managing the economy between member states and the ECB

    2. Reduces the number of tools for member states to combat national economic problems

    3. Stringent convergence criteria (particularly an annual budget deficit of 3 percent of the GDP) mean less flexibility for member states

    4. Creates a three-tier Europe: those who are in, those who are out but want to be in, and those who want to stay out

    5. A single currency does not require a single market

    6. One currency is not necessarily appropriate for a region with hugely dissimilar economic structures

    7. ECB and ECOFIN might pull in different directions

parameters of the Eurozone, decides when intervention in foreign exchange markets is required, and offers broad guidelines for the fiscal policies of member states. It also has the right to impose fines when member states violate the Stability Pact and, as seen in the Greek crisis, was actively involved in enforcing budget cuts. The objective of the ECB is clear-cut, but the same cannot be said of ECOFIN. Tax policies are still set and decided upon at the national level, which means that ECOFIN's guidelines have no force of law. Moreover, to avoid friction between European partners, so far it has not issued fines for violations of the Stability Pact. Up to now, no one can say that the two organizations are working hand in hand, and though the Eurozone undoubtedly has a monetary government (the ECB), ECOFIN still falls short of being described as a unified economic government.

13

Justice and Home Affairs

The Maastricht Treaty added a further dimension to the construction of Europe: Justice and Home Affairs (JHA), which brings together the member states' ministries of justice and the interior. JHA allows for dialogue and cooperation between justice departments, the police, customs as well as immigration services. The areas JHA covers are vast and include all internal security issues. Among the most significant are matters related to EU citizenship, asylum, immigration, and police and judicial cooperation. Those areas are examined in this chapter by addressing the following questions:

1. *Why do member states cooperate in JHA?*
2. *How meaningful is the concept of EU citizenship?*
3. *How unified are asylum and immigration policies across the EU?*
4. *How has the EU responded to the events of 9/11?*
5. *What were the effects of the "big bang" enlargements of 2004 and 2007?*

Reasons for Establishing JHA

Arguably the main achievement of the EU was the establishment of a Single Market founded on the free movement of goods, services, capital, and people. The Schengen Agreement,[1] which came into force in 1985, removed internal border controls between participating countries and helped to further cement this privilege. While the Single Market and Schengen undoubtedly gave many benefits to European citizens, there was a downside to the ability to move freely across the continent. Terrorists, drug and human traffickers, money launderers, and organized crime could take advantage of a more open Europe. Ultimately one member state's security problem could become a security challenge for others. Improvements in police and judicial cooperation, therefore, have often been seen as a functional spillover of the Single Market program and the single currency.

Greater integration in these fields was also needed following a number of political developments beginning with the social and political upheavals following the end of communism in Central and Eastern Europe and the Balkans. By the mid-1990s new transit routes through these countries had been established and greatly facilitated the flow of drugs. Illegal trafficking of humans was also on the rise, as was the establishment of transnational mafia networks. Military conflicts following the breakup of Yugoslavia resulted in significant waves of refugees entering Western Europe and exacerbated the new security challenges confronting the EU. Adding to the challenges, the terrorist attacks on the United States on September 11, 2001, greatly accelerated political decisions at the EU level. During that time public concern over illegal immigration and the subsequent success of several right-wing parties also encouraged member states to advance cooperation in the JHA field. Lastly, the enlargement to twenty-seven member states in 2004 and 2007 necessitated further reconsideration, as it integrated countries that did not share the same prosperity levels as did Western European states, which raised concerns over the potential rise of organized crime, drugs, and human trafficking.

JHA prior to Maastricht

In the 1970s terrorism in Western Europe increased sharply. The Irish Republican Army in Northern Ireland, the Baader-Meinhof Gang in West Germany, and the Red Brigades in Italy shocked the political establishment. The hostage taking and murders of the Israeli team at the Munich Olympics in 1972 revealed that Europe was not immune to the political upheavals in the Middle East. To meet these threats, the Trevi Group[2] of interior and justice ministers began to meet regularly starting in 1976. These Trevi meetings were conducted ad hoc, outside the EU framework, and strictly among national governments. Also, the Trevi Group did not set up any institutions or policy structures, but concentrated purely on the exchange of information and communication on how best to combat transnational crimes.

JHA in the 1990s: From Maastricht to Amsterdam

The dramatically changing international political climate of the 1990s, including the emerging security vacuum in Central and Eastern Europe and the conflicts in the former Yugoslavia, demanded a swift response from the EU. At Maastricht, in addition to setting up a second pillar focusing on the Common Foreign and Security Policy, the EU also established Pillar III, called Justice and Home Affairs. Within this pillar, the member states agreed on areas of common concern including asylum, external borders, immigration, drug addiction, and judicial cooperation on civil and criminal matters, customs, and the policing of drug trafficking, organized crime, and terrorism.

But despite the ever growing security challenges, concerns over sovereignty remained and slowed progress in this area. When the Amsterdam Treaty was signed in 1997, the member states agreed to establish an "area of freedom, security, and justice" in the EU. As a first step, Amsterdam integrated the Schengen Agreement; it then moved policy making on visas, asylum, and immigration from Pillar III to Pillar I, giving Community institutions a greater role in the policy-making process. Limitations to this shift of sovereignty remained, however, as the role of the Commission, the European Parliament, and the European Court of Justice continued to be more restricted than in the policy areas of Pillar I. What was left in the third pillar was police and judicial cooperation in criminal matters.[3] Although the Amsterdam Treaty represented a distinct move toward more supranational decision making in matters relating to internal security, little progress was made in arriving at a common approach to asylum and to visas and immigration, where different standards prevailed across the EU.

Protecting the EU in the Twenty-first Century

The terrorist attacks on the United States in 2001, on Madrid in 2004, and on London in 2005 brought security concerns to the top of the agenda of decision makers. In addition, the integration of ten more member states from Central and Eastern Europe in 2004 and 2007, as well as the enlargement of the Schengen area in 2007 to twenty-five signatory states, only exacerbated the potential risks to the lives of European citizens. The EU responded to these challenges with the ratification of the Lisbon Treaty in 2009. For a start, the treaty abandoned the awkward three-pillar structure and confirmed the right of the Commission to initiate legislation. In addition, Lisbon stated that a group of nine member states could also submit legislative proposals. For the first time the treaty also guaranteed the full involvement of the European Parliament, and also for the first time the European Court of Justice assumed judiciary authority in all JHA matters. In its so-called Stockholm Programme of December 2009 the member states outlined their vision for the period 2010–2014. The program concentrated on the following points:

- Promoting citizenship and fundamental rights
- Establishing a European area of justice that unifies different national approaches
- Developing a security strategy that tackles organized crime, terrorism, and other threats
- Unifying access to Europe for business people, tourists, students, scientists, workers, and persons in need of international protection
- Guaranteeing security for EU citizens through integrated border management and visa policies
- Developing comprehensive European migration and asylum policies

The area of justice and home affairs is vast and covers such issues as free movement of persons, visa policy, EU external borders policy, the Schengen Area, drug policy coordination, EU data protection, racism and xenophobia, crime prevention, the fight against organized crime, external relations, and enlargement that could not be addressed in a publication of this size. The following analysis therefore concentrates only on citizenship, asylum, and immigration, as well as judicial and police cooperation.

Citizenship

EU citizenship, as with any relationship between a government and its citizens, entails rights, duties, and political involvement with the purpose of creating a European public domain and some form of a European political identity (see Table 13.1). Access to EU citizenship is granted through the member states; one must first gain citizenship in one of the member states, which then automatically grants that person EU citizenship.[4] Thus EU citizenship is not regulated by EU laws but is determined by differing national regulations. For instance, the children of an immigrant from Turkey might receive German citizenship, and thus the rights of EU citizenship, only after a naturalization process that could take ten years or more, as Germany has traditionally relied on the principle of *jus sanguinis* (law of kinship), which grants citizenship in line with that of one's parents. But if the Turkish immigrant had chosen Ireland as his destination and would start and raise a family there, his children would automatically be granted Irish and EU citizenship, as Ireland broadly follows the principle of *jus soli* (law of the land), which grants citizenship based on one's birthplace.

The differences in national laws have therefore resulted in a patchwork of EU citizenship across Europe. An example is the right to schooling. In the UK, Muslims have the right to be educated according to their faith. But Muslims in Luxembourg do not have this right, as that country does not have a sufficiently large Muslim population to make religious public schooling practical. Although some unifying features did emanate from the Maastricht Treaty, the entire agenda

Table 13.1. EU Citizenship as Defined by Maastricht

- Right to move freely and to reside on the territory of the EU
- Right to vote and stand in local and EP elections
- Right to diplomatic protection by a member state of one's choice
- Right to petition the European Parliament and ombudsman
- Principle of nondiscrimination on grounds of nationality, gender, race, religion, disability, age, and sexual orientation
- Equal access to the EU's civil service

of citizens' rights and responsibilities is largely determined by different national sets of citizenship.

On the other hand, some positive and notable developments associated with the incorporation of the Schengen Agreement have included a common approach in the EU on how to handle non-EU foreigners. Non-EU visitors can travel freely across the Schengen Area for a period of up to three months if they have a valid travel document and sufficient money to cover their living costs. Furthermore, the Schengen countries have integrated their visa rules, and there is now a single list of countries whose citizens require a visa.

The citizenship agenda was further enhanced with the Lisbon Treaty which gave the EU a legally binding and enforceable Charter of Human Rights. Already envisaged in the preamble of the Amsterdam Treaty, the Charter contains fifty-four articles under the headings of dignity, freedoms, equality, solidarity, citizens' rights, and justice.[5] The Charter forces the EU and its institutions to legislate and act in line with its principles and objectives, while giving the European Court of Justice the judiciary authority on these matters. Alas, human rights provided yet another area for asymmetry within the Union, since the Charter is not applicable in Poland and in the UK.

Asylum and Immigration

In 2010 the EU accommodated around 30 million foreigners, which is 6 percent of its total population.[6] Out of these, 12.3 million (38 percent) were citizens from another EU member state. Citizens from Turkey and Romania were the most numerous of foreigners living on EU territory with just over two million people each, followed by citizens from Morocco (1.9 million), Poland (1.5 million), Italy (1.3 million), and Albania (1 million). Regarding illegal migration, reliable figures are hard to obtain, but in 2009 European border agencies detected over one hundred thousand illegal crossings. Asylum seekers constitute a significant number of foreigners entering the EU annually.[7] The right to asylum is generally governed by the Geneva Convention of 1951 to which all member states are signatories. The Convention states that "no one may be removed, expelled or extradited to a state where there is a serious risk that he or she would be subjected to death penalty, torture or other inhuman or degrading treatment or punishment." But apart from this general prerogative, the status of immigrants and asylum applicants is still determined by different national regulations and standards. Throughout the 1990s the flow of persons seeking international protection in the EU increased substantially, mainly following the breakup of the former Soviet Empire and Yugoslavia, which dramatically necessitated a common solution in line with each member state's capacities for absorbing immigrants.

At the JHA summit in Tampere, Finland, in October 1999, the member states agreed to develop a single EU asylum system, which aimed to create unified procedures and a uniform status for those granted asylum. Member states also asked the Commission to produce more specific proposals on the precise nature of a common approach to asylum and immigration. A response came in November 2000, when the Commission issued a "road map" for an EU-wide policy calling on member states to both secure the rights of long-term foreign residents and asylum applicants, and combat illegal immigration and trafficking by reinforcing partnerships with the countries of origin. Regarding asylum, the Commission did not propose a new EU agency but agreed to a set of principles governing how each member state would assess asylum cases.[8]

The Tampere summit differentiated two phases: the first, ending in 2004, would lay the foundation for integrating border controls and requiring police and judicial cooperation in the recognition of judicial decisions; the second, based on the initial groundwork, would guarantee fundamental rights, access to justice for third-country nationals, and protection under the Geneva Convention, as well as regulate migration, control external borders, and combat organized cross-border crime and threats of terrorism. Over the past years EU leaders managed to agree on a limited number of legislative proposals in this area. Vital stepping stones included the 1995 resolution on minimum guarantees for asylum procedures, the 1997 Amsterdam Treaty that established a common European asylum system, the 2002 agreement regarding a common definition for persons eligible for refugee and subsidiary protection status, and the September 2003 directive on family reunification.

A key innovation resulting from the Tampere summit was the European Refugee Fund (ERF) established in 2000. Jointly funded by member states, the ERF allocates financial aid to member states to balance the burdens borne by providing for asylum and displaced refugees. The fund also supports special projects for the reception, integration, and repatriation of refugees and displaced persons. Financially speaking, the ERF is the largest EU program on asylum and immigration. For the period from 2000 to 2004, when its first funding cycle came to an end, the ERF had disbursed a total of 216 million Euros. Between 2005 and 2010, the fund's size had tripled to accommodate the ten new member states. The EU maintained that level of financial support for the period from 2008 to 2013, when 630 million Euros were at the ERF's disposal.

At a summit meeting in The Hague in November 2004, EU leaders emphasized that the EU's common asylum policy should be based on a fair sharing of responsibility and costs, and on closer cooperation between member states. In an ambitious move, the summit also envisaged a uniform status for people granted asylum, joint processing of asylum applications outside EU territory, and a single assessment procedure. At a subsequent meeting in The Hague in May 2005, member states agreed to change the governance rules that would thereafter apply to EU policy making in this area. The changes included a move to qualified majority voting, a closer involvement of the European Parliament through the introduction of the co-decision procedure, and an enhanced role for the European Court of Justice in asylum and immigration matters, except for economic migration.

In 2005 another remarkable step was the establishment of FRONTEX (with the cumbersome official name of European Agency for the Management of Operational Cooperation at the External Borders).[9] Even candidate and accession countries started to tackle migration in a structurally more coherent manner; MARRI (the Migration, Asylum, Refugees Regional Initiative) was formed in 2004 and included as its members Albania, Bosnia and Herzegovina, Croatia, Macedonia, Serbia, and Montenegro.[10]

Clearly asylum and immigration have become top priorities for the EU. The JHA Council holds as many as eight meetings per year, and summit meetings devoted to the subject took place, such as in Tampere in 1999 and Seville in 2002, demonstrating the political urgency of these matters. Considering that member states remained reluctant to transfer powers over their borders, the amount of authority they did transfer to the EU was remarkable. This was largely owing to the recognition that unilateral responses in this policy area were often ineffective in an increasingly interdependent world and the realization that intergovernmental decision-making procedures were often too slow and therefore incapable of providing effective policy solutions. It is important to remember, however, that asylum and immigration policies are not applicable in all EU member states. Denmark opted out of JHA treaty provisions, and the UK and Ireland decide on their involvement on a case-by-case basis.

Judicial and Police Cooperation

Judicial cooperation in civil matters concerns, for example, problems that arise over the mutual recognition by different member states of court judgments in divorce or child custody cases or commercial questions such as bankruptcy, where two or more member states are involved. The EU established the principle of mutual recognition of court rulings across member states at the Tampere summit in 1999 and, as a consequence, has adopted legislation relating to divorce and parental responsibility, as well as for settling cross-border disputes involving civil claims. Legislation on legal aid for cross-border litigants is also in place, as are rules relating to insolvency proceedings.

Judicial cooperation in criminal matters concerns, for instance, extradition and other cross-border crimes such as drug and human trafficking, terrorism, or crimes concerned with computer security. Further legislation ensures that court orders in one member state—for instance, imposing fines or confiscating assets—are implemented throughout the EU. Legislation relating to the compensation of crime victims, where the victim lives in one member state but the crime occurred in another—have also been developed. Noteworthy, too, is the establishment of the European arrest warrant that came into force in January 2004 and resolved the problem of cumbersome and often lengthy extradition procedures between member states.

Again the European Council meeting in Tampere in October 1999 represented a breakthrough for cooperation between the judiciary and police. The summit proposed the harmonization of criminal law in some areas, and also created a host of new agencies to help police authorities. The most important agency, the European Police Office or Europol, had already been agreed upon in 1995 but was not fully functional until 1999. Between 2010 and 2013 Europol had a budget of 80 million Euros and more than seven hundred staff members, including seconded European Liaison Officers (ELOs) from all the member states. Europol provides information exchanges, coordinates multinational operations, maintains a database, and analyzes crimes. In addition, Europol was made responsible for preventing Euro counterfeiting, and it is also authorized to conduct specific investigations at the request of national law-enforcement agencies (see Table 13.2).

Moreover, the Tampere summit created a European judicial unit (Eurojust) based in The Hague and comprised of a high-level network of national criminal prosecutors with the task of fostering judicial cooperation. The summit also set up a European Police College (CEPOL) and the Police Chief's Task Force, which brings together senior officials for frequent meetings.[11] Despite this impressive number of institutions, progress in the field of police and judicial cooperation has remained sluggish and dominated by deep divisions between member states, as many are reluctant to relinquish authority over one of the most crucial aspects of a country's national sovereignty.[12] Not surprisingly, the 9/11 attacks on the World Trade Center and the Pentagon in the U.S. resulted in a political urgency to equip European countries with mechanisms to counter potential terrorist threats. Although 9/11 did not bring about any completely new policy proposals, it did accelerate the approval of four proposals that had originated two years earlier, around the time of the Tampere summit:

- an anti-terrorism task force within Europol
- a European arrest warrant replacing the traditional method of extradition
- a list of thirty-two extraditable crimes, including terrorism
- a common definition of terrorism and specific minimum sentences for various terrorist offences

Table 13.2. Europol

- Support service for law-enforcement agencies of member states
- Budget: 334 million Euros (2010–2013)
- Staff: 700 (2012)
- Functions:
  -providing information exchanges to prevent international organized crime
  -coordinating multinational operations
  -maintaining transnational databases
  -preventing Euro counterfeiting
  -analyzing intelligence

Hence there was a remarkable turnaround from the sluggishness of the early 1990s to speedy action after 1999 as a result of the combined external pressure of the terrorist attacks in New York, Madrid, and London, as well as the security problems emanating from Central and Eastern Europe. The ultimate authority over police and judicial cooperation, however, still rests with national governments, although the emerging institutions such as Europol did allow greater cooperation and communication between member states.

Outlook

The EU can look back on a decade of impressive developments in the area of justice and home affairs. The summits in Tampere (1999) and The Hague (2004) introduced far-reaching policies regarding asylum and immigration, as well as judicial and police cooperation in both criminal and civil matters, all supported by new institutional structures such as FRONTEX, Europol, or Eurojust. The Lisbon Treaty of 2007 further boosted the JHA agenda by establishing a Charter for Fundamental Rights. Lisbon also introduced qualified majority voting for judicial and police cooperation in criminal matters, and asylum and immigration. In addition, previous restrictions on the European Court of Justice to rule in JHA cases were lifted. Granted, Lisbon also brought opt-outs for the Fundamental Rights Charter (Poland and the UK), as well as for asylum, visa, and immigration (Denmark, with Ireland and the UK deciding on a case-by-case basis on whether to opt in). Nonetheless, justice and home affairs has come a long way since its introduction in the EU agenda at Maastricht in 1991.

JHA, however, has not reached an endpoint in its development. The Single Market and Schengen gave European citizens the right to move freely. Globalization and technological innovation have made EU borders—whether internal or external—more porous, and an ever increasing number of Europeans, for personal or business reasons, will operate outside their national domain. This trend alone demands the need for greater cooperation between national police forces, customs services, and legal hierarchies, which is further exacerbated by the threat of terrorism. Given the aggravation that the bombings in Madrid and London have caused on the psyche of the European public, it seems bewildering that JHA continues to be organized in an intergovernmental fashion. In the aftermath of 9/11 discussions took place on whether to establish a supranational intelligence authority along the lines of the CIA in America. Alas, only Belgium and Austria were in favor of such a setup. Supranational intelligence and police agencies would arguably be more efficient in combating terrorism, yet such developments would seriously compromise the national sovereignty, if not identity, of the member states. Intergovernmental cooperation, even with the introduction of qualified majority voting in certain areas, will therefore most likely continue to be the name of the game.

14

Common Foreign and Security Policy

Discussions on foreign and defense policies in the European Union have often been nebulous, more pretence than substance. Crucial questions of whether and how to move beyond national interests toward a truly supranational authority in foreign policy have hardly been considered throughout the EU's sixty-year existence. The early failings in the 1950s of French Prime Minister Renee Pleven to establish the so-called European Defence Community testified to the political reality that Europe's agenda, up until the 1990s, was dominated by the overwhelming influence of the Cold War, trapping Europe within the global power struggle between the United States and the Soviet Union.

In the end indecisiveness and conflicting opinions over the precise nature of the European project contributed to shortcomings in the sphere of foreign and security policy. Granted, in 1997, the EU established the post of High Representative for CFSP, which was followed up in 2007 with the High Representative of the Union for Foreign Affairs and Security Policy (which merged the two previously existing roles of High Representative for CFSP and the External Relations Commissioner). Nonetheless, the bitter debate over Europe's involvement in Iraq in 2003 offered a reminder that the member states still have not reached a convincing consensus over the EU's scope,

*direction, and aspirations: Should it be a federal union with far-reaching suprana-
tional political, economic, and social powers or merely a "trading union" whereby
supranational integration would be confined to an economic agenda? Because the
EU continues to be more than an international organization but less than a coherent
polity, it is lackluster in the areas of foreign and security policy. In this context, this
chapter addresses five important questions:*

1. *Why have developments in foreign and security policy been so slow
   compared to, for instance, the Single Market initiatives?*
2. *Does Europe have a coherent foreign policy?*
3. *What instruments does the EU employ to pursue its common foreign policy?*
4. *What are the Union's geographical spheres of activity?*
5. *Who represents the EU abroad?*

Security in the Post–Cold War Era

During the Cold War security was synonymous with the defense of territory, with
NATO and the Warsaw Pact as its guarantors. After the breakup of the communist
empire, security acquired a new and complex dimension: nonterritorial threats
increasingly dominate the international agenda, including terrorism, drug trafficking, nuclear waste, ethnic conflicts, economic and social imbalances, environmental problems, and human disasters. A new threat has been the emergence of
new actors in international politics other than states that act without any reference
to national interests (Al Quaida, of course, is the most prominent example). Hence
security post-1989 seems to be linked to issues rather than to states (albeit Saddam
Hussein's Iraq represents a notable exception).

To face the challenges of this new world order, the United States relies on an
enormous military capacity. The U.S. spends more on defense than France, the
UK, Germany, Japan, China, Russia, and India combined. The U.S. also is the only
country worldwide that can intervene at will at any time, anywhere on the globe.
U.S. technology enables the country to wage war with limited (American) casual-
ties. This prime military position will continue long into the future, since the U.S.
also spends five times as much money on military research and development as
all of Europe combined.

It is in this context that one must assess the changing role of the North Atlantic Treaty Organization (NATO). The events of 2002 witnessed major changes for
the Alliance. In that year a new NATO–Russian Council (NRC) was established
to achieve cooperation in missile defense and in the fight against terrorism and
nuclear proliferation. The NATO summit in Prague, in November 2002, also paved
the way for integrating former Warsaw Pact countries from Central and Eastern
Europe.[1] However, fundamental problems persist. NATO remains a large and

conservative organization with decision-making procedures still based on consensus, requiring the agreement of all of its twenty-eight members. In military matters the Alliance continues to rely heavily on the United States. Ironically, though, the U.S. does not necessarily involve NATO in its military operations, as seen in Iraq, where the U.S. forged ahead without NATO. Further questions also remain regarding NATO's future objectives. With Russia now a possible partner, who is the next enemy? And with Europe on the verge of taking on new responsibilities with the establishment of the EU's Rapid Reaction Force (see below), where does NATO fit in the new world order?

An answer to that question was proposed by the former U.S. secretary of defense Donald Rumsfeld at the NATO summit in Prague in 2002, when he convinced the European partners to mount a Rapid Response Force of up to twenty-one thousand troops, to be deployable within five to thirty days and for relatively brief operations against terrorists anywhere in the world. Some commentators judged this move as a cynical attempt by the U.S. to use NATO for its war against Al-Quaida, but the end result, in any case, was a remarkable change in NATO's envisaged function: a transformation from a defense organization into a force capable of preemptive military action. Undoubtedly Rumsfeld bred at least momentary life into the Alliance, with the welcomed side effect of satisfying American national interests. But this could not hide the fact that NATO is an ailing patient, struggling to find a coherent purpose and objective.

Chronology of the Common Foreign and Security Policy

The first attempt to establish a coherent foreign and defense policy at the European level emerged in the ambitious plan by French Prime Minister Rene Pleven for a European Defence Community (EDC). The outbreak of the Korean War in 1950 had prompted widespread fears that the Cold War might intensify and that Korea was merely a prelude to a showdown between the world's two ideological camps. Harry S. Truman, U.S. president at the time, made it quite clear to his West European colleagues that he expected Europe to share the burden of global confrontation, particularly to provide for its own security. American demands grew more urgent during the debate over the future of West Germany's military complex. Clearly any defense force could only benefit from the economic and technological might of Western Europe's most populous country. However, the lesson learned from two world wars was that a coherent strategy had to be found to satisfactorily and safely integrate West German forces into the community of Western democratic states. Pleven's EDC offered just that: a European army composed of national contingents, with a supranational foreign minister, in which all participating states, except for West Germany, could maintain command of their own national units. Britain was the first country to veto the plan, favoring instead the looser intergovernmental Western European Union (WEU), which was merely an extension of the 1948

Table 14.1. Developments in the Fields of Foreign and Security Policy

1948: Brussels Treaty Organization (later to be named the West European Union (WEU)
1952: Pleven Plan to establish the European Defence Community (EDC)
1954: French Parliament refuses to ratify the EDC
1969: The Hague summit establishes European Political Cooperation (EPC)
1992: Maastricht Treaty introduces CFSP as Pillar II of the EU
1997: Amsterdam Treaty introduces position of High Representative
1998: St. Malo Initiative (France, UK) aims at giving Europe capacity for autonomous action
1999: Helsinki summit agrees to set up Rapid Response Force by 2003
2007: Lisbon Treaty introduces the position of High Representative for Foreign Affairs and Security Policy

Treaty of Brussels that Italy and West Germany were invited to join in 1954.[2] Nevertheless, despite Britain's refusal to join, the original EU-6 embraced the EDC in 1952, but Pleven's bold plan failed ratification in France where political sentiment was largely opposed to such ambitious supranational ideals. With hardly an option left, the original Six, along with Britain, settled on the WEU. But without armed forces, the WEU was only an administrative and consultative organ that merely added a European perspective to NATO's decisions.

The next proposal to foster foreign policy at a European level came at the summit in The Hague in 1969, and was termed European Political Cooperation (EPC). An initiative by the newly elected French president Georges Pompidou, EPC turned out to be simply an intergovernmental and bilateral forum for foreign ministers and heads of governments. Supported by a network of national officials and committees, and fiercely guarding its independence from the European Community, EPC established the so-called common position as a political means to establish foreign policy consensus. However, common positions were not binding on the member states, although national governments did agree to avoid actions that might undermine common positions. The result of all this was some degree of streamlining of European foreign policies, albeit outside the realm of the community.

Not until the negotiations for the Maastricht Treaty, which was ratified in 1992, did a more coherent approach to European foreign policy emerge. The treaty, as a result of the negotiations, introduced the three-pillar structure to the newly termed European Union,[3] which meant that the Common Foreign and Security Policy (CFSP) was now regarded as an official EU policy. Maastricht also added "joint actions" as another diplomatic weapon to the arsenal of the CFSP. Once adopted by consensus, common positions and joint actions were binding to the member states. Regarding defense, the treaty mentioned the "eventual framing of a common defence policy, which might in time lead to a common defence," for the purpose of building up the WEU as the defense component of the EU, but also

Table 14.2. Objectives and Instruments of the CFSP

The Maastricht Treaty sets out the following objectives of the CFSP:

- Strengthen common values and interests, and the independence of EU security
- Preserve peace and strengthen international security
- Promote international cooperation
- Develop and consolidate democracy as well as the rule of law, human rights, and fundamental freedoms

In order to achieve these objectives, the EU has the following types of decisions at its disposal:

1. *Common Positions:* adopted by consensus and binding to all member states
2. *Common Strategies:* adopted by consensus and binding to all member states
3. *Joint Actions:* adopted under qualified majority voting in the Council of Ministers after prior unanimous agreement at the European Council

citing the WEU's future development as a way to strengthen the European pillar within NATO.

The Amsterdam Treaty further fleshed out the gradually developing defense plan by stating that the EU was now willing to launch the Petersberg Tasks, to be implemented by the WEU.[4] The CFSP also introduced the post of High Representative—a position held by the former NATO secretary general Javier Solana. Another political step forward was to set up "common strategies" to give clearer focus to EU negotiations on the international stage. The newly introduced "constructive abstention" also allowed member states to voice disapproval of a particular position, strategy, or action without jeopardizing its overall implementation. One has to keep in mind, however, that the European Commission, the European Court of Justice, and indeed the European Parliament are largely sidelined from the foreign policy and security agenda.[5] CFSP is strictly the business of the Council of Ministers and the European Council, which is a purely intergovernmental approach to handling these matters.

The Franco-British St. Malo Initiative of 1998 added further strength to the CFSP. With the violent breakup of Yugoslavia still on their minds, Prime Minister Tony Blair and President Jacques Chirac agreed that the EU must have the capacity for autonomous military action through a credible military force of member states operating within the EU framework. St. Malo thus brought about the establishment of a European Security and Defence Policy (ESDP) that would be used for military missions where the United States did not intend to get involved, and that would freely use national military assets previously committed exclusively to NATO. The Helsinki summit of December 1999 formalized these ideas; it set a deadline for mounting a Rapid Reaction Force of fifty thousand to sixty thousand troops by 2003 that would be responsible for crisis management, peacekeeping, peacemaking, conflict prevention, and humanitarian and rescue missions.[6] The EU also agreed to establish a nonmilitary response capacity that today can provide the

Table 14.3. The Rapid Reaction Force

The EU summit in Helsinki in December 1999 agreed to strengthen CFSP and to add a concrete military wing to the European Union. In detail, the Response Force, ought to

1. Be capable of being deployed within 60 days

2. Be ready to carry out its mission for at least one year

3. Have a strength of 50–60 thousand troops

4. Be responsible for humanitarian and rescue missions, conflict prevention, peacekeeping and peacemaking

civilian component of crisis management with up to five thousand police officers, one thousand of whom can be deployed within thirty days (see Table 14.2).

The Nice summit in December 2000 formalized the institutions of the ESDP, including a political and security committee, a military committee, and military staff. In December 2003 the member states adopted a European Security Strategy giving top priority for action to the fight against terrorism, the strategy for achieving peace in the Middle East, and Bosnia-Herzegovina.

One must keep in mind, however, that the Rapid Reaction Force is not a European army, since it relies only on the deployment of national troops. Further, as stated in the Berlin Plus agreement of 2002, the EU can only act independently from NATO if the Alliance itself does not want to get involved, and the EU must obtain the approval of all NATO members to gain access to NATO's planning capabilities and other resources. In any case, one has to question the military effectiveness of a force comprised only of fifty thousand or sixty thousand troops. The UK, in fact, has argued that the force needs to be expanded in light of developments in the aftermath of the bombing of the World Trade Center in 2001.

Despite the organizational and structural impediments, the ESDP has made its mark in international politics. In January 2003 an EU police mission of five hundred officers relieved the UN International Police Task Force in Bosnia-Herzegovina. In further action, in April of that year, the NATO force in Macedonia was replaced first by an EU military force and then by a two hundred-strong EU police mission. In December 2004 an EU military force (EUFOR) of eight thousand troops replaced the NATO-led Security Force in Bosnia-Herzegovina (SFOR).In 2006 the EU sent thirty-five hundred troops to the Democratic Republic of Congo to help maintain stability during the presidential and parliamentary elections. Following the Israeli-Hezbollah clash in Lebanon during July and August 2006, a number of member states, led by France and Italy, contributed seventy-five hundred troops to strengthen UNIFIL, the UN's Interims Force in Lebanon.

Another advance in foreign policy came with the development of the European Neighbourhood Policy (ENP) in 2004.[7] The ENP offers financial assistance to entities beyond the frontier of the EU, provided they meet the strict conditions of government reform, economic reform, and other issues surrounding positive transformation. The sixteen entities that comprise the ENP are Algeria, Armenia, Azerbaijan, Belarus, Egypt, Georgia, Israel, Jordan, Lebanon, Libya, Moldova, Morocco, the Palestinian Authority, Syria, Tunisia, and Ukraine.[8] The ENP focuses on the objectives of democracy and human rights, the rule of law, good governance, the market economy, and sustainable economic development. In return for a commitment to these goals, ENP countries receive substantial financial support from the European Neighborhood and Partnership Instrument (ENPI), which, between 2007 and 2013, dispenses 12 billion Euros.[9] By 2007 the EU (more precisely the European Council and the Council of Ministers) had agreed on specific plans of action with twelve entities (all but Syria, Belarus, Algeria, and Libya). A new eastern partnership was launched in May 2009 and aimed for deeper bilateral agreements with Armenia, Azerbaijan, Belarus, Georgia, Moldova, and Ukraine in the fields of legislative approximation, economic integration, and democratic reforms, supported by a further 600 million Euros until 2013.

The Lisbon Treaty brought a major institutional overhaul in the way the CFSP is implemented. With the treaty entering into force in December 2009, Baroness Catherine Ashton assumed the position of High Representative for Foreign Affairs and Security Policy. The role combines the previous posts of Commissioner for External Relations and the High Representative for CFSP in an attempt to increase coherence in the way the EU is represented abroad. Part of Ashton's remit also included the establishment of a European External Action Service (EEAS). The service integrates the Commission's 136 offices and representations into a diplomatic network of EU embassies, staffed with some 5,000 officials from the Commission, the European Council secretariat, as well as from the member states. The Lisbon Treaty, however, did not alter the decision-making process, which remained under the member states' domain, and also left untouched the requirement of unanimity for common positions and common strategies.[10] Furthermore, Lisbon explicitly stated that the treaty does not give the Commission the right to initiate legislation. The European Parliament also continues to be largely excluded from CFSP proceedings, and the European Court of Justice still has no jurisdiction over foreign policy matters.

Assessment

The Lisbon Treaty aimed to solve Henry Kissinger's dilemma when, in the 1970s, he asked: Who do I call when I need to speak with Europe? Indeed, prior to Lisbon, a number of different institutions and individuals represented the EU abroad, strongly suggesting that the Union did not speak with a single authoritative voice on the international stage. What the non-European world saw were at least three different actors within the EU, none with central authority. The Commission, for example, exerted international influence as the EU's negotiator at the World Trade Organization by conducting enlargement processes and managing economic relations with third countries; the Council Presidency informed the world of the EU's positions, while also acting as a driving force behind enlargement negotiations. Lastly, the High Representative for CFSP was the spokesperson for the General Affairs Council within the Council of Ministers but only if all member states had decided on a specific course of action. The question on the minds of EU analysts, therefore, was whether Lisbon had ended these institutional rivalries once and for all and provided the needed coherence.

Although still in its infancy, one can safely assume that the network of EU embassies is responsible for the EU's external representation, a function previously held by the rotating Presidency. The limited involvement of the European Parliament is worrisome, however. Given that the Lisbon Treaty granted the EEAS autonomy in budget and staffing matters, the EU would have been well advised to allow the EP to scrutinize the EEAS for the sake of greater transparency and democratic accountability. Nonetheless, and despite the creation of the new High Representative, other actors within the EU will continue to speak for and on behalf of Europe. Only in the field of external trade does the Union have one voice, since it is the Commission that negotiates trade agreements at the World Trade Organization. But in other international contexts the EU hardly represents a uniform front. At the Copenhagen summit for climate change in December 2009, the EU was represented by eight different actors.[11] France and the UK have permanent seats at the UN Security Council, but the EU does not. France, Germany, Italy, and the UK are members of the G20, but the rotating Presidency was invited only in 2009. Lastly, Lisbon not only gave us the new High Representative, it also created a new President of the European Council. The Council frequently reaches decisions on matters that have an external dimension, and it is therefore part of the President's role to express any foreign policy objectives and actions. Hence Lisbon did not necessarily create coherence but only added to the problem of overrepresentation. Therefore Henry Kissinger, and indeed anyone else who wishes to engage with the EU in foreign and security matters, would be well advised to adopt a twenty-first-century mode of communication. Send an email to the High Representative but make sure to copy in the President of the Commission, the President of the European Council, the rotating Presidency, and also the big member states France, Britain and Germany.

People's expectations of the EU's foreign policy may be too ambitious. The simple fact is that the Union is not a global superpower, although it certainly possesses the economic muscle to be one. The CFSP complements but does not replace the foreign policies of its member states, and this became all the more evident in 2003, when the EU could not agree on a strategy toward Saddam Hussein's Iraq. Although the UK, Spain, Poland, Italy, and Portugal supported George Bush's war effort, the other member states were reluctant to send troops, and the European Council of March 2003 could agree only on the wish for a "speedy conclusion to the hostilities."

Nonetheless, the EU has had a significant impact on a number of important world events. Not to be underestimated were the trade sanctions against apartheid South Africa, Slobodan Milosevic's Yugoslavia, or Robert Mugabe's Zimbabwe. The commercial attractiveness of the EU's Single Market exerts a discipline on the economies of non-EU countries that do not want to jeopardize their access to prosperous European markets. In relations with its eastern neighbors, including Russia, Ukraine, Moldova, and other countries in the south Caucasus and central Asia, the EU signed agreements covering trade, political cooperation, environmental protection, and scientific and cultural collaboration. With neighboring countries on the southern and eastern shores of the Mediterranean, the EU seeks to establish a free-trade area as part of the so-called Euro-Mediterranean partnership (EuroMed).[12] The EU also remained a highly active player in Afghanistan (where member states made up the majority of the NATO-led international force), as well as in Palestine. Finally, the Union's progressive enlargement has played a role in persuading the candidate countries of Central and Eastern Europe to adhere to the Copenhagen criteria, especially the promotion of democracy and human rights. In all the projects noted here, the EU has played a role in international politics, although often through quiet, yet persistent, processes. The ultimate test of this assessment will come in the shape of Turkey's envisaged integration into the Union. No foreign policy or diplomatic effort could prompt such sweeping economic, social, political, and cultural transformations as those accession criteria that Brussels expects its easternmost candidate to fulfill.

Future Challenges Facing the CFSP

European states are no longer global powers. Today, at best, only Britain and France would risk an engagement abroad, whereas most other states, notably Germany, the economic power house of the EU, prefer a low-key approach to global affairs. However, the crises in Kosovo and in Macedonia showed that political and military activism by European states, particularly the UK, cannot necessarily be ruled out. It seems that an involvement by any EU member state or by the EU as a whole depends on where one draws the borders of Europe and the EU's sphere of influence. In the context of today's global security, the prospects of grand-scale external threats, like those experienced during the Cold War era, are likely a scenario of the past. Nowadays security threats emanate from ethnic animosities, aggressive nationalism, or terrorism. Hence there is a profound need for peacemaking and peacekeeping facilities that overrides the former notions of traditional warfare. Specially trained police and paramilitary forces will gain greater importance over traditional armies and weaponry. For the EU, this requires a clearer definition of "regional interests" and a more precisely defined agenda of CFSP goals. Specifically an urgent need has emerged for a clear delineation of powers and responsibilities for NATO versus the EU, as well as a potential European army. Otherwise the ongoing arguments and negotiations over responsibilities and strategies will prevail: systematic confusion will continue over peacekeeping versus peacemaking, concerted action versus unilateral action, and whether NATO or a European army ought to take responsibility.

The breakup of Yugoslavia showed that the EU had failed to act promptly and responsibly because it lacked political cohesion, as well as efficient institutions and cogent instruments. The United States had had to step in, most notably in Bosnia and Herzegovina, and finally achieve stability through the Dayton Peace Agreement in 1995. Yugoslavia posed a severe test to the political rationale of the EU. Is it more than an economic union? Does it have a political and moral agenda? And, if so, how far is it willing to impose it? Is the EU ready to match its economic might by assuming global political responsibilities? The Union's tentative response in Yugoslavia, and NATO's bombing campaign against Milosevic's Serbia in 1999, brought these questions to the fore and caused mixed reactions and often disillusionment among the European public. The problem of Serbia clearly resulted in a loss of credibility for both NATO and the EU, and its member state governments. On one hand, the Alliance dallied for a long time before finally intervening militarily, and, on the other, a swift and decisive intervention was undermined by aspects of the cumbersome decision-making process such as the requirement to agree unanimously on bombing targets.

The EU intended to address these shortcomings through the establishment of the Rapid Reaction Force. It remains to be seen, however, whether the intergovernmental nature of this force and the requirement for unanimity might stand in the way of the much-needed proactivity on the part of the EU in the international sphere. At the moment it seems unlikely that the intergovernmental structure of the CFSP will ever result in a supranational European army. In fact, the CFSP could show us one of the end points of European integration, in which some form of cooperation between the member states is institutionalized, albeit without threatening national sovereignty. The Lisbon Treaty, and particularly the establishment of a new High Representative, might look good on paper, but it has no effect on the fundamental characteristic that continues to underline any EU action in the spheres of foreign and security policies: the requirement for unanimous approval by the member states.

15

Trade and the Common Commercial Policy

Shoes, pullovers, and food are just three areas of trade policy that have reached the headlines in recent years. The controversy over shoes and pullovers has concerned the effects of opening trade with China and the massive increase of cheap Chinese imports that are said to threaten the European shoe and textile industries. Food became an issue as a result of a trade dispute with the United States about whether genetically modified food can be allowed to enter European markets. Trade is not just an unimportant niche subject but goes to the heart of international relations, and especially relations between citizen and state when public health concerns are involved. Trade, of course, also affects relations between developed and developing countries: Should European farmers receive subsidies and be protected by trade barriers that "block" imports from developing states?

When the Treaty of Rome established the European Economic Community in 1957, all member states agreed to a common external tariff that largely ruled out national trade policies such as quotas. With the establishment of the Single Market in 1986, the Common Commercial Policy (CCP) became crucial; without a CCP, non-EU exporters potentially could enter the EU market via the member state with the lowest tariff, and then exploit the free movement of goods to ship their products anywhere within the Union. Clearly the Single Market had a spillover effect on the CCP necessitating a uniform approach to how European states trade with the rest of the world.

The EU is the world's biggest trader and at the same time has become an advocate of multilateral trade. Although different member states have different traditions in their approach to international trade, the EU's basic orientation has always been liberal, aiming to achieve relatively harmonious developments in world trade and the progressive abolition of trade barriers. The fear that a common external tariff for the EU would lead to high trade barriers and would make it difficult for outsiders to enter the European markets has not been justified so far. In fact, the overall effect of establishing the European Community as a customs union has broadly created trade rather than diverting it; that is, it has reduced tariffs among member states to a larger extent than it has deterred third-country imports because of tariff barriers. Given this history of EU trade policy, this chapter aims to address the following issues:

1. *What explains the development of EU trade policy?*
2. *What impact does the EU have on the international economic system?*
3. *Who are the EU's main trade partners, and what is its relationship with China, India, and other emerging economies?*
4. *What are the future challenges for the CCP?*

The Global Trade Regime

The international trade regime was one of the key pillars of international economic cooperation after the Second World War. A significant step toward global free trade was the Uruguay Round Agreement (1986–93), which resulted in the latest version of the General Agreement on Tariffs and Trade (GATT) that brought agriculture and textiles under a multilateral regime. GATT also regulated services through the General Agreement on Trade in Services (GATS), intellectual property rights through the General Agreement on Intellectual Property Rights (TRIPS), and trade relations through the Trade Related Investment Issues (TRIM), while also establishing a system whereby signatory countries agreed to a binding settlement of disputes. The Uruguay agreement yielded a single package that for the first time organized bilateral trade relations between countries within a uniform set of regulations that did not grant opt-outs. Russia, China, and Switzerland, however, chose not to sign the agreement.

As part of the Uruguay Round, GATT was transformed into the World Trade Organization in 1995. Located in Geneva, the WTO regulates trade in goods, services, and intellectual property rights based on negotiations between the signatory countries. In 2008, 153 countries had joined the WTO, including all EU member states. Russia and Switzerland continued to stay outside the WTO, but China joined in 2003. As in GATT, trade partners agree to the binding settlement of disputes, but in the WTO this includes official rulings by WTO law chambers.[1] Should a dispute between trade partners arise—for instance, public health concerns over food imports—the EU has to defend its position before the WTO and face potential sanctions for noncompliance with its rulings.

The Doha Development Round

The next round of trade negotiations took place in 2001, in Doha, the capital of Qatar. Some states, particularly the U.S., aimed for further liberalization in agriculture and services. Developing countries, however, sought increased liberalization not only of agriculture but also of textiles, whereas the EU concentrated on environmental concerns, health and safety standards in the workplace, and the recognition of the socio-cultural dimension of its agricultural sector. The subsequent summit in Cancun, in 2003, exposed the difficulties in moving global trade further. The U.S. had just raised tariffs on steel, while also increasing agricultural subsidies. On the other hand, the EU struggled with the reform of its Common Agricultural Policy, and here, in particular, access of non-EU producers, and this resulted in a premature end to negotiations. The next global trade summit was held in Hong Kong in 2005. As in Cancun, it fell short of achieving tangible results, which were partially prevented by U.S. American unilateralism that expressed itself through export subsidies for farmers and protective tariffs for the domestic cotton industry. Hong Kong therefore was an example that trade negotiations are not necessarily about free trade but are often also about how domestic industries can be protected from global competition.

Ever since 2005 the Doha Development Round has been on hold (or, in the words of the European Commission, "has entered a period of reflection"). Richer nations certainly have to accept responsibility for this. On the one hand the First World wants to abolish tariffs on cars and pharmaceuticals, for instance, but, on the other, the U.S. and the EU are reluctant to open up their agricultural markets. Without doubt, free trade is beneficial to consumers around the world, but trade is also a highly charged political issue and therefore subject to special interests. It is no surprise that EU farmers often complain the loudest whenever the possibility of a new global deal on agriculture appears on the horizon. Doha is further complicated by the impact of non-democratic and often criminal regimes, which prevent a further extension of free trade. A telling example here is Cameroon, which imposes import tariffs of a staggering 60 percent. These revenues do not necessarily benefit its population but instead tend to end up in the pockets of the ruling elites. Lastly, we have seen the emergence of new power players in the global trade arena. Countries such as China, but also India, Brazil and Russia, have become more confident and do not always go along with Western proposals. Hence, although the U.S. and the EU can still break a deal, they now need other partners to make a deal happen.

Table 15.1. Decision Making within the CCP

1. Setting objectives: Commission, together with the Trade Policy Committee
2. Negotiating: Trade Commissioner
3. Adopting results: Council of Ministers and European Parliament

Decision-Making Process

The overall decision-making process comprises three steps: setting objectives, negotiating, and adopting the results (see Table 15.1).

1. *Setting objectives.* The Commission is required to present its trade objectives to, and have these endorsed by, the Trade Policy Committee, which includes trade officials from the member states and usually meets with the Commission weekly.[2] During these meetings the full range of trade policy issues is discussed, and it is here that the Commission presents its specific trade objectives and secures endorsement for these. In contrast to the U.S. Congress, the European Parliament is not actively involved in trade policy, and it debates trade issues only after the mandate has already been adopted by the Council of Ministers. The Commission, however, encourages interest groups to offer feedback and input during the development of the mandate.

2. *Negotiating.* The Commission, represented by its Trade Commissioner, is the negotiating authority at the WTO. Again, the Trade Policy Committee is deeply involved in discussions and consultations during negotiations with third parties, thus reflecting the fundamental nature of the EU as a balance between intergovernmental and supranational forces.[3]

3. *Adopting results.* The results of negotiations must be approved by the European Parliament and the Council of Ministers (in this case, the GAERC—the General Affairs and External Relations Council—which brings together foreign ministers of member states). Results are adopted by applying the ordinary legislative procedure with qualified majority voting in the Council for the majority of issues. Unanimity however is reserved for cultural and audiovisual services, for social, educational and health services, as well as for those policy fields where the EU applies unanimity in its internal legislative processes (for instance tax). In practice, however, member states try to obtain consensus, particularly during the conclusion of WTO negotiations or when sensitive national issues are at stake.

But negotiations and the adoption of results are not always straightforward, as demonstrated by the Treaty of Nice. The treaty entered into force in 2003, with a list of items that remained under national authority and where the member states and not the Commission were the negotiating parties at the WTO. Among the notable exclusions were that France could continue to protect its national film industry. Other exclusions concerned certain cultural and health-care issues and matters of social policy and transport. Nice produced a compromise: the CCP integrated

Table 15.2. The Role of the European Commission (DG Trade)

- Define EU interests
- Negotiate agreements on behalf of EU member states
- Monitor implementation of international agreements
- Liaise with other departments within the Commission with a trade dimension (environment, competition, agriculture, etc.)
- Inform the public

obligations that had been established in the Uruguay Round, including trade in services and intellectual property rights, but the nature of the exclusions indicate that the member states themselves, not the Commission, determine the contractual basis for international negotiations (Table 15.2).

Instruments of the CCP

The CCP uses various tools to implement the EU's trade agenda, for example, tariffs, quotas, voluntary export restraints (VER), anti-dumping measures, and trade sanctions (see Table 15.3).

1. *Tariffs.* The average EU tariff is about 5.1 percent.[4] For agriculture, the tariff jumps to 12 percent and is even higher for specific products such as sugar, wheat, and dairy products. As much as 30 percent of imports, however, has no tariff and is therefore allowed to leave or enter the EU without any customs duties. These goods include construction materials, computers, and telecom equipment. Sensitive imports such as cars, clothing, or footwear have a 10 percent surcharge.

2. *Quotas.* The EU sets import limits on certain goods, primarily bananas, sardines, tuna, iron, and steel.

3. *Voluntary export restraints (VER).* Quantitative export restrictions are agreed upon jointly by exporters and importers. A well-known VER is the 2005 agreement limiting the quantity of Chinese textiles that can enter the EU.

4. *Anti-dumping measures.* Dumping refers to the practice of selling goods below the market price in order to gain a higher market share with the goal of harming competitors. The WTO allows for countervailing measures, such as the imposition of custom duties that are equivalent to the dumping margin. The Commission's responsibility is to check for evidence of dumping and decide the type of counteraction to take. An example of this is the Commission's response, in the 1980s, to the import of semiconductors and chemicals from the United States.

5. *Trade sanctions.* The most obvious sanction is where the EU simply stops trading with a country altogether, mainly for political reasons. Notable examples are sanctions against apartheid South Africa in the 1980s, Milosevic's Yugoslavia in the 1990s, and Robert Mugabe's Zimbabwe a decade later. The Trade Barrier Regulation of 1994 gave WTO members the opportunity to act against unfair

Table 15.3. Instruments of the CCP

1. Tariffs
2. Quotas
3. Voluntary export restraints
4. Anti-dumping measures
5. Trade sanctions

trade measures by, for example, preventing access to a particular market. A country can impose sanctions if it receives permission from the WTO. In the case of the EU, there is, however, the added requirement of an approval by QMV in the Council of Ministers.

Trade Patterns

In 2010 the European Union accounted for 15 percent of the world's exports and for 18.8 percent of its imports, making it far the leading global player.[5] Some 35 percent of the EU's trade outside its own boundaries was with its leading partners: the U.S., China, Russia, and Switzerland. Trade with European countries that are not members of the EU accounted for 28.7 percent; 9.2 percent of trade is with Africa as a whole; and only 5.2 percent is with the poorest states in the world—those in sub-Saharan Africa, the Caribbean, and the Pacific (the so-called ACP countries). From a regional perspective, we recently witnessed the growing influence of Asia, and here, in particular, China whose exports to the EU rose from 81.3 billion Euros in 2002 to 282.5 billion Euros in 2010. By that year the negative trade balance with China had reached 169 billion Euros (see Table 15.4).[6] When looking at individual member states, Germany has the highest trade surplus in the EU with 157 billion Euros, and the UK has the highest deficit with 118 billion Euros. Still, one has to keep in mind that a staggering 62 percent of the EU's overall trade actually happens between EU member states.[7] Accusations that the EU has established a European fortress that is difficult for outsiders to enter are therefore not necessarily unfounded.

Bilateral Trade Agreements

Most of the trade relations with the EU's major trading partners, including China and the United States are managed under the WTO rules. Beyond the WTO, the EU has negotiated specific trade relations with other countries that are too numerous to mention.[8] This complex trade agenda could be organized into five areas: agreements with the European Economic Area (EEA); agreements with the Euro-Mediterranean Partnership; association agreements with view to EU membership; agreements reached with developing countries; and preferential trade agreements.

1. *The European Economic Area.* This is a bloc of small European states that have decided to forsake EU membership but are nonetheless accepting all directives

Table 15.4. The EU's Leading Trading Partners in 2010

EU Exports to:	Billion Euros	Percent	EU Imports from:	Billion Euros	Percent
World	1349.2	100	World	1509.1	100.0
1. U.S.	242.2	18.0	1. China	282.5	18.8
2. China	113.3	8.4	2. U.S.	170.4	11.3
3. Switzerland	105.2	7.8	3. Russia	160.1	10.6
4. Russia	86.1	6.4	4. Switzerland	83.2	5.5
5. Turkey	61.3	4.5	5. Norway	79.4	5.3
6. Japan	43.8	3.2	6. Japan	65.8	4.4
7. Norway	41.9	3.1	7. Turkey	42.3	2.8

Source: Eurostat, 2012.

and regulations emanating from the EU's Single Market program. In this respect, Norway, Iceland, and Liechtenstein implement EU law to gain access to the EU's Single Market and its 485 million consumers.[9] Because these states are not EU countries, they cannot participate, for instance, in the formulation of product regulations. Instead, they simply follow EU regulations for ease of trade relations.

2. *The Euro-Mediterranean Partnership (Euromed).* Euromed was launched in November 1995 at the Barcelona conference of EU foreign ministers and eleven non-EU counterparts from Mediterranean countries.[10] The objective of the partnership, referred to as the Barcelona Declaration, is to foster free trade between the EU and the southern Mediterranean, but also among the participating states and entities,[11] without any tariff barriers, agricultural barriers, or any obstacles to services. Euromed received a boost in 2004 with the launch of the European Neighborhood Policy (ENP) which provided financial support from the EU in return for political and economic reforms.[12] At first glance this agreement looked promising for the region, as it offered preferential access to rich European markets. The agreements focused mainly on trade in goods, but have in recent years been complemented by a range of additional negotiations that aimed to open up access for agricultural products and liberalization for trade in services and financial products. Indeed, between 2000 and 2010 exports to the EU had increased by about 10 percent every year. On closer inspection, however, the industrial base of the Barcelona countries is rather small and does not pose a significant threat to EU producers. It is no surprise, therefore, that the Euromed countries only account for about 10 percent of the EU's total external trade.[13]

3. *Association Agreements.* These agreements aim for a smooth integration of candidate countries into the EU. They are negotiated with each individual country and accommodate the acquis communautaire, as well as market access. Of the current candidate countries, Turkey has by far the most significant trade relations with the EU. As early as 1963 Turkey signed a Customs Agreement, which was upgraded in 1996 to a Customs Union that nonetheless focused mainly on industrial goods and excluded the vital sectors of agriculture, services, and public procurement.

The start of official negotiations for EU membership in October 2005 saw a further boost to trade between the two partners. The importance of the EU for Turkey is unquestionable, with nearly two-thirds of the country's exports going to Europe and more than half its imports coming from an EU member state. Similarly, in 2010, Turkey ranked fifth for exports from the EU and seventh for imports to the EU (see Table 15.4).

4. *Development Policy.* For nearly thirty years, trade relations with developing countries were dominated by the Lomé Conventions, named after the capital of Togo where the first convention took place. Initiated in 1975, the agreement brought together the EU and forty-five states from Africa, the Caribbean, and the Pacific, the so-called ACP countries, as noted above. Lomé aimed for an equal partnership and sought for a more just and balanced economic order. In the fields of agriculture, industrial development, and regional cooperation, the EU offered special aid for the least-developed countries. The Commission admitted that the Lomé Conventions had been a failure, mainly because the policy was incapable of strengthening the industrial base of the developing world and also failed to deliver on the promise of easier access to affluent European markets.

Lomé was replaced, in 2000, by the ACP-EU Partnership Agreement, often also referred as the Cotonou Agreement (named after the capital of Benin), which, like its predecessor, concentrated on ACP countries that, by 2012, had numbered seventy-nine. Unlike its predecessor, the Cotonou Agreement provided for a transition to free trade through regional economic partnerships between developing countries. Access to Europe was still restricted for ACP countries, particularly in agriculture, although a new program that was launched in 2001 granted the forty-nine poorest countries duty-free access to Europe. Cotonou was complemented by "Everything-But-Arms" (EBA) agreements that promised special aid and trade privileges to these countries once they met objectives of good governance and democracy. Thus an evident shift occurred in how the EU related to the developing world. At Lomé, the EU looked at development criteria such as GDP per capita and infant mortality rates; with Cotonou, the EU advocated general principles such as trade access, good governance, and political dialogue, as well as economic diversity that can be achieved regardless of a country's economic development.

Cotonou is set to continue at least until 2020 with a major review taking place every five years. However, the EU was increasingly criticized for granting privileged access to Europe for ACP countries, which is illegal under WTO rules, Hence, in 2008, the EU set up the so-called Economic Partnership Agreements (EPA) with the aim of establishing free trade with the ACP countries. As a result, the EU began to phase out all trade preferences from which the ACP countries had benefited ever since the start of this process in 1975. EPAs also differ from country to country taking on board specific characteristics, whether geographical and climate- related, or economic and structural. The EPAs, however, placed the EU in a difficult position: How could trade and development be fostered among the world's poorest countries without preferential treatment? One way would have been to strengthen competitiveness and productivity among the ACP countries before trade preferences are abolished and the stiff wind of global competition could affect developing producers in a detrimental fashion.

A good example of such a process is provided by the EU's banana wars. One of the longest-running trade disputes was finally settled in December 2009. For fifteen years, banana producers in Latin America felt disadvantaged by the high import tariffs charged by the EU, as well as the preferential treatment offered to African and Caribbean countries. The agreement stated that, by 2017, the EU will cut its import tariff on bananas from Latin America from 176 Euros per ton to 114 Euros. But to assist poorer countries, the EU pledged to mobilize up to 200 million Euros to help African and Caribbean producers improve their competitiveness in what in the future will be a much less restricted global market. In return, Latin American countries agreed to drop any other pending WTO disputes. This settlement might serve as a blueprint on how developing countries could be eased into global competition. As yet unknown is how other WTO members respond to this approach, a decision that will ultimately be made as part of the ongoing, yet momentarily stalled, Doha Development Round.

Despite the shift in the EU's development policy through Cotonou and EPAs, exports from the ACP countries to the EU have actually declined over the last thirty years. According to the European Commission, some of the countries struggle to keep up with ever-changing EU regulations (for instance in such areas as food safety or animal welfare). Many ACP countries also lack the infrastructure to trade with their neighboring countries, which results in very low levels of intra regional trade. Lack of competition and red tape are also factors that undermine a speedier economic development.[14]

On the other hand, some African countries have achieved impressive growth figures over the last decade; a process which was also accelerated by investment from the EU but also from China. Most notably, the service sector (and here in particular tourism, information technologies and health) has undergone a dramatic transformation and in the forty-one least developed countries, more people now work in the service sector than in farming. Given these positive developments of recent years, cautious optimism seems justified, given that the EU has moved on from the ineffective legacy of earlier development approaches to one that has the potential to act as a catalyst for economic development and higher standards of living.

5. *Preferential Trade Agreements*. The majority of EU trade is governed by the WTO. Beyond this regime, however, the Union has also established partnerships with individual or groups of countries that offer tariff concessions or other preferential treatment. Beyond the groups of countries mentioned above, the EU had reached agreements with Chile, Columbia, Costa Rica, Mexico, Peru and South Korea. As of 2012, preferential trade agreements were being negotiated amongst

others with Canada, India, Singapore, Malaysia, Ukraine, Brazil, Argentina, Uruguay, and Paraguay, while the start of negotiations had been considered with for instance Japan and Vietnam. Going into any further specifics however, would be beyond the scope of this publication.[15]

Future Challenges to the CCP

With trade expanding across the globe, the Common Commercial Policy has now reached center stage in the EU's approach on how to deal with the outside world. Once a spillover policy to safeguard the functioning of the Single Market, the CCP has now become a powerful tool in shaping international affairs. If the goal of foreign policy is to change a country's behavior—whether through diplomacy or by military means—then the CCP represents a crucial weapon for the world's most powerful economic bloc. Ever since the WTO came into existence, the EU has tried to impose political and social objectives through economic means, whether it is the acceptance of global health standards in return for removing agricultural barriers or political reform in developing countries in return for market access. But external trade relations are very much in flux, and many challenges still lie ahead. So far, a coherent global environmental agenda has not been included, as evidenced by the disappointing outcome of the Copenhagen climate summit in 2009 (see chapter 16). The protection of intellectual property rights is complicated by, among other things, the profusion of counterfeited products in China, which has created dangerous loopholes for the global trade regime. In return, the rise of China, India, Brazil, and Russia as serious economic forces might in the future further undermine the agenda-setting power of the EU and also of the U.S. Hence the current stalemate in the Doha Development is much more than a trivial bickering over tariffs and quotas. It is also about a new hierarchy that has emerged in international trade, with new emerging players introducing new demands and objectives that are a testimony to the radical transformation of global politics in the twenty-first century.

16

Environment

Environmental damage arguably represents the most pressing issue of modern times. Global warming, natural catastrophes, or food shortages can endanger prosperity and global peace, challenges further aggravated by the industrial rise of China, India, Brazil, and Russia. The environment presents specific threats that, perhaps more than any other issue, require coordination across borders. Pollution does not respect boundaries, as was aptly demonstrated during 1986, when a reactor in Chernobyl in the former Soviet Union released radioactive pollutants across Europe, during a time when the member states debated the Single European Act. In addition, a common environmental policy is crucial for a market's effective operation. Environmental regulations can distort trade and have both the appearance and effect of trade barriers. They must therefore be harmonized and coordinated at a level that fits the market. The key issues in this debate are:

1. *What are the reasons behind the establishment of the EU's Environment Policy?*
2. *What is the scope of the Environment Policy?*
3. *How did the EU and other international actors respond to the challenge of global warming?*

The Development of the EU's Environment Policy

An environment agenda was not part of the founding treaties of the EU of the 1950s. Rather, it emerged from separate initiatives beginning as late as 1972. These were broadly coordinated as action programs that passed some two hundred pieces of legislation, chiefly concerned with limiting pollution by introducing minimum standards, notably for waste management, water pollution, and air pollution. Political pressure from the Green Party in the European Parliament, as well as from Germany, the Netherlands, and the Scandinavian states, in the 1980s and early 1990s led to greater demand for a coherent policy at the European level. As a consequence of this shifting political paradigm, the EU agreed on a series of so-called Environmental Action Plans (EAPs). Whereas the first two (1973 and 1977) were merely measures to correct already existing and environmentally harmful legislation, the third EAP of 1982 stipulated that environmental action can contribute to economic growth and the creation of jobs. The fifth EAP (1993) advocated sustainable growth, and also listed as priorities waste reduction, lower energy use, change in consumption patterns, pollution control, and environmentally friendly transport by specifically targeting such sectors as industry, energy, transport, agriculture, and tourism.

The sixth EAP (2001–10) aimed to improve the implementation of existing legislation by integrating environmental concerns into other policies, while also concentrating on citizens and suggesting more environmentally friendly consumer behavior. Land-use planning decisions had to take the environment into account. At its core, the sixth EAP had four objectives.

- Climate change and global warming
- Natural habitat, wildlife, and biodiversity
- Environment and health
- Natural resources and waste management

Regarding treaties, the "greening" of European politics was first recognized in the Single European Act of 1986. However, given the significant prosperity increase which the establishment of the Single Market had promised to governments, industry, and the business community,[1] the EU had missed a great opportunity, as tighter environmental regulations and guidelines would most likely have been acceptable as a necessary by-product. But instead of introducing an environmental agenda in parallel with the opening of markets across Europe, environmental policy during the subsequent years had to catch up with ever more detailed Single Market regulations. A more formal inclusion arrived with the Maastricht Treaty (1992), which linked the promotion of sustainable growth to environmental protection. The Amsterdam Treaty (1997) gave the European Parliament considerable influence by giving it veto power for environmental legislative proposals through the application of the co-decision procedure. The Cardiff process of 1998 stated that an environmental dimension must be added to most policy areas (and not just to the obvious ones such as agriculture or transport). Furthermore, the Gothenburg strategy (2001) declared environmental protection one of the key elements of the Lisbon Process which aimed to establish the EU as the world's most competitive and knowledge-based economy by 2010.

The Roles of the Commission and Other Institutional Players

The Commission is the main driver for the EU's environmental agenda, both in terms of administering policies and regulations and in prioritizing key areas for activity. DG Environment employs around 500 officials, a far cry from the six staff members who dealt with such issues in 1970. After the introduction of initial environmental regulations in 1973 the Commission took only a partial interest, and implementation of environmental regulations across the EU became more of a distant focus than a political reality. As such, complaints of non-implementation from citizens, NGOs, governments, or industry actors doubled between 1988 and 1992, finally forcing the Commission, in 1996, to lay out a strategy on how to solve this issue. Nonetheless, non-implementation of environmental rules remained a severe problem, and over the years the Commission has adopted a new strategy, assuming the role of mediator between complainants (such as Greenpeace) and polluters.

In recent years, and given the very complex nature of environmental policy, the Commission has set its priorities as follows:

- Environment and health (air and water pollution, nuclear safety, and genetically modified organisms [GMOs])
- Chemical policy, including the so-called precautionary principle which places the burden of proof that no environmental damage has taken place with the industry before a license to produce or trade is issued

Apart from the Commission, other EU institutions also had an impact on the development of an environmental agenda. The European Court of Justice has played an important role in promoting the legal foundations of environmental policy, deciding, for instance, in the 1988 Danish bottle case,[2] that environmental protection may override the free movement of goods, and ensuring member state compliance. The ECJ is especially able to perform this function because of the role of environmental groups that help to enforce policy by prosecuting malpractice. As an additional institutional player, the European Environmental Agency (EEA) has produced information on how to standardize behavior since 1994. Unlike the Environmental Protection Agency in the U.S., however, the EEA lacks legal powers to take polluters or non-implementers to court. The agency is also decentralized

Table 16.1. Fields of EU Environmental Activities

Specific Policies:

Air, Biotechnology, Chemicals, Civil Protection and Environmental Accidents, Climate Change, Environmental Economics, Environment and Enlargement, Health, Industry, International Issues, Land Use, Nature and Biodiversity, Noise, Soil, Sustainable Development, Waste

Environmental Elements in:

Agriculture, Development, Economic and Financial Affairs, Employment, Energy, Enterprise, Fisheries, Internal Market, Research, Cohesion, Trade, Transport

and linked to national environmental bureaucracies, which raises concerns over its independence. Nonetheless, the provision and standardization of information is important in setting methodologies for evaluating environmental impact which in turn are essential for establishing an objective starting point for discussions and policy decisions between member states and Brussels.

The Scope of EU Environment Policy

The environmental agenda of the EU is vast. It did not develop as a single, coherent strategy but instead developed in a piecemeal fashion and is often added on to other existing EU policies. This add-on principle is referred to as Environmental Policy Integration (EPI), which means that each economic activity has to be seen in light of its environmental impact. A look at DG Environment's website reveals the scope of its activities and is listed in Table 16.1.

In addition to the many issues that form environmental policy, the whole agenda is further complicated by the need to persuade the member states of the appropriateness of both agreeing to and implementing coordinated environmental policy. Member states have different positions and cultural attitudes toward the environment.[3] The resultant discrepancy in positions was once neatly described as "leaders" and "laggards," but it also reflects different ways of perceiving and measuring environmental damage and risk.[4] As a compromise, member states were to focus on the technical measures, such as BAT (best available technology), that should be used. Yet with the recession of the 1990s and the perception that environmental protection costs money, even Germany lost its leadership position in the environment debate and the UK government, under Tony Blair and Gordon Brown, pushed forward newer policy approaches.

The March 2007 Summit

Much was expected of the German Presidency during the first half of 2007. Indeed, with Chancellor Angela Merkel (a physicist and former Environment Minister) as a pivotal figure, the EU came up with a striking agreement (see Table 16.2) that caught many observers by surprise and even won praise from the environmental

Table 16.2. March 2007 Summit: Key Points

- Cut greenhouse gases by 20 percent of the 1990 level by 2020
- Take 20 percent of energy from renewable sources
- Ban traditional light bulbs by 2009
- Equip every power station with carbon capture technology by 2010
- Compel farmers to grow bio fuel plants on land that was previously subsidized under land-set-aside programs

lobby. The key target was the reduction of greenhouse gases by 20 percent (compared to levels reached in 1990) until 2020. The target of 20 percent, however, referred to the entire EU (although every country had to have at least a 10 percent use of bio fuels). Hence every member state had to draw up so-called National Allocation Plans (NAPs) which determined the total quantity of carbon dioxide emissions that companies were allowed to produce.[5] These NAPs were organized into three periods: the first running from 2005 to 2007; the second, from 2008 to 2012; and the third, from 2013 on. The Commission then scrutinized these plans and made adjustments to these targets.

A further innovation was the development of the Emission Trading Scheme (ETS) which covered 11,500 energy-intensive installations, representing half of the EU's carbon dioxide pollution. These installations included, among others, oil refineries, power plants, and steel mills or factories producing cement, bricks, or paper. The novel aspect of the ETS was the ability of participating companies to buy or sell emission allowances, whose prices were subject to the usual market forces of supply and demand. Hence a company with low emissions could sell some of its emission quota to another company that might be about to exceed its pollution limits.

Not surprisingly both the NAPs and the ETS quickly came under fire. Slovakia was the first EU member state to open a case against the European Commission, arguing that the imposed obligations to reduce carbon dioxide pollution as set by the Commission were too severe. The case paved the way for other countries in Central and Eastern Europe[6] to object to the targets sets by the Commission, claiming that the limits were too low and would undermine economic development, which was still significantly behind Western European levels. These controversies were representative of the wider debate that engulfs environmental protection. How should a commitment to reduce pollution be executed? On the one hand, one could argue for a flat-rate reduction which all countries must adhere to. This, however, would greatly impede economic development in poorer areas intent on catching up with the richer, western parts of Europe, which in the past experienced higher economic growth (but also higher levels of pollution).

A further twist in the battle over emission levels came in September 2009, when the European Court of First Instance sided with Estonia and Poland and annulled the Commission's decision to lower the carbon emission quotas of both countries. Adding insult to injury, the Court also stated that carbon limits ought to be set by the member states and not by the Commission. This caused much consternation, since the protection of the environment—a natural phenomenon that transcends national boundaries—from now on depended on national commitments without the Commission as a supranational entity calling the ultimate shots.

International Cooperation: From Kyoto to Copenhagen

The EU has become a major player in advancing international environmental protection given its harder stance on this issue than that of the U.S. or developing nations. But it has also been forced to change its policies in response to international norms. The Kyoto Protocol established a very different set of criteria for climate emission control compared to the EU's policy of best available technology. Kyoto put in place economic measures that sought to share the burden of managing climate. In 1997 the signatories agreed to a widespread reduction (from 1990 levels) in the emission of greenhouse gases by 2010. As such, the EU agreed to 8 percent, the U.S. administration under Clinton to 7 percent, and Japan and Canada to 6 percent. Alas, President George W. Bush's refusal to sign the Protocol endangered its implementation, since Kyoto stated that at least 55 percent of global emissions had to be covered by the signatory states. With the U.S. having 36 percent of global emissions, it was Russia's decision in 2004 (with 17 percent of global emissions) to sign the agreement that brought Kyoto up to this required quota.

But in addition to Kyoto souring relations between the EU and the U.S., trade conflicts over hormone-treated beef and genetically modified food were ongoing. No surprise, therefore, that in the environmental field the EU looked beyond America. Through the European Neighbourhood Policy the Union not only promotes human rights and good governance but also encourages environmental sustainability. The same can be said of the Euro-Mediterranean as well as the entire EU Trade Policy.[7]

With the Kyoto Protocol due to expire in 2012, twenty-nine governments gathered at the Copenhagen Climate Change Conference in December 2009, with the aim of agreeing to a far-reaching international solution capable of addressing the challenge of global warming. But after two weeks of intensive negotiations, the summit failed to agree on binding commitments to cut greenhouse gas emissions. China, in particular, was widely accused of filibustering discussions, while domestic political constraints undermined President Obama's ability to aim for an ambitious agreement that many environmental activists judged to be a last opportunity to reverse global warming. In a disappointing outcome for the EU, the Copenhagen Accord established a goal to keep global temperature increases below two degrees Celsius. Two years later, in Durban in December 2011, 194 states agreed on the "Durban platform," a commitment to negotiate a legally binding climate deal by 2015 which would then enter into force by 2020. What at first glance looked promising, however, revealed a serious flaw. Until 2020, there is no international agreement on greenhouse emissions. After the expiration of Kyoto, cuts in emissions are now based purely on nationally set targets, which on top of it are only on a voluntary basis. It is by no means certain, that countries such as the United States, China, and Canada will in the future manage to even reach their previous Kyoto levels. In the end, the EU was left as the only economic powerhouse willing to reduce its emissions.

Assessment

Is the EU good for the environment? In its favor the EU has developed a range of new initiatives and principles for environmental management and enforcement. The environmental agenda is also extraordinarily comprehensive and has a very broad range. With the help of Environmental Action Plans the EU established an environmental angle to the entire EU policy-making process and therefore has boosted the environmental performance of some previously laggard member states. Without a doubt, when it comes to the environment, the EU is a global leader.

On the other hand, the precautionary principle (which establishes that new technological developments should not proceed if environmental damage might result) has been mainly rhetorical. A sizable implementation gap is still evident, as the EU's most dynamic sectors such as pharmaceuticals and biotechnology are themselves potential creators of biohazards. The EU still produces vast emissions, not helped by the traditional car and transport lobby. Although the dissemination of information and the provision of standards has undoubtedly had a major impact on our understanding of environmental damage and our ability to manage it, that on its own may not be enough.

With the ongoing sovereign debt crisis, some analysts argued that the imposition of tougher environmental standards would unjustifiably impose a heavy burden on member states struggling with ailing economies. On the other hand, more stringent EU emission targets might force European businesses to invest even further in environmental technologies, a process that might lead, for instance, to the development of solar power stations not just in Europe but potentially also in Africa and other developing areas, making the EU less dependent on fossil fuels from Russia or the Middle East. What might seem as undermining economic recovery could in the end turn out to be an invigorating force within the global economy of the future.

As such, the environment might represent the "next big thing" for the EU. The period between the 1950s and 1980s focused on the establishment of the Single Market, arguably the EU's biggest achievement so far. What began as a vehicle to bring peace to hostile states has turned into one of the world's economic powerhouses. The 2004 and 2007 rounds of enlargement made significant progress in the unification of a once-divided continent. But the sovereign debt crisis seriously undermined the credibility of the European project. EMU was planned as a vehicle to move the continent to an ever closer union, as stipulated in the Maastricht Treaty. In sharp contrast, the malfunctioning of the Eurozone brought deep hardship to many Europeans. A comprehensive environmental agenda, however, could once more make a positive impact on the lives of Europeans and, in the process, provide the Union with much-needed legitimacy. Still, despite the surprising and comprehensive 2007 agreement, the EU has a long way to go to transfer itself into the clean and sustainable knowledge economy. Then again, only monumental efforts can meet a monumental challenge, which is what the environment represents.

17

The Sovereign Debt Crisis in the Eurozone

A mere ten years after its introduction, Economic and Monetary Union was rattled to its core by the large public deficits and faltering economies of some of its members. The severity of the economic downturns prompted some commentators to predict the end of EMU and indeed of the entire European integration project, arguing that the union could no longer sustain the strains imposed by the working mechanisms of the single currency. While the EU might be able to avert such a doomsday scenario, it is unquestionable that a policy that was trumpeted as a bold achievement went spectaculary wrong and caused hithero inconceivable hardship to millions of European citizens. The key issues surrounding these extraordinary developments are the following:

1. *How severe were the economic downturns and which states were most affected?*
2. *Why did these crises develop?*
3. *To what extent did the working mechanisms of EMU contribute to these crises?*

4. *What were the responses by EU institutions to improve economic and fiancial conditions and were these successful?*
5. *What lies ahead for EMU and European integration?*

The Economic Downturn in the "PIIGS" Countries

The sovereign debt crisis that shook the Eurozone affected in particular the so-called PIIGS—Portugal, Ireland, Italy, Greece and Spain. By the end of 2011, the economic and financial situation in these countries indeed revealed a grim picture (see Table 17.1). Greece's public debt was a staggeringly high 165.3 percent of GDP, which was particularly dramatic when compared with the Eurozone's benchmark of 60 percent as set out in the Maastricht Treaty's Stability Pact. Furthermore, all the PIIGS countries had annual account deficits that violated the Stability Pact's guideline of 3 percent. Ireland's annual debt of 13.1 percent was the highest, although this figure was a marked improvement to the 32.4 percent for 2010, when the country was forced to bail out its entire banking sector. Turning to GDP growth, the figures were equally sobering. Greece's economy had contracted by 6.2 percent, having shrunk by 7.4 percent in the previous year. As to unemployment, the PIIGS were suffering worse in comparison with the EU average. The governments in Spain and Greece in particular had to confront the prospect of intensified social unrest, since a quarter of their populations (and up to half of their youth population) was out of work. These dramatic circumstances were exacerbated by international financial markets that were reluctant to lend money to the PIIGS and only did so by charging punishing interest rates. While the governments of Germany and the UK had to pay a relatively modest 2 percent in order to refinance their debts, the figures for others, for instance for Greece (31.0), heavily undermined the chances of a coherent economic recovery (see Table 17.2). The money markets' lack of confidence in the PIIGS, however, affected the whole of the Eurozone. By May 2012, the credit rating agency Standard & Poors granted its triple A status only to four states: Finland, Germany, Luxembourg, and the Netherlands. Just a couple of years previously, this accolade had been granted to all members of the single currency.

Greece: The New Sick Man of Europe

The attribute of Europe's sick man had originally been given to the United Kingdom in the 1970s. Some forty years later, Greece proved to be a worthy successor to this title. Prior to the introduction of the Euro, the country had become accustomed to high inflation (for instance 11 percent in 1994) and a currency—the drachma—to which international investors hardly flocked. With the introduction of the Euro in 2001 (two years after the currency was originally launched), interest rates fell to below 2 percent. Greeks for the first time had the benefit of a stable and

Table 17.1: Economic Downturn in EU and Selected Member States

Country	Debt 2011 (% of GDP)	Account deficit 2011 (% of GDP)	Growth Q1 2012 (% of GDP)*	Unemployment March 2012
Greece	165.3	9.1	-6.2	21.7
Portugal	107.8	4.2	-2.2	15.3
Ireland	108.2	13.1	1.0**	14.5
Spain	68.5	8.5	-0.4	24.1
Italy	120.1	3.9	-1.3	9.8
EU 27	82.5	4.5	0.1	10.2
Germany	81.2	1.0	1.2	5.6
France	85.8	5.2	0.3	10.0
UK	85.7	8.3	0.0	8.2

*Figures in comparison with the first quarter of 2011
**Figures for fourth quarter of 2011
Source: Eurostat

solid currency. Unfortunately, the country used this newfound stability to fund wage growth rather than to pay off its existing debt. Salaries in the public sector skyrocketed and nearly doubled within ten years. During the same time, 75,000 additional civil service jobs were created, while pensions in the public sector rose to an incredibly generous 92 percent of pre-retirement salary rates. This spending spree could only be described as madness with an irresponsible political class using financial hand-outs to win over the electorate.

These generous gifts stood in marked contrast to the performance of the Greek economy. The country was known for its rather reluctant taxpayers, and successive governments lost about thirty billion Euro each year because of uncollected tax receipts. Although the country had the second longest working hours among OECD countries (with 2,120 hours per year only trailing South Korea), productivity was well below European standards. On top of this, Greeks enjoyed very early retirement levels, since it released its work force at an average age of 61.4 years.

Clearly, Greece had an unsustainable economic model. The country simply spent more than it earned, resulting in steadily growing public debt levels, which by 2009 had hit 127 percent—more than double the benchmarks of the Eurozone's Stability Pact. Add blatant corruption to the mix—for instance in the assignment of lucrative EU-funded projects—and the spiraling debt caused by staging the Athens Olympics in 2004, it became evident that Greece was heading for a disaster. It was down to the newly elected Socialist government of George Papandreou to confront Greeks with the shocking yet unavoidable truth: only the combination of radical spending cuts and tax increases could save the country from financial collapse. In December 2009 and two months after assuming office, Papandreou admitted that previous Greek governments had "cooked the books" and had presented falsified figures in order to gain entry into the Eurozone in the first place and to avoid

Table 17.2. Ten Year Bond Yield, November 2011 (in per cent)

Greece	31.00
Ireland	8.21
Portugal	14.01
Spain	6.67
Italy	7.04
Germany	2.04
France	3.68
UK	2.13

Source: Bloomberg

potential fines from the EU in the subsequent years of Euro membership. It came as little surprise that Papandreous's disclosure was met with disbelief—both in Europe and in Greece itself—and his imposed tax rises and spending cuts resulted in widespread social unrest, often violent demonstrations, and general strikes.

EU Responses to the Crisis in Greece

In March 2010 and with the international financial markets becoming ever more concerned about the growing possibility that the country might not be able to meet its financial commitments, Papandreou announced an austerity package. Being a member of the Eurozone, such speculation started to have an overall effect on the reputation of the single currency. The pivotal figure was German Chancellor Angela Merkel, who wanted to delay an EU response until the time after regional elections were held in the German state of North Rhine Westphalia. Merkel and other European leaders rightfully calculated that any rescue package for Greece was hugely unpopular among their citizens, who argued that they should not foot the bill for excessive Greek spending patterns. Alas, international markets were becoming ever more jittery and in April 2010—and just a week before the elections (which her party incidentally lost)—Merkel under pressure from French President Nicolas Sarkozy agreed to a thirty billion Euro rescue package. This bailout came with the following conditions:

- Thirty billion Euro in loans up to a maximum of 110 billion Euro
- Interest rate of 5.2% (which was reduced in March 2011 to 4.2%)
- Widespread cuts in government spending

- Privatization of fifty billion Euro worth of public assets
- Raise of the retirement age to sixty-seven for men and sixty-five for women
- Tax increases on cigarettes, alcohol, and fuel
- Higher sales tax
- Demands to tackle tax evasion and to cut health care and pensions provisions
- Involvement of the EU's statistical office Eurostat in monitoring Greek accounts
- Loss of control over tax and spending should Greece fail to meet these conditions by March 2012

By spring 2011, Papandreou had failed to reduce the rapidly accumulating public debt. Ever since his announcement in December 2009, social unrest had intensified, exacerbated by powerful unions that organized two general strikes. In a desperate attempt to reschedule some of its debt, Greece issued a two-year bond which traded at an astonishing rate of 23.6 percent. But the government could do little about the key design flaw of EMU. Membership of the Eurozone automatically eliminated the option to devaluate a country's currency. Hence, Greece did not have a shortcut for dealing with its debt, or a path to regain, at least temporarily, competitiveness by offering its goods cheaper on the international markets. A devastating conclusion was starting to emerge: Given the economic parameters that the country was finding itself in, where could growth (and consequently an economic recovery) have come from?

The EU responded to the deteriorating situation by making even more funds available. In July 2011, the initial thirty billion Euro rescue was enlarged to a staggering 109 billion Euro. Apart from this cash injection, private banks were asked to write off 21 percent of the credit they had given to Greece. A longer time frame and lower interest rates to pay off debt had already been agreed to in March 2011. This deal, at least in the short run, prevented the country from defaulting on its 350 billion Euro debt burden. On the other hand, analysts quickly pointed to a number of shortcomings. First, the so-called haircut of 21 percent by private banks was only on a voluntary basis. While 90 percent of creditors signed up to the deal (including Deutsche Bank, HBSC, BNP Paribas, Allianz and Axa), others, including Unicredit, Credit Agricole and the Royal Bank of Scotland, did not. There was also uncertainty over hedge funds and their willingness to write off such substantial debts. In any case, the package did not address the underlying malaise of the Greek economy, and the question remained how the country would be able to raise productivity levels and gain competitiveness.

The July agreement therefore only provided the EU with some momentary breathing space, and it was not long before another emergency summit had to be called to appease financial markets, which continued to charge unsustainably high

Table 17.3. Time Line of the Eurozone crisis

June 2009	ECB's liquidity injection of 442 billion Euro
December 2009	Greece announces extent of its financial situation
March 2010	Greek austerity measures begin
April 2010	EU bail out for Greece: 30 billion Euro
May 2010	EU and IMF establish European Financial Stability Fund (EFSF) of 750 billion Euro
November 2010	Bail out for Ireland: 85 billion Euro
December 2010	European Stability Mechanism (ESM) established
March 2011	Intergovernmental Euro Plus Pact
May 2011	Bail out for Portugal: 78 billion Euro
July 2011	Bail out for Greece raised from 30 to 109 billion Euro
Oct 2011	Euro Rescue Deal
December 2011	ECB's offers cheap three year loans worth 489 billion Euro
January 2012	Intergovernmental fiscal compact
February 2012	ECB's offers cheap three year loans worth 529 billion Euro
February 2012	EU agrees second bail out for Greece: 130 billion Euro
June 2012	Bail out to rescue Spanish Banks: 100 billion Euro
June 2012	EU leaders agree to set up a supervisory system for Eurozone banks

interest rates on Greece's government bonds. In October 2011, EU leaders agreed on yet another Euro rescue which consisted of a voluntary write down of 50 percent of the country's debt. In an attempt to add a popular mandate to his negotiations with the EU, Papandreou announced a referendum on the conditions of the bail out: a move that was met with fury by Merkel and Sarkozy, who threatened to stall the next tranche of rescue money.[1] In the end, and amid growing political unrest, the beleaguered prime minister resigned and a caretaker government of technocrats under Lukas Papademos (a former vice president of the European Central Bank) was put in place.

But despite the unprecedented financial support, there was no sign of Greece turning the corner. By the beginning of 2012, the country found itself in its fifth successive year of recession. Economic output in 2011 had fallen by 6.8 percent in comparison with the previous year. The GDP drop in the last quarter of 2011 ran to 7 percent. It became ever more apparent that Greece needed yet another rescue, and EU leaders agreed in February 2012 to the second bailout, this time even higher, with 130 billion Euro. The terms of the deal were harsh and included the following:

- Acceleration of privatization of state-owned businesses
- Slashing of 150,000 public sector jobs by 2015

- Cut in the minimum wage by 22 percent for new employees
- Public spending cuts of 3.3 billion Euro in 2012

The Sovereign Debt Crises in Other Eurozone States

The reasons behind the downfall of so many of the Eurozone's economies were startlingly similar. Across the region, the arrival of the Euro resulted in low interest rates and a stable currency, which prompted an economically hyperactive spending and consumer boom. In Spain, greedy banks handed out ever-cheaper mortgages. At one stage the Spanish construction industry accounted for a quarter of the country's GDP and was counting on the illusion that an ever-increasing number of foreigners and affluent Spaniards would snap up more and more holiday and retirement homes. With the sub-prime mortgage crisis of 2008 and 2009, this economic model proved to be shortsighted and foolish. As of 2012, one out of five Spanish workers was without a job, and in a country of forty million, one million families had no steady source of income. Not surprisingly, the government of Socialist Prime Minister José Luis Rodríguez Zapatero experienced an electoral meltdown. In November 2011, Zapatero was replaced by the conservative Mariano Rajoy, who (like Papandreou in Greece) embarked on a brutal austerity course in order to cut the public deficit to 3 percent by 2013.[2] But the conundrum for Spain remained the same as it had been for Greece: where could growth have come from? The country suffered from extremely high unemployment which prompted widespread social unrest. Furthermore, Spain's banks were shackled by the excesses of the previous property boom with balance sheets that were full of properties no one wanted to buy. The markets reacted accordingly. Bond yields rose steadily to over 7 percent, a rate widely regarded as unsustainable. The Spanish bailout of one hundred billion Euro to shore up the country's financial sector therefore did not take the EU by surprise.[3]

In Ireland, it was once again banks—working cosily in tandem with the political establishment and the construction industry—that failed to read the signs on the wall and foolishly believed in a never ending economic miracle fueled by low Eurozone interest rates. At the prime of the property boom, Dublin had become Europe's most expensive city. Irish people were now paying the price for this megalomania. In November 2010, the EU bailed out this small country of some 4.5 million people to the tune of 85 billion Euro (at an interest rate of 5.8 percent), thirty-five billion of which was spent on recapitalizing failing banks, ten billion was needed to pay for ongoing commitments, and forty billion was set aside to keep the country afloat for the next three years. In the meantime, the government had embarked on massive spending cuts (a notable 18 percent pay cut for civil servants) and tax increases, with the aim of bringing the annual public deficit which ran at 13 percent at the end of 2011 in line with the Stability Pact's target of 3 percent.

Table 17.4. Changing governments in the EU: 2011–2012

June 2012	Greece
May 2012	Slovakia, France
April 2012	Romania, Netherlands
November 2011	Spain, Italy, Greece
June 2011	Portugal
April 2011	Finland
February 2011	Ireland

In Portugal, for once property speculation could not be blamed. Instead, a laggard economy, which was already found to be difficult to compete within the Eurozone and the Single Market, was further exposed by the credit crunch. The EU came to the rescue in May 2011 with a package of seventy-eight billion (at an interest rate of between 5.5 and 6 percent) and demands for widespread privatization.

In Italy, massive public debt had been a fixture of the country's public finances for a long time, at least since the expansion of the welfare state from the 1970s onward. But Prime Minister's Berlusconi's inability (or unwillingness) to implement much-needed reforms to support Italy's competitiveness within the EU's Single Market resulted in a sudden loss of confidence by the international financial community. Some structural economic characteristics were simply appalling: a vast black market accounting for around 20 percent of the country's economic activity; endemic corruption which meant that goods and services sold to the public sector were subject to "side payments" that were siphoned off by the political establishment; widespread tax evasion to which successive governments turned a blind eye; poor school and university systems with a substandard research output; and a web of vested interest groups and closed professions, which severely undermined innovation.

In the end, it was of considerable irony that the markets imposed ever-higher interest rates on Berlusconi, which ultimately led to his downfall, caused by an industry of which he once had assumed to be a master. In the run up to an EU summit in October 2011, Berlusconi received a firm demand from other Eurozone leaders to commit to firm spending cuts and other austerity measures. The Italian government responded with a "letter of intent." In a press conference, Merkel and Sarkozy were asked about the likelihood of Italy being able to stick to its promises. Both leaders were only able to muster an embarrassed smirk. In the following days it became ever clearer that Berlusconi had lost the support of his coalition partners. Given his devastatingly poor record and economic policies that shamelessly benefited his personal business interests, it was with great relief among investors and EU leaders, that Berlusconi resigned in November 2011 to be replaced by yet another un-elected government of technocrats led by the highly respected former EU commissioner Mario Monti.

Growing Euroskepticism

With the resignations of Berlusconi and Papandreou, all of the five prime ministers of the PIIGS had been forced to leave the political stage (see Table 17.4). Ireland had voted in a new government in February 2011. Portugal followed suit in the summer while during the autumn of that year a new centre-right government came to power in Spain. Most remarkable however was the fact that at one stage we had two un-elected care taker governments (in Italy and in Greece) which placed serious questions over the democratic legitimacy of the Eurozone project.

The frenetic developments left their mark on other countries as well. Demonstrations across the continent protested against austerity measures, and an ever-growing number of citizens called into question the very legitimacy of the European project. Across the continent, governments were voted out of office in a clear sign that the path of austerity which had been prescribed to bring budgets under control, as well as the massive increase in bailout funds (which after all were funded from taxpayers' contributions) were met by an ever-growing Eurosceptic public. During the first round of the French presidential elections in April 2012, the far-right candidate of the *Front National,* Marine le Pen took the party's highest tally ever in such polls with 17.9 percent of the votes. Le Pen had campaigned on leaving not just the Euro, but the EU altogether. On the left of the political spectrum, Jean-Luc Melenchon, who passionately argued against austerity measure, achieved eleven percent of votes. The eventual winner, the Socialist leader François Hollande heavily criticized the austerity policies of the incumbent president Nicholas Sarkozy and argued for a series of growth measures that ought to replace the budget cuts that had been in place in France.

Greece was forced to hold two elections in quick succession after the first poll did not produce a clear winner. In the second run-off in June 2012, Syriza—the "Coalition of the Left"—was the runner-up with 27.1 percent of the vote. Its leader Alex Tsipras argued that Greece should renounce the conditions attached to the bail-out and stop austerity altogether. When asked how the EU would respond to such a violation, Tsipras simply argued that the EU would do everything to keep Greece in the single currency, for fear of contagion spreading to other members of the Eurozone. The established parties on the centre left and centre right—the only ones who campaigned on keeping the E-prescribed course—won only 41.8 percent of the votes. This result was even more astonishing in light of the fact that opinion polls placed continued support for Greek membership of the Euro at seventy percent. Hence, the elections presented a picture of a nation that had high reservations about the rescue deals but was unwilling to give up the single currency. A clear case of having the cake and eating it at the same time. The country's new prime minister was Antonis Samaras, leader of the center-right party New Democracy, who led a coalition that also included members from Papandreou's Socialist Party (Pasok) and the smaller Democratic Left party.

In the Netherlands, the Freedom Party under its flamboyant leader Geert Wilders left the coalition—and thus brought down the government—in April 2012 in protest over austerity measures that were designed to bring the country's budget deficit down to the limits set by the Stability Pact. Wilders had recently added an anti-Euro and anti-austerity rhetoric to his usual anti-immigration platform. Another far right Freedom Party—this time in prosperous Austria—had long been campaigning against the EU and immigration, and in the spring of 2012 stood at the top of the polls. Even in Germany, one of the few countries that had continued to enjoy growth during the crises, the Pirate Party, a rather odd collection of people arguing for internet freedom was able to galvanise protest votes and secured seats in three successive state elections during the spring of 2012.

EU Responses to the Crises

The credit crunch of 2008 and 2009—which after all was caused by a massive contraction of the world's banking system—already forced European leaders to reconfigure economic and monetary institutions even before the extent of the Greek malaise became known. As such, at the March 2009 summit, EU leaders discussed new mechanisms to regulate and supervise the financial sector. Credit agencies, solvency of insurance companies, capital requirements for banks and cross-border payments, and electronic money were high on the agenda. More important than these discussions, however, was the establishment of a High Level Group on Financial Supervision under the chairmanship of the former French central banker Jacques de Larosière. At the end of their deliberations, the group advocated the establishment of a European Systems Risk Council (ESRC), an early-warning unit that operates under the guideline of the ECB and with the entire EU-27 as members.[4]

The Larosière plan would have resulted in a supranational setup that would not only have offered advice and guidelines but would also have formed a coherent supervisory body with direct powers to regulate the banking and insurance sectors of the member states. The plan prompted instant criticism from some member states, most notably Great Britain, which saw its highly lucrative hedge fund industry under threat. At first, the EU only partially agreed with Larosière: the Systems Risk Council as a supranational authority was indeed put in place. But Larosière's idea of granting this body the supranational power to supervise national financial markets was downscaled to mere supranational advice, thus giving the member states the final say in the regulation of their national banking, insurance, and securities sectors. It was not until the summit of June 2012, when Eurozone leaders finally agreed to establish a supranational supervisory system for banks, which might pave the way for a European banking system in the years to come. UK Prime Minister Cameron however stated that his country would not be part of such a set-up which provided further evidence of the growing policy and institutional asymmetry within the EU.

With regards to the sovereign debt crises, the first thirty billion Euro rescue package to save Greece resulted in the establishment of the *European Financial Stability Fund* (EFSF) with a volume of 750 billion Euro (see Table 17.5). Agreed in May 2010, the fund included contributions of sixty billion Euro from all EU members (even those that do not have the Euro), 440 billion Euro from Eurozone members, as well as 250 billion Euro from the International Monetary Fund.[5] It is important to note that the fund offered loans, not grants. Hence, countries contributing to the fund would receive their money back (default permitting), including interest.

In December 2010, the EFSF was placed on a firmer, long-term footing with the establishment of the *European Stability Mechanism* (ESM). Operational since July 2012 and with a lending capacity of five hundred billion Euro, the fund could be tapped into but only as a last resort. The ESM required a change to the Lisbon Treaty. It was set up as an intergovernmental institution located in Luxembourg and gave future bail-out mechanisms a firm legal base. It was not however, a stimulus package, as countries in financial distress first had to look for other refinancing sources, such as international money markets.

Beyond bail-out mechanisms, the EU—and here in particular the tandem of Angela Merkel and Nicolas Sarkozy—convinced their European partners to agree to a set of structural reforms which aimed to prevent a recurrence of the unsustainable economic models as witnessed above all in Greece. Negotiated in March 2011, the *Euro Plus Pact* addressed three key elements: sustainable public finances, financial stability and tax policy co-ordination.[6] The *Euro Plus Pact* was yet another example of the ever increasing asymmetry within the European Union, as not all countries signed up to it which henceforth turned the pact into merely an international treaty. Sweden, Hungary, the Czech Republic and the UK—all of which are outside the Eurozone—decided for yet another opt-out. All other countries, including the non-Euro users Bulgaria, Denmark, Latvia, Lithuania, Poland and Romania, however, signed the pact and abided to what could cynically have been referred to as Merkel's and Sarkozy's dictum on sound economic governance.

Given the continued liquidity crisis in Greece and increasingly also in Italy and Spain, the autumn of 2011 was characterized by much discussion on the next necessary steps to prevent the European house from collapsing. After frenetic consultations, an emergency summit in October 2011 agreed on the *Euro Rescue Deal,* which further wrote down Greek debt by 50 percent. The agreement also gave specific guidelines for the re-capitalization of European Banks, while also asking state investment funds (and here in particular those in China) for a boost to the EFSF.[7]

As ambitious as the deal sounded, analysts were quick to point out a number of uncertainties. First, the Greek write down to which the Institute for International Finance (IIF, the global umbrella organization of the banking industry) was bullied

Table 17.5. EU Agreements during the Sovereign Debt Crises

April 2010	First Greek Rescue: 30 billion Euro
May 2010	European Financial Stability Fund (EFSF)
	EU and IMF as partners
	volume of 750 billion Euro
December 2010	European Stability Mechanism (ESM) established
	Successor to EFSF
	Intergovernmental institution located in Luxembourg
	Start date of July 2012
March 2011	Euro Plus Pact
	Rules related to economic governance, including public finances, financial stability and tax co-ordination
October 2011	Euro Rescue Deal
	Writing down of Greek debt by 50 per cent
	Recapitalisation of banks
	Increase of EFSF
January 2012	Fiscal Compact
	Debt reduction to 60 percent of GDP by end of 2013
	Violation results in automatic fines
	Enforced by European Court of Justice

into, represented a voluntary commitment, and it was not clear how many of the IIF's members would subscribe to it. Second, in the immediate aftermath of the summit, the response by global investment funds, in particularly those of China to become involved in the EFSF was at best lukewarm, which made the target of 1.5 trillion Euro look rather ambitious. Third, the summit discussed a further involvement of the International Monetary Fund but failed to give any specifics details. Hence, it remained unclear, if and to what extent the IMF would become involved in the re-capitalization process, and if so, whether this would be restricted only to the Eurozone—a move which might cause consternation amongst non-Eurozone IMF members.

The almost perpetual summitry of the previous two years continued with the gathering in Brussels in December 2011. Merkel and Sarkozy (by then often simply referred to as Merkozy) aimed to enforce tighter budgetary rules on Eurozone members in order to appease financial markets which continued to threaten to undermine the performance of the single currency. After the usual acrimonious negotiations lasting long into the night, the so called *Fiscal Compact* allowed EU institutions to enforce austerity measures should a Eurozone country overspend its budget. Countries were now obliged to get their debt to below 60 percent of GDP by the end of 2013. If not, automatic fines would be imposed. Moreover, in order to reach the 60 percent mark, Eurozone members had to have an annual reduction of 1/20th of the difference between that target and their actual debt. At a follow-up summit in January 2012, when the *Fiscal Compact* was signed, member state governments further agreed to empower the European Court of Justice as the enforcer of these fiscal rules. The Court therefore received the entitlement to impose fines against countries that continued to breach the agreement.

The summit became notorious for the veto used by UK Prime Minister Cameron.[8] President Sarkozy very much wanted this agreement to be part of a new EU treaty. However, Cameron in return insisted on concessions for the UK's finance industry in the wake of potentially stricter EU regulations. His demands were flatly refused, although in the run-up to the summit Merkel had already sensed that the UK might not sign up to any agreement. In the end, Cameron pleased the sizeable Eurosceptic wing in his own conservative party, avoided a potentially acrimonious ratification process at home and henceforth stabilized his premiership.

The *Fiscal Compact* marked the true arrival of a two-speed Europe. While opt outs (for instance for the Human Rights Charter or Schengen) have been common for twenty years, the Eurozone was now moving towards a fiscal union with uniformed budget rules. The Stability and Growth Pact of the Maastricht Treaty was toughened up by imposing a regime of fiscal discipline that further undermined fiscal and monetary national sovereignty.

But not only European leaders tried in an increasingly desperate fashion to prevent the crises from spinning out of control. The performance of the *European Central Bank* also came under intense scrutiny. The ECB had reacted slowly in lowering interest rates when the first effects of the credit crunch started to come to the fore. While the U.S. Federal Reserve lowered rates for the first time on September 18, 2007, it took the ECB a further three weeks (October 8) to respond. Also, while both the U.S. Fed and the Bank of England used quantitative easing as a widespread method to add liquidity to struggling economies, the ECB's hands were tied in this respect.[9] Quantitative easing in the EU however was more complicated given that the ECB had to look after the monetary well-being not just of one, but of seventeen entities. This meant that if the ECB had decided to help for example Greece, then countries such as Portugal, or Ireland justifiably would have argued for help too. Furthermore, quantitative easing had to be agreed by all Eurozone members, and it therefore came as little surprise that this financial vehicle was only used to limited effect.

On a more positive note, the ECB made three very significant liquidity injections. In June 2009, the bank set aside 442 billion Euro worth of cheap loans for EU banks which had to be repaid within one year. This was during the height of the credit crunch when banks had stopped lending to one another and to businesses, resulting in a shortage of cash. An even more ambitious injection took place in December 2011 under the tutelage of newly appointed ECB president Mario Draghi.

On this occasion, 489 billion Euro were made available. Given the very low interest rate of one percent and a generous repayment period of three years, 523 financial institutions across the continent applied. In contrast to the first injection two years earlier, some of the money was invested straight away in buying government bonds from distressed Eurozone members, such as Spain or Italy. Hence, Draghi's move not only helped banks and businesses, but also the struggling under performers of the Eurozone. A couple of months later, in February 2012, Draghi made available a further 529 billion Euro under the same conditions in what the ECB referred to as its long-term repo operation (LTRO). Again, as in December borrowing costs on the international markets fell for the crisis-ridden states, as banks bought up sovereign debt which offered higher returns.

Lessons Learned

The crises in particular in Ireland, Greece and Spain demonstrated that a number of countries had embarked on utterly unsustainable economic models. Easy access to cheap money and low interest rates proved too much of a temptation for politicians and citizens alike to embark on a spending and consumption spree without looking at the fundamental working mechanisms and potential flaws of their national economies. Instead of improving economic parameters, of investing in research and education, of building up coherent infrastructures, of establishing conducive industrial relations, the order of the day was spend, spend, spend without worrying how countries would fare during an economic downturn. This behavior was irresponsible and the political establishment in the PIIGS had much to answer for.

But irresponsible behavior was not only confined to the governments in the countries affected by a sovereign debt crises. Across the continent, other governments but also EU institutions turned a blind eye to what was going on. What had been agreed at Maastricht, when the key principles of Economic and Monetary Union were set out in the Stability Pact represented a worthless piece of paper that no one felt obliged to adhere to. Ever since the start of EMU in 1999, France and Germany had persistently violated the Stability Pact by accumulating more debt than was allowed. The Commission would have been entitled to impose fines, but failed to do so, fearing a tarnished reputation for the young currency on the international markets. So if France and Germany regarded the Stability Pact as more of a guideline than a legal obligation, why should other countries have obeyed? And given that the start of EMU coincided with a time of calm economic conditions, why would anyone indeed have bothered?

The financial sector too enjoyed a period where regulation was shockingly neglected. How else can one explain the arrival of the now infamous 110 percent mortgages given out to bank customers with an insufficient capital collateral? The Euro worked fantastically well in a time of economic plenty. The realization, that

EMU was shockingly ill-equipped to handle a financial crisis came—for many countries and their citizens—too late. EMU ought to have been a firm prescription on how to keep spending and inflation under control but turned into a temptation to give in to easy access to cheap money. It all ended in unsustainable economic models, unbalanced growth, wage and spending excesses and a reliance on bubble revenues.

The rationale of politics and of politicians is to improve people's lives, to guarantee peace and safety, to secure standards of living and increasingly to offer environmentally sustainable conditions. For a great part of its existence, the European Union and member state governments did precisely that. The founding treaties of the 1950s ushered in a period of peace amongst former enemies. Free trade across borders brought a remarkable level of prosperity. The Maastricht Treaty of 1993 paved the way for the reunification of a once-divided continent. But Economic and Monetary Union? It conveyed potentially irreparable damage to the European idea and a loss of moral authority. What started out as a project to achieve an ever closer union brought hardship to great many people. Behind the unemployment statistics and falling GDP levels are people who had lost their livelihood, whose businesses went bankrupt, whose pensions had been eroded, whose welfare state had become sclerotic. Who would have thought that eighty years after the implosion of the Weimar Republic in Germany—one of the historical memories which after all prompted European governments to found the EU, we saw the return of Fascists marching in the streets (of Athens). Austerity measures are never popular and always seem to offer political opportunities for demagogues and political insanity could yet return to Europe with even greater force should politics fail in its attempt to bring the economic and financial situation under control. What leaves a sour taste is also the fact that Greece and Italy were governed by unelected officials during the height of the crises—hardly a ringing endorsement for legitimacy and democratic accountability.

In the run-up to the start of EMU, many analysts and in particular the economists of the German *Bundesbank* warned that the Eurozone would not be an optimum currency area (OCA) where economic structures and financial parameters of the participating countries are by and large in line with one another. The *Bundesbank* warned repeatedly against the inclusion of such countries as Greece or Italy. Both were allowed to join despite the fact that one of the key ingredients of EMU—that of an overall budget deficit of no more than 60 percent of GDP—was not met. Furthermore, an optimum currency area relies on labor mobility. In the United States, a recession in one part of the country might be offset by workers moving to a more prosperous one. Labor mobility in the EU though, is very limited and only 3 percent of citizens live in a member state other than their country of birth. An OCA also requires some form of mechanism to transfer funds from one region to another. The EU budget however is very limited (only about 1 percent of each member state's GDP), while Germany agreed to EMU under the explicit condition that fiscal union would not be part of it. In the US, monetary union took place alongside a political (and thus fiscal) union. German and other leaders, howeverm argued that a monetary union could be established without the accompanying unifying political measures. They proved to be wrong.

A decade later and the doomsday preachers of the *Bundesbank* had won the argument. The key point here is that with a single currency, countries lose their monetary autonomy. It seems too obvious to mention, but once you are a member of the Eurozone you lose a crucial instrument on how to keep your economy competitive: that of devaluating your currency. Hence, once a country adopted the Euro it could no longer compete by offering lower prices. It had to compete on quality and innovation, which turned out to be next-to-impossible given the high levels of efficiency, expertise and productivity of northern European economies such as Germany, the Netherlands, Luxembourg or Finland. In return, these countries enjoyed a benign competitive advantage based on the exchange rate parity. EMU allowed countries such as Germany to build up a vast trade surplus on the back of consumption-hungry yet less competitive southern European Eurozone partners.

Blaming irresponsible governments and greedy citizens in the PIIGS would not have solved the Euro crisis. The fact remained that the PIIGS were not in a position to get out of their economic and financial mess by themselves. The option of devaluation does not exist in EMU. Defaulting on debt would have affected banks and governments across the EU, while a collapse in demand would have consequences for export orientated member states such as Germany. The EU therefore had no choice but to stay the course.

The Future of EMU

If one believes in European integration, in giving up certain aspects of a country's national sovereignty for the sake of European solidarity, in improved relations amongst neighbors, in shared and sustained prosperity across the continent, then Economic and Monetary Union had the potential to form a vital cornerstone for such an idea. However, EMU in its present shape dramatically undermined and jeopardized European integration and threatened the very viability of such a vision, unless—of course—it undergoes a process of drastic reform.

What if Greece—or indeed other countries—had decided to leave the Euro, as was advocated by a growing number of politicians and commentators? Economic meltdown and a financial collapse would almost certainly be the outcome. Proponents of a Greek exit often cited the example of Argentina, which at the beginning of this century unpegged its Peso from the US Dollar which resulted in a massive devaluation of its currency. It worked for Argentina, chiefly because the country possessed significant deposits of minerals, which it could now sell cheaply within a booming world economy. In short, the country unlike Greece had something viable to offer.

If Greece had left the Euro, the value of a reinvented Drachma would almost certainly have collapsed in relation to the Euro, maybe by as much as 50 percent. The country would have found it impossible to meet its credit commitments (which are in Euros). This would have brought about more bank collapses and subsequent nationalizations across the EU as Greek debt was now worthless. Surviving banks, which throughout the crisis were reluctant to lend, would have to reduce their exposure even more, resulting in a further credit crunch. Investors would have to pull out of Greece, the European Central Bank would have to intervene by buying up Greek drachma in order to keep that currency at an artificially higher level which would have hit the ECB's currency reserves hard. Capital controls would have to be imposed and borders would have to be closed down in order to prevent money from pouring out of the country. There might also be have been a run on the Euro as investors began to speculate which country would be the next victim.

Given this apocalyptic scenario the only viable alternative is to reform EMU; for the sake of the financial and economic survival (not just of Greece but of all EU countries), as well as the moral sake of the entire European integration project, which after all rests on the notion of European solidarity, of a mind set which can transcend a focus on purely national interests. The EU therefore has no choice but to move ever closer towards fiscal and economic harmonization. *The Euro Plus Pact* of March 2011, as well as the *Fiscal Compact* of January 2012 already prescribes a narrowly-defined path on how national economies ought to be organized. The former introduced tighter rules on public finances, pensions, health care and other welfare provisions which now have to be translated into national law. The latter concentrated on a balanced budget rule, which if violated would result in automatic fines and a loss of budgetary sovereignty.

What EMU needs is a mechanism that can facilitate the transfer of money from richer European states to their poorer southern partners. The *European Stability Mechanism* which emerged from the Bail Out Fund offers a last-resort credit facility for countries in financial peril. However, this might not be enough. One might want to look at the example of German unification, where a poorer entity (eastern Germany) was shored up by a richer one (western Germany). The government organized this by imposing a so-called solidarity tax which was deducted at source from the pay slips of western employees. More than twenty years after unification, workers in the west continue to pay this tax and the total money the country spent on rejuvenating the east now stands at over 1500 billion Euro (which incidentally is about one eighth of what Germany has granted Greece in loans).

But having a straightforward fiscal transfer from richer northern taxpayers to poorer southern citizens might be impossible to achieve given the growing EU scepticism amongst European electorates. The fact is that the EU already transfers money—albeit in a limited fashion—through its cohesion and agricultural policies. The EU budget is financed through member state contributions, and this pot of money is then handed out in large parts to farmers, and to economically backward regions. It is therefore not unimaginable that the next seven year budget (which enters into force in 2014) might see a significant boost for such funds, designed to finance infrastructure and other programmes in struggling countries in order to stimulate growth. After assuming power in May 2012, French President Francois Hollande called on other leaders to agree to precisely that. The chorus for growth-stimulating measures grew louder with Spanish Prime Minister Mariano Rajoy and Italian Prime Minister Mario Monti backing Hollande's call. Even ECB President Mario Draghi argued that the *Fiscal Compact* ought to be complemented by a "Growth Compact." A little tweaking of the EU budget, however, would not be enough. The EU spends about ninety billion Euro per year on redistributive programmes. Such an amount would merely represent a drop in the ocean given the severity of the economic crises. Budgets however have to be agreed on a unanimous basis by all member states. Therefore there is every reason to doubt a massive increase in the EU's next financial perspective which runs from 2014 to 2020.

Given the limited options available to the EU, it was only compelling that commentators and political leaders frequently called upon the European Central Bank to assume a more pivotal role. Granted, ECB President Mario Draghi embarked on a more proactive course than his predecessor Jean-Claude Trichet when we injected liquidity into southern Europe by offering one trillion Euro in bank loans. But again, these measures only offered a temporary remedy. What the EU needs is a central bank that is capable of buying up government debt. The idea is to introduce Eurobonds issued by the ECB but guaranteed by the Eurozone members which would enable countries like Greece to access money at a cheaper rate than those offered by the international financial markets. Germany however was vehemently opposed to such an idea as it would undermine the ECB's independence; a sacrosanct relic which had its origins in the way the German *Bundesbank* was set up which in itself was a reflection of the financial collapse of the Weimar Republic that resulted in the rise of Nazi Germany. However, if Germany (and indeed other EU countries) is committed to a supranational economic and monetary union, then supranational mechanisms ought to be put in place to alleviate discrepancies in the economic structure of other Eurozone members. Simple rules on how to run an economy are not enough. These ought to be complemented by financial mechanisms that allow for a transfer of funds. A straight forward solidarity tax along the lines of German unification might be a step too far for the mind sets of European citizens. But call it fiscal federalism or call it financial solidarity, the EU has to find ways of transferring money from richer to poorer parts for Economic and Monetary Union to succeed.

Outlook:
The Future of European Integration

Looking back on sixty years of European integration, the EU has clearly transformed the political and economic landscape of Europe. These six decades have witnessed some remarkable successes. The creation of an internal market resulted in one of the world's richest economic blocs with some 485 million consumers. Through its Common Commercial Policy the EU emerged as one of the most powerful actors within the international trade agenda. A sustained transfer of funds through the Cohesion Policy greatly aided the economic development of a number of previously laggard states. As to environmental protection, the EU assumed the role of global leader, although concerns over profits, and political haggling over emission standards have often resulted in sub-optimal outcomes whether at European or at international level. In contrast, the union also developed policies that have been widely criticized over the years. After many reforms, the Common Agricultural Policy, for instance, still accounts for most of the EU's spending, while in foreign and security policies, the EU still has not assumed the role of a pivotal player that would flex its political muscle in line with its economic might. Nonetheless and despite some setbacks, up until the first years of the twenty-first century, the European Union had delivered on its initial objectives of promoting economic prosperity and establishing peace on a war-ravaged continent.

In recent times, however, fundamental differences of opinion have appeared over the future of the EU. The failed 2005 referendums in the Netherlands and France on the constitution, as well as the controversial ratification process of the Lisbon Treaty, caused much consternation among the European political elites with voters, sending out the clear message that European integration either had gone far enough or had already gone too far. The lowest turnout ever in the elections to the European Parliament in 2009 and the worrying rise of far-right parties also pointed to an EU that seems out of touch with its electorate. The issue of Turkey's future accession resulted in a further rift, as some member states are concerned about the political, economic, and institutional implications of integrating such a large country that is not only substantially below EU levels economically but also has distinctively different cultural and social standards. The sovereign debt crises in the PIIGS countries dramatically undermined the most striking symbol of European integration, and the ambition to use EMU as a vehicle for an ever closer union resulted in rising unemployment numbers, faltering economies, and ever-growing Euroskepticism which made citizens question the very rationale of the European project.

Upcoming Challenges

The next decade will mark a turning point for the EU. EMU—if it can survive the strain of integrating hugely divergent economies—needs drastic reform. With the next rounds of enlargement and the integration of Croatia, Montenegro, Iceland, Serbia, Macedonia, and Turkey, EU membership will rise to thirty-three, as long as all countries are committed to far-reaching reforms; a process which in the case of Turkey at best remains uncertain, given the comments by the Turkish political establishment on the doubtful prudence of joining a club that due to the sovereign debt crisis seems to stand on rather shaky economic foundations.

But other policy areas are also in need of major adjustments. The Lisbon process of the Single Market for instance, which aimed to establish the EU as the world's most competitive and knowledge-based economy by 2010, was quietly cast aside in favor of the so-called EU 2020 strategy, whose catchphrase is the development of a "smart, sustainable and inclusive economy." The strategy centers around five targets. First, the EU aims to have 75 per cent of people aged twenty to sixty-four in a regular job. Second, member states ought to invest 3 percent of their GDP in research, development, and innovation. Third, environmental protection ought to be enhanced further. As such, the EU envisages the reduction of greenhouse gases by 20 percent (in comparison with levels reached in 1990). Renewable energy and energy efficiency ought to be boosted by 20 percent. Fourth, the EU aims for a reduction in school dropout rates to less than 10 percent, while 40 percent of people

Table O.1. Policy Asymmetry in the European Union, 2012

Policy Area	Opt-Out	Other Form of Asymmetry
Schengen Agreement	Ireland, UK	Bulgaria, Romania, and Cyprus set to join in the future
Charter of Fundamental Rights	Poland, UK	
Asylum, Visa, and Immigration	Denmark	Ireland and UK decide on a case-by-case basis on whether to opt in
Single Currency	Denmark, Sweden, UK	Bulgaria, Croatia, Czech Republic, Hungary, Latvia, Lithuania, Poland, and Romania set to join in the future
Euro Plus Pact	Czech Republic, Hungary, Sweden, UK	
Fiscal Compact	Czech Republic, UK	

aged thirty to thirty-four ought to be equipped with a university degree. Finally, the strategy intends to reduce the number of people affected by poverty and social exclusion by twenty million.

Despite these noble targets, much doubt over a successful outcome has already been cast. True, the economic downturn could give the strategy a new impetus. Ironically, the Lisbon process was undermined by an economic boom during which member states lacked the urgency to reorganize their economies. Given the current economic climate, policy makers might turn to the *EU 2020 strategy,* as a vehicle that could deliver growth. On the other hand, the strategy is set to run for ten years, a long time, and governments might lack the urgency to implement the strategy's guidelines. Also, while progress is monitored by the European Commission the tools for implementing the reform are held at national level: a design flaw that also undermined Lisbon. Given the precarious state of public finances across the EU, it remains doubtful whether national governments are willing (or indeed capable) of committing to new spending measures.

This leads to the second hurdle which the EU will have to clear soon. The current seven-year financial perspective runs out at the end of 2013. Prior to this date, member states have to agree on a new budget that will cover the years 2014 to 2020. We have already seen that a number of political leaders including Mariano Rajoy (Spain), François Hollande (France) Mario Monti (Italy) and Antonis Samaras (Greece) have called for a growth pact that ought to complement the austerity policies of the EMU's Stability Pact. Such an agreement could boost EU spending on, for instance infrastructure or housing projects. It could also offer financial support in those areas targeted by the *EU 2020 strategy.* However, EU budgets have to be approved in a unanimous fashion, and while southern Europe is desperate for an increase in EU support, such enthusiasm is not met by the likes of David Cameron (UK) or Angela Merkel (Germany). An enlarged EU budget could offer much breathing space for those countries that are financially damaged by the sovereign debt crisis. As an important side effect, it could also add urgency and determination to the *EU 2020 strategy* and could elevate it beyond the status of being mere guidelines. But it would require the EU to embrace a fundamental change: to move from a vehicle that implements EU integration predominantly through regulation, into an organization that actively embraces redistribution and the transfer of tax payers' money from richer to poorer parts.

Any discussion of EU spending cannot ignore the Common Agricultural Policy, and a reorganization of the sector is earmarked for 2014. Between 2007 and 2013, spending on agriculture amounts to fifty-three billion Euro, or 40 percent of the EU's budget (which equals to around 0.3 Euro per citizen per day). Seventy percent of agricultural expenses are taken up by direct payments to farmers. Twenty percent is spend on rural development measures, with the remainder handed out as export subsidies.[1] Dacian *Cioloş*, the Romanian commissioner for agriculture (2010–2014) proposed a small reduction of the CAP money to 36 percent of the overall EU budget. He also placed a greater emphasis on environmental protection with 30 percent of agri-money earmarked for environmental measures, which would enable farmers to instance diversify production for instance. Farmers in Central and Eastern Europe would also see their levels of income brought closer to that of their western counterparts. Co-funding between the EU and national budgets was also on the cards, as was a reduction of the maximum financial support that farmers could receive.

The proposal cannot be described as radical and leaves plenty of room for the EU's institutional actors to define their negotiating position. In contrast to previous CAP reforms, the European Parliament is now involved under the new ordinary legislative procedure which—although adding much needed democratic legitimacy—will complicate negotiations further. In any case, we can already anticipate much haggling between those countries that would like to maintain the status quo (such as France and Spain), those that would support an increase in the CAP, potentially combined with specific cohesion measures (such as governments in Central and Eastern Europe) and those that are disappointed by the timid nature of *Cioloş*'s proposal (such as the United Kingdom) as it fails to lessen the impact the sector has on the EU policy making in general and the budget in particular.

Long-Term Ramifications

In light of these monumental challenges, we ought to remind ourselves that Europe is not the European Union and that the European Union is not Europe. Instead, the EU is the organizational vehicle that aims to make sense of Europe with all its national differences and idiosyncrasies. For much of the second half of the twentieth century, European integration delivered through the EU made sense to the member states and the majority of their citizens, as national governments gave up some of their national sovereignty in order to achieve goals that could not be attained by the states individually. Once national governments no longer see the rationale of working with the EU for the sake of enhancing their own national interests, then the reason for the EU to exist in its current form will become questionable. Given the current doubts over the future course of European integration, one might want to examine other potential avenues. There are four possible options for the future shape of the EU.

United States of Europe. Altiero Spinelli and Jean Monnet's dream of a federal Europe along the lines of the United States has receded as the EU has enlarged. Their idea would call for a division of responsibilities between a central authority and states, regions, or provinces. This would mean closer integration in such fields as taxation, economic, foreign, and social policy. The original six founding states have traditionally advocated this model, although support for it has faded and only remains to some extent among the political elite in Luxembourg and Belgium. It is difficult to imagine a United States of Europe with an EU of twenty-eight or more member states.

Multi-Speed Europe. First introduced in the 1990s by the German politician Wolfgang Schäuble and the former French foreign minister and disgraced IMF boss Dominique Strauss-Kahn, this proposal would allow an inner core of countries (France, Germany, Belgium, the Netherlands, and Luxembourg) to move ahead with closer integration. This asymmetry among European partners already exists on a significant scale (see Table 17.1). In the future it certainly remains possible that some member states will be disappointed by the slow progress of the European project and decide to pursue their own common objectives for economic models more socially oriented than those promised by EU integration. Solving the sovereign debt crises might also necessitate an intergovernmental treaty to which the Eurozone—but not others—would subscribe to. We would then witness the start of a union within a union, thus introducing another organizational tier to the political landscape of the continent.

Free-Trade Europe. This concept has sometimes been called the British model of European integration. It argues that future European cooperation should be kept at an intergovernmental level, preferably with national vetoes. The cornerstone of this model is the Single Market, allowing for the free movement of goods and the removal of trade barriers. But any political form of integration, such as a more coherent foreign policy, is only possible with the unanimous consensus of member states. With the 2004 and 2007 enlargements and the pending integration of six more states most notably Turkey, Britain has won support for this idea, especially among countries such as Poland and Estonia that have more Atlanticist instincts and, at least in recent years, have placed greater emphasis on free markets than on social protection.

Constitutional Europe. This proposal builds on the belief that the EU—although shaken by the Eurozone problems—represents a stable foundation that constantly needs to update policies and institutions in line with internal and external developments. In this view, the treaties of Maastricht, Amsterdam, Nice, and Lisbon are regarded merely as individual bricks in the evolving process of building the European house.

Whatever the outcome of the current reform efforts, Europe needs an organizational framework, whether it is the EU or some other subsequent derivative. The European scene in the twenty-first century is vastly different from the divided world of the emerging Cold War of the 1950s, and the needs of European citizens and their governments have certainly changed. Global warming, technological innovation, the Internet, e-commerce, and other aspects of globalization have increased interdependencies between nations and are widely regarded as calling for close cooperation between states seeking to achieve common goals. Yet a closer and more integrated Europe will have to ensure that it does not undermine national differences and identities in the process and above all does not wreak havoc with the economic and financial situation of its citizens as witnessed with the Eurozone disaster.

The EU's ability to face its numerous challenges, however, is undermined by an ever more prominent mindset among EU leaders and their citizens that elevates domestic political concerns over any notion of European solidarity. In some countries, Europe's biggest asset is acting as a defense wall against unwanted immigration. In the spring of 2011, Tunisian refugees coming from Italy were barred from entering France. In Austria and in the Netherlands, xenophobia had entered the political mainstream. Moreover, European solidarity seemed to have given way to a divisive notion of us-and-them. In Greece for instance, austerity measures imposed by the EU prompted people to hark back to the hegemonic order of World War II with newspaper cartoons and demonstration banners depicting German Chancellor Merkel as Adolf Hitler. At the end of the first decade of the twenty-first century, EU politics is not driven by supranational institutions based around a purposeful commission. Instead we have national leaders, from Merkel to Sarkozy, Hollande, Cameronm and Monti who were calling the shots, none of whom could be described as a high-profile European. Instead the EU is dominated by national leaders, preoccupied with their domestic agenda, who did not construct the EU in its present shape and form but merely inherited it from the previous generation and the likes of François Mitterrand, Jacques Delors, and Helmut Kohl.

The elitist character of Brussels does not help either. Europe's capital hardly interacts with the outside world and European integration has predominantly been constructed "from above." Until the ratification of the Lisbon Treaty, the involvement of the European Parliaments was limited, and most national parliaments showed little interest in European affairs. During the current crisis, this democratic deficit has now erupted and gave way to Euroskeptic attitudes and a growing rejection of the European project. But Europe has much to be proud of. It is still the most prosperous continent in the world. Its states enjoy peaceful relations with their neighbors that were unimaginable just a couple of decades ago. Institutions and policies were created that reach far beyond those of other transnational organizations in South-East Asia, the Middle East or Latin America. But the breadth of the current challenges calls for coherent and authoritative responses. Whether the EU will be able to successfully address these remains to be seen.

Notes

1. Parameters of European Integration

1. It is important to note that the Council of Europe is not an EU institution. Similarly the European Court of Human Rights in Strasbourg, which is related to the Council of Europe, should not be confused with the EU's European Court of Justice, which is located in Luxembourg.

2. Jean Monnet, a rather illustrious character, was born in France in 1888 and spent his early years working in his father's cognac business. He was not drafted in World War I because he suffered from nephritis. During World War II and after the fall of France in 1940, he worked for the UK government and was instrumental in organizing supplies for the French Resistance movement. Monnet died in March 1979 at the age of ninety.

3. The WEU began life as the Brussels Treaty Organisation. The Brussels Treaty was signed on 17 March 1948 by Belgium, France, Luxembourg, the Netherlands, and the United Kingdom, and provided for collective self-defense and economic, social, and cultural collaboration between its signatories. In 1954 the Brussels Treaty was modified to include West Germany and Italy, thus creating the Western European Union. The WEU was primarily concerned with increasing Soviet control of Central and Eastern Europe, and committed all signatory countries to the mutual defense of any member.

4. The initial purpose of EURATOM was twofold: it sought to ensure the creation of the necessary conditions for the development of nuclear energy within the community and also worked to guarantee an equitable supply of ores and nuclear fuels. The treaty created the EURATOM Supply Agency, which had the power to purchase fuels for community use and develop a common supply policy based on the principle of equal access to fuel.

5. The Treaty of Rome also established the institutions of the EEC: an Assembly (renamed Parliament at its first meeting), the Council of Ministers, the Commission, and the Court of Justice. The balance between these institutions would evolve as the EEC developed, but the Treaty set an important precedent in securing a supranational decision-making institution in the Commission, while limiting the role of the Parliament and therefore the involvement of European citizens whom that institution ought to represent.

6. British interest in European integration was largely a product of the country's declining international political prominence, especially in the aftermath of the Suez crisis in 1956. By the end

of the 1950s Britain also had to confront the fact that economic ties were shifting away from the Commonwealth toward the European continent.

7. The European Commission, the EU's key bureaucracy, is analyzed in detail in chapter 3.

8. Charles de Gaulle had been forced to leave office in 1969 at the age of seventy-nine, and his counterpart in West Germany, Chancellor Konrad Adenauer, resigned in 1963 at the age of eighty-seven.

9. According to the country's statistical office, West Germany's exports nearly trebled between 1960 and 1970, rising from 24.5 billion Euros (at 2004 prices) to 64 billion.

10. Luxembourg Prime Minister Pierre Werner was commissioned to write a report on the suitability of an economic and monetary union. The report had a marked impact on the process of establishing the Euro in the 1990s. Chapter 12 offers a more detailed analysis of the Euro.

11. The Merger Treaty, which was signed in April 1965 and implemented on 1 July 1967, integrated the EEC, the ECSC, and EURATOM as the European Community.

12. This system was called "the snake" as the value of a national currency was allowed to fluctuate by 2.25% in either direction in relation to other national currencies. It was this continual fluctuation that inspired commentators to use the metaphor of a snake wiggling its way from one end of the scale to another; more on this in chapter 12.

13. With the election of Ronald Reagan in 1980, the U.S. underwent a drastic transformation of its macro-economic approach. The neoliberal agenda of "Reaganomics" advocated tax cuts for big business and high-income earners, based on the premise that the subsequent savings would help boost productivity and employment levels. Through a "trickle-down effect," Reagan contended, the generated wealth would eventually reach broader segments of society. Reagan also argued for a limited role of the state in addressing and managing economic problems. Reagonomics was based on the monetarist philosophy of Milton Friedman, of the University of Chicago, who called for the state to be a passive actor, merely responsible for organizing and safeguarding the parameters within which economic activity and the free flow of market forces ought to take place. Reaganomics, therefore, was in stark contrast to prevailing European approaches that still relied to a significant extent on Keynesianism and its reliance on a much more interventionist and proactive role of the state.

14. The full text of Thatcher's speech can be viewed at http://www.margaretthatcher.org/speeches (accessed 23 June 2010).

15. The "co-decision procedure" was introduced by the TEU. In such policy fields as health, consumer protection, or culture, for instance, the EP now had veto power enabling it to block legislation. The Lisbon Treaty of 2009 replaced co-decision with the so-called ordinary legislative procedure. It is now the most common way of passing legislation. See also chapter 6.

16. During the Cold War the WEU never merged with the EU largely because the latter integrated member states that did not belong to NATO and considered themselves as neutral. At the Amsterdam summit in 1997, the EU adopted the WEU's so-called Petersberg Tasks of peacemaking, peacekeeping, and humanitarian missions as the basis of a European security and defense policy. With the gradual development of the CFSP, the WEU lost its rationale and, by 1999, a gradual process of integrating the organization into the EU had started. See chapter 14.

17. With the Labour Party winning the elections in 1997, one of the first acts of Prime Minister Tony Blair was to sign the social charter.

18. At a summit meeting in the Luxembourg town of Schengen, Belgium, the Netherlands, France, Luxembourg, and West Germany decided to remove all border controls between the signatory countries. The so-called Schengen Agreement came into force in 1985, and over the next years Spain, Portugal, and Italy joined up. Denmark, Ireland, and the UK, however, chose not to ratify the Agreement. In the case of the latter two, this decision was mainly prompted by fears of terrorism in Northern Ireland. By 2012 all EU member states, with the exception of Britain, Ireland, Cyprus, Bulgaria, and Romania, had ratified Schengen. Four non-EU states—Iceland, Norway, Liechtenstein, and Switzerland—are also enrolled in the program.

19. EU citizenship is granted to those who have obtained citizenship status in one of the member states.

20. The so-called IGC consists of representatives of the governments of EU member states who meet at length to prepare the agenda for summit meetings. This system was first used during the negotiations over the Single European Act. The IGC for the summit meeting in Nice began on 7 February 2000 and ended with the agreement on the Treaty of Nice (7–11 December 2000).

21. The specific institutional changes are addressed in the individual chapters on the Commission (chapter 3), the Council of Ministers (chapter 5), and the European Parliament (chapter 6).

22. Estonia, Latvia, Lithuania, Poland, the Czech Republic, Slovakia, Hungary, Slovenia, Malta, and Cyprus joined in June 2004. The integration of Bulgaria and Romania was completed in January 2007.

23. The Convention of Europe consisted of 105 representatives from all 15 member states, as well as from the 10 countries that were about to join in 2004.

24. In return, legislation can be blocked by at least four countries representing 35% of the EU population. This new system, however, will not come into effect until 2014.

25. For a more detailed discussion on the President of the European Council, see chapter 4.

26. The High Representative's responsibilities are discussed in more detail in chapter 3.

27. For a detailed discussion on the European Parliament and the changes brought to this institution by the Lisbon Treaty, see chapter 6.

28. The Czech Republic also secured a concession. Fearing a legal avalanche of claims from Germans who were expelled from Czech territory in the aftermath of World War II, the charter cannot be activated retrospectively.

2. Enlargement

1. The initial membership of EFTA in 1960 included Britain, Denmark, Portugal, Austria, Sweden, Norway, Switzerland, Finland, and Iceland. Liechtenstein joined later on.

2. After the ousting, in Portugal, of the Caetano regime in 1974 and the death of Spain's General Franco in 1975, both countries applied for EU membership in 1977.

3. With the accession of Sweden, Austria, and Finland, and disregarding the microstates of Liechtenstein, Monaco, the Vatican, Andorra, and San Marino, only three West European countries remained outside the EU: Iceland, Norway, and Switzerland. Iceland considered membership at the time of the British accession in 1973 but concluded that policy differences, regarding fishing, in particular, were simply too great. Norway applied for membership in 1972 and 1992, but each time a negative referendum voted to stay outside the EU, mainly because Norwegians thought that their country was already quite prosperous and well served by the existing free-trade agreement with Brussels. Like Norway, the Swiss government also applied to the EU in 1992 but had to withdraw its application after a negative referendum. Thus EFTA continues to exist, with Iceland, Norway, Switzerland, and Liechtenstein as its members.

4. For more information, see chapter 10.

5. After the integration of Bulgaria and Romania in 2007, financial support for candidate and accession countries is delivered through the so-called Instrument for Pre-Accession (IPA) with five subheadings, namely, transition assistance and institution building, cross-border cooperation, regional development, human resource development, and rural development. Before 2007, however, the EU had a number of programs designed to assist applicant countries in their development prior to joining the EU. These programs included the following:

- ISPA (Instrument for Structural Policies for Pre-Accession); invested around 1 billion Euros annually in transportation and the environment
- SAPARD (Special Programme of Pre-Accession for Agriculture and Rural Development); invested around 500 million Euros annually
- PHARE (Poland/Hungary Assistance for Reconstruction of Economies); invested around 1.5 billion Euros annually
- TAIEX (Technical Assistance Information Exchange Instrument); provided information exchange on all aspects of the acquis communautaire

- Twinning; provided full-time secondment of advisers from the EU-15
- CARDS (Community Assistance for Reconstruction, Development and Stabilisation designed for Western Balkan countries)

6. These programs are discussed in greater detail in chapter 10.

7. For a more extensive discussion, see Christopher Preston, *Enlargement and Integration in the European Union* (London: Routledge, 1997).

8. Detailed accounts of the institutional changes brought forward by the Treaty of Nice and the Lisbon Treaty can be found in chapter 3 (Commission), chapter 5 (Council of Ministers), and chapter 6 (European Parliament).

9. The chief disagreement over British membership was the country's contribution to the EU budget. Successive prime ministers, particularly Margaret Thatcher, argued that Britain paid too much into Brussels' coffers, based mainly on the fact that the UK had a limited agricultural sector, the sector on which the EU spends most of its money. The issue was finally resolved at a summit meeting in Fontainebleau in 1984, which granted Britain a rebate of 60% of the difference between the money it paid into the budget (as a share of its GDP) and the money it received from redistributional programs. By 2005 this rebate came to more than 8 billion Euros. In light of the accession of much poorer states, the rebate became the subject of much controversy, with Central and Eastern European countries, Sweden, and the Netherlands, in particular, calling for an end to this preferential treatment. During the summit meeting of December 2005, Prime Minister Tony Blair eventually gave in to mounting diplomatic pressure and agreed to reduce the rebate to 1 billion Euros.

10. One element of these principles is the EU's commitment to the prohibition of the death penalty.

11. A rare exception to this rule was the integration of Austria in 1995, when concerns were voiced that the Single Market would allow Germans, in particular, to purchase second homes in tourist areas. Austria feared that the livelihood of some communities might be in jeopardy given that holiday homes are only occupied for a limited number of weeks. Ultimately a compromise was reached, stating that foreign second-home owners have to make their property available for rent to other holidaymakers.

12. The aims of the Stabilisation and Association Process are the following:

- The drafting of Stabilization and Association Agreements (SAAs), with a view to accession
- The development of economic and trade relations with the region and within the region
- The development of the existing economic and financial aid
- Aid for democratization, civil society, education, and institutional development
- Cooperation in the field of justice and home affairs
- The development of political dialogue

13. Until the arrival of the unifying Instrument for Pre-Accession (IPA), financial assistance was given as part of a program called the Community Assistance for Reconstruction, Development, and Stabilisation (CARDS), for which the EU had earmarked 5 billion Euros for the period from 2000 to 2006. CARDS was mainly used for infrastructure, institution building, and matters related to justice and home affairs.

14. As of 2010 visa regulations are still in operation for Kosovo. Four EU members—Cyprus, Greece, Slovakia, and Spain—have not recognized the country and thus cannot process Kosovan passports.

15. Ethnic tensions between Greek and Turkish Cypriots reached a violent climax in 1974, forcing the Turkish army to intervene. The invasion resulted in the de-facto division of the island, with Greek Cypriots in the southern part and Turkish Cypriots in the northern part, where the Turkish Army continues to have a sizable military presence. Aside from Turkey, no other country has ever given diplomatic recognition to the self-styled Turkish Republic of Northern Cyprus (TRNC).

16. More detailed information on the Schengen Agreement can be found in chapter 13.

17. The EU's trade agreements with the European Economic Area are analyzed in chapter 15.

18. According to estimates by the International Tribunal for the former Yugoslavia, some one hundred thousand people lost their lives during the war, which lasted from 1991 to 1995 and

involved three ethnicities: Bosnian Serbs, Bosnian Croats, and Bosnian Muslims (also referred to as Bosniaks).

19. Republika Srpska is the official name of that entity. It translates into "Serbian Republic" but, to avoid confusion with the state of Serbia, whose official name in English is the Republic of Serbia, the Bosnian wording is used on the international stage.

20. For instance, at the moment the EU spends around 80% of its cohesion money on countries that have 75% of the EU's average GDP. Should this formula be kept in place after Turkish accession, most of the cohesion money would then end up in Turkey (and to some extent in Bulgaria and Romania).

3. The European Commission

1. Before the accession of Central and Eastern European states in 2004, the Commission was comprised of twenty individuals: nineteen commissioners and one Commission President. In a union of fifteen members, the five biggest states—France, Germany, the UK, Spain, and Italy—each had two commissioners, and all the others had one. The Treaty of Nice, which was designed to prepare the Union for enlargement, developed a new formula whereby each member state now only has one commissioner. The treaty also stated, however, that there could be no more than twenty-seven commissioners. Thus, should the Union integrate additional members, some states might have to share a commissioner, but the treaty did not specify how such a rotating system might work. The most recent Lisbon Treaty of 2007 would have reduced the number of commissioners to fifteen. In a referendum held in June 2008 Ireland rejected the treaty partially because of fears that the country might subsequently lose its commissioner. To win over the Irish public, the final version of the treaty therefore reverted back to the formula used at Nice of twenty-seven commissioners. Lisbon, however, came up with another formula: in 2014 the number of commissioners should be no more than two-thirds of the number of member states, which at current count would reduce the College of Commissioners to eighteen.

2. The European Parliament also must approve the entire Commission (see chapter 6).

3. The appointment of France's former foreign minister, Michel Barnier, to the Single Market portfolio in 2010 illustrates this point.

4. A telling example was the appointment of the Hungarian candidate Laszlo Kovacs in 2004. The member states decided that Hungary should be given the Energy portfolio, and the Hungarian government appointed Kovacs to this post. During his confirmation hearing before the European Parliament, however, it emerged that Kovacs had a rather thin knowledge of energy matters, and he was subsequently transferred to the portfolio of Taxation and Customs.

5. Walter Hallstein from West Germany, the first Commission President (1958–67), and Jacques Delors from France (1985–94) arguably have been the most influential individuals chairing this institution. Both had a clear vision. Hallstein argued for a more federal Europe for which he was passionately opposed by French President Charles de Gaulle. Delors envisioned a "social Europe" which, in addition to the Single Market, also offered protection for workers; more than once, this vision resulted in acrimonious confrontations between Delors and Margaret Thatcher.

6. In addition to the Commission's services, there are eighteen European Community agencies, for example, the European Food Agency Authority, the European Railway Agency, and the European Environment Agency. Furthermore, there are three CFSP agencies, including the European Defence Agency, the EU Institute for Security Studies, and the EU Satellite Center. The responsibilities of all these services are to accomplish specific technical, scientific, or managerial tasks. Regarding JHA, two other agencies work to enhance cooperation between customs, police, immigration, and justice departments in all member states.

7. The Prodi Commission (1999–2004) embarked on an ambitious program to reform the organization. Its key objective was the implementation of a new career development structure in which promotion is exclusively based on merit and performance. The new staff regulations took effect under the Barroso Commission in November 2004.

8. For a more detailed analysis of the Commission's powers and responsibilities, see D. Dinan, *Ever Closer Union* (London: Palgrave, 2010), chapter 7.

9. Over the years the Commission has met with severe criticism because of its authority to issue rules, for example, deciding on the precise shape and size of cucumbers or the length of a sausage. The institution is perceived by many as overly bureaucratic, and this has resulted in growing public hostility.

10. Budget contributions could be raised to 1.27% of the GNP, but member states have decided that currently 1.045% is sufficient.

11. It is important to note that although the member states first give the Commission the negotiating parameters, the final agreement at WTO negotiations must still be endorsed by the member states (see chapter 15) based on the system of qualified majority voting (see chapter 5).

4. The European Council

1. Until 2003 the Summit always met in the country holding the Presidency, which explains why EU treaties often had the name of a town attached to them, such as Amsterdam or Maastricht, as it was in those locations where the Summit took place.

2. The term of the President of the European Council lasts for 2½ years. One reelection is permitted under the Lisbon Treaty, which would bring his total tenure to a maximum of five years.

3. Van Rompuy convened his first summit in February 2009, which, upon his request, dealt with the economic crisis in Greece that threatened to undermine the Euro.

4. Some meetings of the European Council stand out as definitive turning points in the history of the Union, for example, Bremen 1978, with the launching of the European Monetary System; Fontainebleau 1984, where the British budget rebate was resolved; and Maastricht 1991, Amsterdam 1997, Nice 2000 and Lisbon 2007, where agreements were reached on the respective treaties.

5. The meeting in Nice in December 2000, however, surpassed all previous summits in length and political controversy. Instead of the usual two days, member states bargained for four days, especially, in view of enlargement, over the future of policies involving cohesion, the budget, and agriculture. The reweighing of national votes and the configuration of majority voting in the Council of Ministers was another important item on the agenda.

6. With a Union of so many members, all with diverging opinions over the precise course for European integration, a unanimous communiqué might be impossible to reach. Therefore, some member states now commonly issue explicitly stated reservations.

7. For a more detailed discussion, see D. Dinan, *Ever Closer Union* (London: Palgrave, 2010), chapter 8.

5. The Council of Ministers

1. The Council of Ministers is officially called the Council of the European Union. The name is an unfortunate choice, as it is similar to the Council of Europe, an international organization, not part of the EU, that deals with human rights, and to the European Council, the summit where twenty-seven heads of government gather.

2. COREPER is an acronym for the French name of the committee, which is Committee des Representatives Permanentes.

3. This rather complicated procedure was decided at the Nice summit in December 2000 under the chairmanship of French President Jacques Chirac. In lengthy bargaining processes, the member states tried to establish a formula that would allocate votes for every new member state that joined the EU in 2004, as well as for Romania and Bulgaria, which joined in 2007. With twenty-seven countries casting their votes, a fine balance had to be established safeguarding the interests of smaller member states while also guaranteeing significant progress toward greater European integration. Particular attention was paid to ensure that a country's population was reflected in the number of votes allotted. Germany, the most populous country in the EU and home to some 80 million citizens, argued for a higher number of votes compared to France, with a population of only some 60 million. However,

President Chirac argued that France should have identical voting powers in order to symbolize the equality between the two traditional driving forces of Europe. Poland, which had been invited to attend the summit though not yet a member state, felt short-changed when a proposal was circulated giving the country fewer votes than Spain, although both have nearly identical populations of some 40 million. In the end, after many late-night bargaining sessions, a resolution was reached. The Polish delegation was appeased by being granted the same number of votes as Spain, and German Chancellor Schröder backed away from his initial demand for the sake of European cooperation.

4. The Council of Ministers also has exclusive executive authorities over issues relating to the Euro and EMU (see chapter 13), where the ECOFIN Council is effectively the economic government of the EU. Other councils, however, such as the Agriculture or Environment Council, have generally delegated all executive power to the Commission and merely fulfill their legislative duties by voting on proposals that emanate from the Commission.

5. Institutional jealousies emerged quickly in the aftermath of the Lisbon Treaty. Only weeks after its ratification, the Spanish Presidency announced its intention to hold a U.S.-EU summit in Madrid and proudly invited President Obama. The U.S. administration however, declined to attend, citing an abundance of EU summits which proved to be a stinging embarrassment to Spanish Prime Minister Zapatero. Even worse for him, other EU member states, as well as Herman van Rompuy, the President of the European Council, criticized the Spanish government for exceeding its competences in calling the summit in the first place. It is hoped that the future will establish a more conducive working relationship between the President of the European Council and the Presidency over who chairs what and when, which might help to keep the political vanities of prime ministers in check for the sake of a more efficient summitry.

6. A telling example of the opportunities given to a country that holds the Presidency was the summit in Lisbon in March 2000. Later termed the "Dot.com Summit," the EU agreed on a complex set of measures with the aim of becoming the world's most competitive, knowledge-based economy by 2010.

7. The concept of a "troika" was introduced in 1981, whereby the foreign ministers of the current Presidency, of the one immediately preceding it, and of the immediate successor would meet to discuss political matters. Initially these meetings were merely briefings and lacked political substance, but since the Treaty of Amsterdam, in 1997, a great deal of coordination has been seen between successive presidencies.

6. The European Parliament

1. The most influential committees are the Committee on the Environment, Public Health, and Food Safety, the Committee on Internal Market and Consumer Affairs, and the Committee on Budgetary Control, since the EP exercises considerable power in these policy areas. On the other hand, the Committee on Transport and Tourism has always been marginal.

2. Legislation under a single majority is passed when the majority of parliamentarians present are voting in favor of a proposal. However, the EP applies a system of absolute majority, where the majority of all MEPs (whether present or absent) must vote in favor in order for the legislation to pass. With the current membership at 754 MEPs, the absolute majority is 378. In the past the EP was often ridiculed for its often sparsely attended plenary session. In 2000, for instance, the attendance record was 75%. Against the backdrop of this relatively low figure, the EP introduced sign-up procedures and cut the daily allowances of MEPs who failed to attend sessions. As a consequence, attendance between 2006 and 2009 rose to 93%.

3. The procedures included consultation (which gave the EP the right merely to be consulted on legislation), cooperation (which gave the EP the authority to amend legislation), co-decision (when the EP had the final veto power), and assent (during which the EP had to give its approval to international and accession agreements).

4. The ordinary legislative procedure is a carbon copy of the co-decision procedure, which was introduced by the Maastricht Treaty in 1993.

5. More information on the special legislative procedure can be found on the EU's website, and specifically at http://europa.eu/scadplus/constitution/procedures_en.htm (accessed 19 June 2012).

6. Other commentators, such as Moravcsik and Majore, contend that the notion of a democratic deficit in the EU is a myth, arguing that, because the EU is not a state, it should not be subject to the same democratic demands as traditional states are. Moreover, both authors point to the fact that the EU specializes in areas in which direct democratic accountability is generally limited (for example, EMU and the role of the European Central Bank).

7. The European Court of Justice

1. For example, the ECJ caseload jumped from 79 in 1970 to 433 in 1985, and the average length of proceedings for a ruling rose from six months in 1975 to fourteen months in 1985. As a result, the backlog of cases increased from 100 in 1970 to 527 in 1985.

2. For a more detailed analysis of the impact of EC case law, see D. Dinan, *Ever Closer Union: An Introduction to European Integration* (New York: Palgrave, 2010), chapter 10.

3. Fundamental rights can be categorized roughly into three groups: civil rights, such as respect for private life, freedom of religion, and freedom of expression; economic rights, such as the right to own property or the right to carry out economic activities; and rights of defense, such as the right to effective judicial remedy or the right to legal assistance.

4. Yvonne van Duyn was a Dutch national who had come to the UK to accept an offer of employment with the Church of Scientology. Van Duyn was refused entry to the UK on the grounds that the British government regarded the Church of Scientology as socially harmful, although no legal restrictions were placed on its practices. Mrs. van Duyn took the UK Home Office to court, but, unfortunately for her, there was an EC directive giving the member state a degree of discretion, if the activity in question was contrary to public order. In effect, Mrs. van Duyn was not permitted to work in the UK on the grounds that the British government considered the Church of Scientology to be harmful and antisocial, and thus against the public order. With this ruling, however, the ECJ was able to advance its case law with numerous references to the free movement of people. In fact, this case enabled the Court to establish a precedent by upholding an individual's right to take up employment in another member state under the same conditions as a national of that state.

5. The German supermarket chain Rewe intended to import the French liqueur Cassis into Germany. But the German authorities refused to allow it, because the drink was not of sufficient alcoholic strength to be marketed as a liqueur. Under German law, liqueur had to have an alcoholic content of 25%, whereas Cassis only had between 15% and 20%. Rewe argued that the rule was a quantitative restriction, which runs counter to Article 30. The ECJ ruled that once a product has been lawfully produced and marketed in one member state it should be admitted into any other state without restrictions.

6. Gabrielle Defrenne—an airhostess with the former Belgian airline Sabena—brought an action for compensation on the ground of discrimination of pay. Sabena did not dispute that male employees earned more money for the same type of work. The question referred to the ECJ was whether Article 119 (equal pay for equal work) had a direct effect on the airline. Of course, Van Gend en Loos already showed us that it had. The ECJ stated that the aim of Article 119 was the elimination of all discrimination, not only regarding individual undertakings but also entire branches of industries and even of the economic system as a whole. Subsequently the Court's rulings on equal pay enabled the Commission to implement a series of directives on women's issues that forced the member states to end blatant discrimination in the workplace. This case was then followed by a series of cases dealing with pensions, training, part-time work, and so forth.

7. The Lisbon Treaty granted the ECJ powers in the field of criminal and police cooperation. However, the court still is not entitled to review the validity or proportionality of operations carried out by the police or other law-enforcement agencies of a member state. Regarding foreign and security policies, the ECJ is still largely excluded but at least now has the right to review the legality of so-called restrictive measures (for instance, trade sanctions) imposed by the European Council.

8. Checks and Balances

1. The Italian candidate Rocco Buttiglione was heavily criticized for remarks about homosexuality and single mothers, and Ingrid Udre from Latvia was charged with corruption and deemed unfit. Further, the Hungarian Lazlo Kovacs was judged by the EP as lacking the expertise needed to handle the Energy portfolio. As a result of these censures, the EP threatened to disapprove of the entire Commission. Ultimately the Barroso Commission relented to the pressure: Buttiglione was replaced by Italy's former Europe minister Franco Frattini; Kovacs was moved from Energy to Taxation; and Udre was replaced by her compatriot, Andris Piebalgs, who assumed responsibility for the Energy portfolio.

2. A good example may be seen in the former British Commissioner for Trade Peter Mandelson, a close political ally of former prime minister Blair. Mandelson's position as a national politician became untenable after he was forced to resign twice as a government minister.

3. The failed constitution of 2005 proposed that television cameras be allowed at Council meetings.

4. See also chapter 5.

9. The Single Market and Competition

1. The Commission acknowledged that uniformity across the EU in sensitive issues such as drugs, terrorism, and tax regimes was not on the agenda.

2. Member states, in the end, agreed on a minimum rate of 15% and a maximum rate of 25%. There are also reduced rates of varying degrees which the member states can impose in line with their tax objectives. For instance, the UK reduces VAT to 0% for educational material. At the moment Cyprus has the lowest VAT rate with 15%, whereas Denmark opted for the maximum of 25%.

3. In terms of realistic consumer behavior, however, substantial national differences remained. For example, a Dutch person is far more likely to purchase goods in a Dutch shop than in a German shop, even if he or she lives on the Dutch-German border within equal walking distance from a Dutch and a German supermarket.

4. Prompted by the deregulation and privatization of key industries, the Commission estimated the following price reductions:

> Airfares: 41% between 1992 and 2000
> Electricity prices: 15%
> National telephone calls: 50% since 1998
> International telephone calls: 40% since 1998

5. In 2002 the EU had a population of 360 million people. This meant that geographical mobility was still rather limited, since only 4.6% of EU citizens lived in member states other than their country of origin.

6. The source for this figure is the European Commission, DG Internal Market, Internal Market Scoreboard No. 22 (November 2011).

7. One can follow the progress of the Single Market by accessing the website of the DG Internal Market: http://www.ec.europa.eu/internal_market/score/ (last accessed 22 June 2012).

8. The open method of coordination was based on benchmarking and targets. Member states had not only agreed on wide EU targets but had also reported on the progress of their national programs in achieving those targets. This method also allowed for policy learning through comparison. The Lisbon Strategy therefore relied on voluntary compliance by member states to targets which they themselves had set. The role of the European Commission had been marginalized to that of an overall secretariat. Given this approach, Lisbon hardly threatened an invasion into sensitive national policies through further European legislation.

9. The Directive was originally drafted in 2004 by the Dutch Commissioner Frits Boltkestein, who served under the Prodi Commission from 1999 to 2004.

10. A wide range of services are free from regulatory restrictions and can be offered anywhere

in the EU, regardless of where the business is registered, for instance, tourism and leisure businesses or business services such as consultancy work. Industries that already have EU legislation in place, including telecommunications, transport, and financial services, are not at all affected by the Boltkestein Directive, as are labor or criminal laws that are specific to certain member states. A decision on the service directive was reached in November 2006, and it became effective at the beginning of 2010.

11. The maximum charges are 0.35 Euro for calls made to one's home country from another EU member state, 0.11 Euro for incoming calls from another EU country, and 0.50 Euro per megabyte for downloading data. The regulation also introduced per-second billing, as well as a cut-off mechanism once a phone bill reaches 50 Euros.

12. Microsoft now offers worldwide interoperability information for a flat fee of ten thousand Euros.

13. L. McGowan and S. Wilks, "The First Supranational Policy in the EU," *European Journal of Political Research* 28, no. 2 (1995): 141–169.

14. More information on the impact of the credit crunch can be found in chapter 12. The sovereign debt crisis within the Eurozone is analyzed separately in chapter 17.

10. Regional Policy and Cohesion

1. The geographical area stretching from London, to Paris, to Milan, and then back via Munich and Brussels roughly resembles a banana, and blue is the official color of the EU; hence the name "blue banana."

2. Before 2007 the cohesion system consisted of a multitude of funds with complex objectives and program guidelines, which could not have been described as user-friendly. Therefore, for the budget period 2007–13, the Commission's goal was to make the system simpler and more coherent.

3. The eligibility for convergence projects is limited to regions with less than 75% of the EU's average GDP.

4. All regions are eligible for this spending category except those that qualify for the convergence category (i.e., below the 75% threshold).

5. Eligible regions include those that have a coast, border another member state, or share a border with a non-EU state.

6. EU cohesion policy also applies to the eighteen "statistical effect" regions that were below the 75% threshold prior to the 2004 enlargement but no longer qualified following enlargement and the subsequent drop in the EU's average GDP. Without transitional funding, these regions would justifiably feel punished for agreeing to the accession of the twelve new members. Hence the European Council agreed to support these regions to the amount of some 22 billion Euros. Furthermore, spending targets were set in order to support the long-term creation of jobs in such areas as research and innovation, the information society, and sustainable development. In the case of the convergence objective, the target is 60%, and in the case of the regional competitiveness and employment objective, the target is 75% of the total available funding.

7. Countries eligible for money from the Cohesion Fund include the twelve new member states that joined in 2004 and 2007, as well as Greece and Portugal. Spain's eligibility is transitional and will gradually be phased out.

8. This became evident during the negotiations for the 2007–2013 budget, which took place in December 2005. The Polish delegation stalled talks by insisting on a larger share of cohesion funding than the other EU partners and the British Presidency were willing to offer. Not until the final hours of the summit was a unanimous agreement reached after German Chancellor Merkel handed over a share of the cohesion money earmarked for eastern Germany to Poland.

9. Notable exceptions to the working mechanisms of this triangle were the so-called Community Initiatives (2001–2007) which dramatically enhanced the Commission's power and responsibility. Here, the Commission, not the Council of Ministers, is responsible for the design of policy measures and the general allocation of money, giving it the sole power to set the agenda. Community Initiatives

included Interreg (interregional cooperation), Equal (gender equality), Urban (urban regeneration), or Leader+ (job creation and rural development).

10. These programs included ISPA, which offered support for investment in transport and the environment; SAPARD, the Accession Program for Agriculture and Rural Development with the aim of improving processing structures, marketing channels, and food-quality control; and PHARE, which, since 1989, has focused on institution building and support for investment.

11. Figures are from Eurostat, 2011.

12. The debate on the positive versus the negative effects of EU Cohesion started as soon as EU funds were increased in the aftermath of the Maastricht Treaty of 1993. See, for example, R. Leonardi, "Cohesion in the European Community," *West European Politics* 16, no. 4 (1993): 492–515; and M. Keating, "A Comment on Leonardi," *West European Politics* 18, no. 2 (1995): 408–412. For more updated sources, please refer to the bibliography.

11. The Common Agricultural Policy

1. As a general rule, all decisions on prices are based on unanimous consensus, although de jure the Council's decision on agricultural measures is by qualified majority voting.

2. For a detailed discussion on the shortcomings of the CAP, see D. Dinan, *Ever Closer Union: An Introduction to European Integration* (New York: Palgrave Macmillan, 2010), chapter 11.

3. In that period, for example, production grew by 2% per annum, whereas the EU consumer purchased only an additional 0.5% of agricultural products.

4. A telling example is the Duke of Westminster, who owns prime real estate in central London and also runs a 1,280-acre farm in northwest England. With an estimated fortune of 4.9 billion£ (around 6.4 billion Euros), the duke, in 2004, nonetheless received a subsidy of 326,000£ (around 425 million Euros) from the EU budget.

5. See also Neill Nugent, *The Government and Politics of the European Union* (New York: Mac-Millan, 2010), chapter 10.

6. ECU refers to the European Currency Unit, a basket of European currencies used as a means of settlement between European central banks. See also chapter 12.

7. In 1994, for instance, agriculture contributed less than 1% to the overall GDP in Luxembourg, Germany, and the UK; the share in France was 2%; and Greece had the highest rate at 7.5% (figures are from Eurostat).

8. In 1992 the EU overproduced 20 million tons of cereal, 1 million ton of dairy produce, and 750,000 tons of beef.

9. For example, the intervention price for cereals dropped by 29%; for beef, by 15%; and for butter, by 5%.

10. Farmers working on a large scale were asked to set aside 15% of their arable land.

11. MacSharry established a program that subsidized farmers for up to twenty years if they set aside land to protect the environment.

12. One hectare equals 100 square meters, or around 900 square feet.

13. Price supports were reduced by 20% from the 1986–1988 figures, and export subsidies were gradually reduced by 36% by 2000.

14. For instance, the price for cereals was reduced by 20% and that of beef by 30%.

15. Ultimately the Berlin summit could only agree on a milk price reduction of 15%, to become effective in 2005. Beef prices were reduced by 20%, instead of the proposed 30%, and the price of cereals was reduced by a mere 7.5%.

16. The EU argued for a worldwide cut in trade-distorting subsidies by 55% and for lowering export refunds by an average of 45%, with a reduction of import tariffs by an average of 36%.

17. Fischler also proposed that rural development measures be introduced, 80% of which would be financed by the EU, including early retirement, afforestation, technical assistance, and environmental programs. He also envisioned the retraining of farmers for other professions to be financed by the

Structural Funds of the Cohesion Policy (see chapter 10). Finally, Fischler offered the governments of the accession countries the chance for national top-ups to match these countries' spending levels on agriculture prior to joining the EU.

18. For 2004, for example, 44.4 billion Euros was earmarked for agriculture and 30.7 billion Euros for cohesion.

19. Specifically the Fischler plan argued for a further reduction in price support. Farmers would now receive a flat rate of direct support based on their previous income, which should be reduced by 20% between 2004 and 2009. Also, under cross-compliance, farmers would receive direct support once they met environmental and food safety standards, with a maximum financial aid of 300,000 Euros.

20. Farmer unions across Europe have been highly critical of the cross-compliance system. Although most agreed that the old price support system was outdated and needed drastic reform, the new system, they felt, imposed a heavy bureaucratic burden with its numerous, detailed rules, for example, specifying the type of taps allowed for milk tanks, and that oil tanks had to be blue and diesel tanks green.

21. The health check abolished the requirements to set aside 10% of arable land. Quantitative restrictions on milk production will come to an end in 2015. Hence, with overproduction now less of an issue, farmers are again allowed to maximize their production potential. In addition, the amount spent on direct aid was reduced. Instead, all farmers who received more than 5,000 Euros in direct aid had their payments reduced by 5%, and the money was transferred to a Rural Development budget. This rate increased even further to 10% in 2012. An additional cut of 4% was made on payments to affluent farmers who received more than 300,000 Euros. The Rural Development budget can be used by poorer member states (below 75% of the EU's average GDP) to address such objectives as climate change, renewable energy, water management, or biodiversity.

22. A group of outside experts appointed by Commission President Prodi (Sapir Report 2003) argued that the CAP should be wound down and re-nationalized.

23. For more on COPA, see http://www.copa-cogeca.eu (last accessed 5 June 2012).

12. Economic and Monetary Union

1. Two power-generation projects of the New Deal were the development of the Tennessee Valley Authority and the building of Nevada's Hoover Dam.

2. Keynesianism has often encountered the problem that, during economic downturns, people may be reluctant to spend, and thereby reinvest in the economy, preferring instead to save their earned money for a rainy day. Similarly a positive investment climate also depends to a significant extent on trust and the belief that governments can manage the economy successfully. But not every government automatically has such support. Moreover, the management of such large-scale projects requires a massive administrative effort, with the potential pitfalls of mismanagement and excessive bureaucracy. Most important is that Keynesian economic policies might require time to come to full fruition. During that lag the economy might pick up, and thus government intervention would only accelerate a boom and cause inflationary pressures.

3. U.S. President Ronald Reagan (1981–89) and British Prime Minister Margaret Thatcher (1979–90), among many, were true believers in monetarism. Both implemented a series of tax breaks while also reducing public spending, which in the case of the U.S., however, was more than compensated by massive investment in the military.

4. For example, private banks can borrow money from a central bank that charges interest at their official rate. The private banks then utilize this as capital to pass on to their customers, thereby making a profit as these consumer loans are charged at a higher rate than the central bank rate. Hence a low interest rate will boost the economy as it allows for cheaper consumer loans, but with the added danger of a rise in prices as more money enters the economy. Conversely, higher interest rates can be used to lessen the inflationary tendencies in a rising economy since consumer spending will be curtailed by higher loan rates.

5. With quantitative easing (QE) a government issues bonds which are then bought up by the country's central bank, a more elegant way than simply printing money. A government then uses the money to inject liquidity into the economy, for instance by offering financial assistance to struggling businesses. QE is therefore often used to jumpstart an economy which is falling into recession, as evidenced by the Obama administration and the UK government under Gordon Brown during the credit crunch of 2008 and 2009.

6. Prior to German unification in 1990 the Deutschmark was already the leading currency in Europe, and countries such as Denmark, the Netherlands, Austria, and Sweden had pegged their currencies to Germany's. A monetary union that integrated Germany's economic might was therefore highly attractive to European countries with weaker currencies, particularly France and Italy.

7. Once the UK, Spain, and Italy decided to participate in the EMS, the margins for these three countries were raised plus or minus 6%.

8. Because of this currency basket, every participating national currency contributed to a constantly changing value of the ECU. Businesses and private individuals could open bank accounts and, for example, invoice their clients in ECU. With some currencies going up and others going down, the currency volatility of the ECU was much less prominent than that of only a single national currency. The EMS also established a European Monetary Fund, which offered loan facilities for balance-of-payment assistance that was backed by 20% of national gold and U.S. dollar reserves, as well as 20% of national currencies.

9. On that day, which has since been named Black Wednesday, the British pound lost some 13% in value compared to the Deutschmark. This happened despite the massive infusion of 30 billion U.S. dollars by the Bank of England to keep up the value of the pound. In the end Britain plunged into a recession, and Black Wednesday was estimated to have resulted in job losses approaching one million jobs, and the UK Treasury estimated the cost of Black Wednesday at 3.4 billion pounds.

10. In 1986 the European Council asked Commission President Jacques Delors to chair a committee consisting of the heads of the member states' central banks. The committee's task was to analyze and identify how and when conversion to EMU could be achieved. The subsequent Delors Report formed the blueprint for the Stability and Growth Pact that emanated from the Maastricht Treaty of 1991.

11. The ECB has an Executive Board, with a president, vice president, and four other leading experts, and is appointed by the European Council for eight years. The role of the Executive Board is to implement monetary policy. The Governing Council of the ECB, comprised of the Executive Board and governors of national central banks, sets interest rates. In addition to this there is the General Council, made up of the Governing Council and governors of other European central banks that are not in EMU, which addresses tasks involving all EU states such as standardized accounting.

12. A negative referendum in Denmark, in 2001, underlined the government's decision not to participate. Similarly, in the UK, public opinion continues to be predominately against the Euro. Although former prime minister Tony Blair supported EMU, his successor, Gordon Brown, always believed that the country's economic structure and cycles were fundamentally different from those of the Eurozone, a view to which conservative Prime Minister David Cameron also subscribed.

13. In February 2009, Robert Zoellick, president of the World Bank, argued that a total of 120 billion Euros was needed to shore up the banking system and get the economy going again. Around the same time the former Hungarian prime minister Ferenc Gyurcsany mentioned an even higher figure of 180 billion Euros.

14. Rescue packages were also agreed to with non-EU countries including Bosnia and Herzegovia, Belarus, Ukraine, Russia, and Serbia.

15. In 2010, Poland was the first country to reach pre-crisis levels of their production, followed by Slovakia and the Czech Republic in 2011. On average, the World Bank predicts 106% of pre-crisis production levels by 2012.

16. Pegging a currency to the Euro implies that national central banks and governments focus their monetary and economic policies on keeping a fixed exchange with the Euro. This, in turn, results in financial stability which could result in an economic boost as foreign investors start to arrive. On

the downside, and in order to keep a currency in line with the Euro, a central bank might have to raise interest rates to keep their national currency attractive to investors. This, however, might dampen economic growth as credit is more expensive to obtain.

17. According to the IMF, some countries in the region fared better than others. Poland, for instance, could rely on a big domestic market and had also diversified its production base, factors that kept the country relatively stable throughout the downturn. On the other hand, the crisis hit those countries first that had unsustainable fiscal policies, such as Hungary or Romania. Again Poland, but also the Czech Republic, both with balanced budgets, escaped relatively unscathed. Finally, those countries with a comprehensive system of financial-sector supervision such as the Czech Republic were also to ride out the storm much more easily (IMF Survey Magazine Online, 28 December 2009).

18. The case of the exchange rate between the British pound and the Deutschmark is a telling one. During the 1990s the value of the pound fluctuated between 2.20 and 3.50 Deutschmarks. Businesses trading in both countries, therefore, were forced to set aside capital to compensate for potential losses arising from negative developments in the exchange rate that, in some cases, could amount to 20% of a business's annual turnover. With EMU, such tied-up capital could now be used to better effect.

19. In Italy, for instance, 1,936 lira equaled 1 Euro. If the price for a cappuccino was now 60 cents instead of 1,200 lira, customers almost automatically perceived this as cheap. In this instance, then, a café owner might have been prompted to raise the price to 80 cents (or 1,548 lira). In Germany the business association for the gastronomical trade defended the price increases, arguing that many of its members had not printed new menus in anticipation of the introduction of the Euro. The association further argued that they would like to spare a further price update, and hence a new printed version of the menu. Therefore prices were raised even further to account for the post-introduction period.

20. An illustration is offered by the economic boom in Ireland. From the early 1980s until the credit crunch of 2008, the country had enjoyed an unprecedented economic expansion accompanied by inflation. With inflation for property, for instance, reaching such high levels that large sections of society were priced out of the housing market, Ireland needed higher interest rates to prevent the economy from overheating. On the other hand, for years after the introduction of the Euro, France and Germany suffered from an economic slowdown and could have done with lower interest rates than the ECB had agreed to. All these countries now had to apply non-monetary means to reach their economic ends.

21. Portugal made drastic budget cuts in order to fulfill the Stability Pact criteria. But between 2002 and 2007 France and Germany have persistently breached the pact with spending levels regularly exceeding 3.5%. Although the Commission can recommend fining a country that violates the Stability Pact, it has refrained from doing so mainly because such action would undermine investors' confidence in Europe's currency.

22. Granted, the EU is trying to offset this negative impact of EMU by financing cohesion. However, the total amount available for cohesion (some 30 billion Euros per year) does not seem overly generous for a union of 485 million citizens. See also chapter 10, this volume.

13. Justice and Home Affairs

1. The Schengen Agreement was signed in 1985 in the Luxembourg town bearing the same name between the Netherlands, Belgium, Luxembourg, France, and Germany, and allowed for free cross-border travel between these countries. One by one, other countries signed up, and the Schengen Area now includes all EU states with the exception of Ireland, the UK, Cyprus, Bulgaria, and Romania. Four non-EU countries—Iceland, Norway, Switzerland, and Liechtenstein—have also implemented the Agreement. The area now includes a population of more than 400 million people. Schengen forms part of the acquis communautaire, and accession states at some stage have to implement the Agreement. Although an opt-out was granted to Ireland and the UK, this is no longer the case for Cyprus, Bulgaria, and Romania. Security concerns in these countries have so far delayed the ratification.

2. The Trevi Group was named after the location where the group first met, a hotel directly opposite the famous fountain in the old town center of Rome. Trevi subsequently became the French acronym for *terrorisme, radicalisme, extremisme, et violence internationale*.

3. Regarding police and judicial cooperation in criminal matters (Pillar III), the powers of the European Court of Justice and the European Parliament were still severely curtailed. The EP was only consulted on legislative proposals without having a proper veto or agenda-setting power, and the ECJ also did not have the same powers that it wielded under Pillar I. For instance, the ECJ had no jurisdiction to review the legality of police operations.

4. This means that an Italian national living in Vienna, Austria, could theoretically be elected mayor. That individual could also vote in local elections in Vienna and for the Viennese representative to the European Parliament. The Italian, however, is not allowed to stand or vote for any Austrian federal or regional government unless he or she assumes Austrian citizenship.

5. "Dignity" refers to the right to life and prohibits torture, slavery, and the death penalty. The section on freedoms cover liberty, privacy, marriage, thought, expression, assembly, education, work, property, and asylum. Equality addresses the rights of children and the elderly. Solidarity refers to social and workers' rights including the right to fair working conditions, protection against unjustified dismissal, and access to health care. Citizens' rights include the right to vote in elections to the European Parliament, as well as the right to move freely within the EU. It also includes several administrative rights such as a right to good administration, the right to access documents, and the right to petition the European Parliament. Justice issues include the right to an effective remedy, a fair trial, the presumption of innocence, and the principles of legality, non-retrospectivity, and double jeopardy.

6. The term "foreigner" is defined as an individual with citizenship other than his or her country of residence (Eurostat, December 2011).

7. Between September 2008 and September 2009 the figure totaled 258,000. (Eurostat, March 2010).

8. Every member state agreed to examine the application of any alien and to pass on an asylum application to the member state that played the most important part in the applicant's entry or residence. Meanwhile, the responsible member state would take charge of the applicant throughout this period and allow the return of an applicant who is in another member state illegally.

9. FRONTEX is located in Warsaw, Poland, and offers a means for member states to cooperate in managing external borders. The agency assists member states in training national border guards, and offers technical and operational support at external borders.

10. MARRI is a regional forum that meets twice a year to enhance state and human security, and to initiate, facilitate, and coordinate developments in the fields of asylum, migration, visas, and border management. The MARRI Regional Center was opened in Skopje, Macedonia, in September 2004.

11. The EU was also set up a series of programs to improve cooperation in combating crime. One of these was AGIS (2003–7), which aimed to set up an EU-wide network based on the exchange of information and best practices. Another was ARGO (2002–2006), which funded cooperation in the areas of external borders, visas, asylum, and immigration.

12. Europol is an illustrative case. Despite its considerable activities that support national law-enforcement agencies, Europol has no executive policing authorities and certainly no power to make arrests.

14. Common Foreign and Security Policy

1. The integration of Bulgaria, Estonia, Latvia, Lithuania, Romania, Slovakia, and Slovenia was formally completed in March 2004. These countries joined three other former communist states (Poland, Hungary, and the Czech Republic) that had been members since 1999. With the integration of Croatia and Albania in 2009, NATO now has a membership of twenty-eight. At a summit in 2008, Ukraine, Georgia, and Macedonia were assured that eventually they, too, could become members. Discussions are also held with Bosnia and Herzegovina, Montenegro, and Cyprus. Macedonia's application has been blocked by Greece over the naming issue of that country, and any potential application of Cyprus has to overcome the hurdle of Turkey's consent. European countries that decided to stay outside of NATO include Ireland, Sweden, Finland, Switzerland, Austria, and Serbia.

2. The WEU began life as the Brussels Treaty Organisation. The Brussels Treaty was signed on

17 March 1948 by Belgium, France, Luxembourg, the Netherlands, and the United Kingdom, and proposed to unite the signatories in collective self-defense and in economic, social, and cultural cooperation. West Germany and Italy joined in 1954, thus creating the Western European Union. The WEU was dormant for most of the Cold War, but it was reactivated in 1984, with WEU foreign and defense ministers agreeing to meet more regularly.

3. The three pillars introduced by the Maastricht Treaty, as discussed in chapter 1, included Pillar I, the Economic Community; Pillar II, the Common Foreign and Security Policy; and Pillar III, Justice and Home Affairs. The pillar structure was abandoned with the ratification of the Lisbon Treaty in 2009.

4. The Petersberg Declaration of 1992 stated that the WEU will engage in peacekeeping missions, crisis management tasks (including peacemaking missions), as well as humanitarian and rescue missions.

5. According to the Amsterdam Treaty, the European Parliament only consults with the Presidency on CFSP matters. The Commission, however, can make CFSP proposals.

6. The Rapid Reaction Force was another example of intergovernmentalism succeeding supranationalism, as the General Affairs Council of the Council of Ministers was charged with its implementation.

7. The EU has also been active in other parts of the world, and between 2000 and 2010, there were twenty-three separate CFSP missions in operation. For instance, in 2008, the EU, concerned by the outbreak of piracy acts off the coast of Somalia, set up Operation EUNAVFOR (European Union Naval Force Somalia—Operation Atlanta) to protect vulnerable vessels cruising off that coast. Between 2008 and 2009 thirty-seven thousand EU troops from twenty-three member states were deployed in Chad on a UN request to protect civilians and refugees. EUCOPPS was formally established in April 2005 to engage in the reform of Palestinian civil policing, and, in July of that year, became EUPOL COPPS (European Union Police Mission for the Palestinian Territories) when EU foreign ministers reiterated their commitment to contribute to the development of Palestinian security capacity through the Palestinian Civil Police and agreed that this should become a European Security and Defence Policy mission. The EU had been particularly active in Congo where five separate missions were completed between 2003 and 2007.

8. Because relations with Russia are governed by a separate program, Russia is not part of the ENP.

9. Prior to 2007 the ENP countries as well as Russia received financial support from several programs. Between 2000 and 2006 the Technical Assistance to the CIS (TACIS) program, with a volume of 3.1 billion Euros, was designed for Russia and the EU's eastern neighbors. The MEDA program, the major financial instrument of the Euro-Mediterranean partnership, targeted Mediterranean countries with an even larger amount, 5.3 billion Euros. The new financial perspective for 2007 to 2013, however, has replaced these funds with a single vehicle, the European Neighborhood and Partnership Instrument (ENPI).

10. However, the Lisbon Treaty changed the way decisions on joint actions are agreed upon; they are now subject to qualified majority voting and not to a unanimous consensus.

11. These eight actors included Denmark, which organized the summit; the Commission President; Swedish Prime Minister Frederik Reinfelt, representing the rotating Presidency; Spanish Prime Minister José Luis Zapatero, representing the future Spanish Presidency; EU High Representative Catherine Ashton; UK Prime Minister Gordon Brown; French President Nicolas Sarkozy; and German Chancellor Angela Merkel.

12. On external trade, see chapter 15.

15. Trade and the Common Commercial Policy

1. The WTO is composed of governments and political entities such as the EU, with the vast majority of member countries from the developing world. All EU member states have joined the WTO and aim to coordinate their positions prior to trade negotiations. However, the European Commission alone speaks for the EU at almost all WTO meetings.

2. The Trade Policy Committee was formerly known as the Article 133 Committe, which derived

its name from Article 133 of the EC Treaty. Made up of national officials, it used to be chaired by the country that holds the EU Presidency, a role that the Lisbon Treaty now reserves for the High Representative for Foreign Affairs and Security Policy. The European Commission conducts negotiations at the WTO on behalf of all member states, but first it must consult the Committee and is bound to act in line with the Committee's recommendations.

3. The issue is complicated because the Commission can only negotiate in those areas where the member states have given it legal competence. In other areas where no WTO agreement has been reached, the member states negotiate individually. An example of the latter is France's protection of its film industry and the quantitative restrictions imposed on Hollywood imports.

4. World Trade Organization, World Tariff Profiles, 2011.

5. The U.S had 11.4% of exports and 17% of imports. The figures for China were 14.1% and 12.0%, respectively (Eurostat, 2011).

6. All figures are for 2010 (Eurostat, 2012).

7. In 2011 the total amount of imports and exports within the EU was 5532.1 billion Euros. With non-EU countries the figure was 3219.6 billion Euros, giving an overall trade volume of 8751.7 billion Euros (Eurostat, 2012).

8. In April 2012, the Commission's website listed specific trade agreements with 156 states.

9. In 1975 and again in 1994 Norway was on the verge of joining the EU, only for negative referendums to halt the ambition of the respective governments in power. Before the credit crisis of 2008 and 2009 Iceland saw little reason for membership, as integration into the EU would have allowed other EU fishing fleets to enter Icelandic waters. Liechtenstein also prefers to stay outside the Union, as this enables this tiny Alpine micro state to maintain its status as a tax haven. Switzerland is not a member of the EEA, since the country is particularly protective of its banking industry and does not follow EU law governing the free movement of services and capital.

10. By 2010 the membership of non-EU entities had increased to sixteen, including, Albania, Algeria, Bosnia and Herzegovina, Croatia, Egypt, Israel, Jordan, Lebanon, Libya, Mauritania, Monaco, Montenegro, Morocco, Syria and Tunisia, as well as the Palestinian Territories.

11. Trade among the Euromed countries is still rather limited. According to the European Commission, total intra-regional trade amounted to only 15 billion Euros in 2009, which means that the area has one of the lowest levels of regional economic integration in the world.

12. For more detailed information on the European Neighborhood Policy, see chapter 14.

13. The figure is for 2009 (European Commission, DG Trade, 2012).

14. The website of the European Commission listed some harrowing examples of trade anomalies. For instance, Ghana sent 49 percent of its exports to the EU but only 3 percent to its neighbor Benin. A lack of competition means that moving a container from the Kenyan city of Mombasa to the Ugandan capital of Kampala cost as much as moving one to Shanghai. In Rwanda, clearing red tape for imports took on average 124 days in comparison with an OECD average of 12 days. Source: European Commission, DG Trade: http://ec.europa.eu/trade/creating-opportunities/bilateral-relations/regions/africa-caribbean-pacific. Last accessed on 27 June 2012.

15. For more detailed information, readers might want to consult the websites of DG Trade and here in particular: http://ec.europa.eu/trade/creating-opportunities/bilateral-relations/countries-and-regions/. Last accessed on 27 June 2012.

16. Environment

1. More information on the benefits of the Single Market as outlined in the Cecchini Report can be found in chapter 9.

2. In the 1980s Denmark obliged soft drink and beer producers to sell their products in reusable containers. The Commission took Denmark to court claiming a violation of the free movement of goods. The Court dismissed the case, however, arguing that regulations regarding the marketing of bottles did not exist at that time, and that in any case environmental protection may have precedence over single market regulations.

3. The UK once argued that it did not need the same amount of environmental regulation because

it had short fast rivers (rather than long, slow, deposit-dropping continental rivers) that carried pollutants into the sea.

4. In Germany the focus was on measuring discharges from sources, whereas the UK would measure the medium holding the pollutant (for instance, ambient air pollution).

5. A key criterion in the setting of the allowance was that every member state's target has to be that agreed upon in the Kyoto Protocol. This means that a member state had to make sure that the allocations they grant to their plants allowed the state to meet its Kyoto benchmark.

6. The Central and Eastern European countries included the Czech Republic, Hungary, Bulgaria, Latvia, Lithuania, and Romania.

7. The European Neighbourhood Policy and the Euro-Mediterranean Partnership are analyzed in greater detail in chapter 15.

17. The Sovereign Debt Crises in the Eurozone

1. Bail-out money was not paid out in one installment. Instead, it was divided into several tranches which were released at certain intervals and subject to the bailed-out country meeting its tax and spend commitments.

2. Rajoy's first budget called for twelve billion Euro worth of spending cuts and fifteen billion Euro of tax increases with the aim of bringing the annual deficit down to 5.5 percent in 2012 and to 3 percent a year later, the latter being an EU-wide benchmark to which Spain had agreed to in the *Fiscal Compact* of January 2012. This amounted to 570 Euro of either spending cuts or tax increases per citizen. Government departments were asked to slash their budgets by 17 percent. The wages of civil servants which had been reduced by 5 percent in 2010 were kept frozen.

3. Shortly after asking for bail-out money, Rajoy announced further spending cuts and tax increases amounting to sixty-five billion Euro in austerity measures. The sales tax was raised by 3 percent and civil servants saw their salaries reduced. The reduction of social security contributions, which had been Rajoy's only stimulus to the economy was scrapped.

4. De Larosière also pressed for the establishment of European Supervisory Authorities (ESA) based on a European System of Financial Supervisors (ESFS). Members of the ESFS are representatives from the twenty-seven national supervising authorities with the objective to oversee micro-prudential risks. The ESFS in itself would consist of three further sub-bodies, namely, the EBA (European Banking Authority), EIOPA (European Insurance and Occupational Pensions Authority), and ESA (European Securities Authority).

5. During the crisis, Christine Lagarde, the Head of the IMF, asked for an increase in contributions from its members. During 2011 and 2012, she managed to raise the Fund's lending resources by 430 billion US Dollars, 200 billion of which came from the Eurozone. The largest shareholder of the IMF, the United States, declined to contribute more money at that particular moment.

6. With regard to public finances, the fiscal rules of the Stability Pact of the Maastricht Treaty had to be written into national law. Pensions, health care, and other welfare state provisions had to be kept at financially sustainable levels. As to financial stability, the debt for banks but also for households and non-financial firms had to be sustainable and were monitored by the recently established European Systemic Risk Board. Lastly, the pact aimed for the development of a common corporate tax base, and the common tackling of fraud and tax evasion, although direct taxation would remain under the competence of national governments.

7. The key points of the *Euro Rescue Deal* were the following:

- The writing down of Greek debt by 50 percent with the remaining debt to be secured by member states.
- A recapitalization of European banks with the requirement to raise their capital ratio to 9 percent. Banks were required to raise their capital by first going to private markets. If this initiative proved to be unsuccessful, banks were then obliged to apply to their national governments for financial support. The European Financial Stability Fund (EFSF) was seen as the last resort in order to reach the 9 percent target.

- Increase the resources of the EFSF: By establishing a so-called Special Purpose Vehicle, EU leaders aimed to raise money by approaching wealthy state investment funds (such as those held by China) to boost the ESFS's capacity to 1.5 trillion Euro.

8. It was not only the UK that did not sign up to the treaty. The Eurosceptic governments of the Czech Republic, Hungary, and Sweden all indicated that they first had to consult their national parliaments. We therefore saw the emergence of the awkward acronym CHUCKS for four countries that did not—at least from the start—committed to tighter budgetary rules. In the end, it was only the UK and the Czech Republic who decided on the latest opt-out of the EU's treaty agenda.

9. Quantitative easing is explained in greater detail in chapter 12.

Outlook: The Future of European Integration

1. Figures according to: http://www.euractiv.com/cap/cap-reform-2014-2020-linksdossier-508393; last accessed on 16 July 2012. France has traditionally been the biggest beneficiary of the CAP and receives about 20 percent, followed by Germany and Spain (13 percent each), Italy (11 percent) and the United Kingdom (9 percent).

Bibliography

For those who wish to deepen their knowledge of the European Union, the EU's official website (http://europa.eu) offers information on policies, institutional affairs, legislative initiatives, and summit conclusions. Given that the site is produced by EU institutions, some of the information, not surprisingly, is slanted rather positively. For a more independent account of recent policy and institutional developments, a valid source of information is the website http://www.euractiv.com.

Numerous textbooks have been published on the EU in recent years, and readers may find the following three helpful in deepening their understanding of EU affairs:

- Arguably the most advanced text in prioritizing academic debates in political science is S. Hix, *The Political System of the European Union,* 2nd ed (New York: Palgrave Macmillan, 2011).
- For a historical overview of European integration and EU institutions, see D. Dinan, *Ever Closer Union: An Introduction to European Integration (European Union)* (New York: Palgrave Macmillan, 2010).
- For the most in-depth analysis of EU policies, see H. Wallace, M. Pollack, and A. Young, eds., *Policy-Making in the European Union* (Oxford: Oxford University Press, 2010).
- For detailed information on history and institutions, see N. Nugent. *The Government and Politics of the European Union* New York: Macmillan, 2010).

More specialized information and analyses can be found in the sources listed below in line with the chapters of this book.

1. Parameters of European Integration

- P. Anderson. *The New World.* London: Verso, 2010.
- D. Dinan. *Europe Recast: A History of the European Union.* New York: Palgrave Mamillan, 2004.
- N. Scicluna. "When Failure Isn't Failure: European Union Constitutionalism after the Lisbon Treaty." *Journal of Common Market Studies* 50, no. 3 (2012): 441–456

2. Enlargement

- O. Dursun-Ozkanca. "The Legitimacy of the European Union after Enlargement." *Journal of Common Market Studies* 48, no. 3 (2010): 767–768.
- H. Grabbe and U. Sedelmeier. "The Future Shape of the European Union." In M. Egan, N. Nugent, and W. Paterson, eds., *Research Agendas in EU Studies: Stalking the Elephant,* 375–397. New York: Palgrave Macmillan, 2009.
- M. O. Hosli, M. Mattila and M. Uriot. "Voting in the Council of the European Union after the 2004 Enlargement." *Journal of Common Market Studies* 49, no.6 (2011): 1249–1270.
- N. Nugent. *European Union Enlargement.* New York: Palgrave Macmillan, 2004.
- C. Preston. "Obstacles to EU Enlargement: The Classical Community Method and the Prospects for a Wider Europe." *Journal of Common Market Studies* 33, no. 3 (1995): 451–463.
- F. Schimmelfennig and U. Sedelmeier. *The Politics of European Union Enlargement.* London: Routledge, 2009.

3–8. Institutions

- J. Alter. *Establishing the Supremacy of European Law.* Oxford: Oxford University Press, 2003.
- D. Chalmers, G. Davies, G. Monti, and A.Tomkins. *European Union Law.* Cambridge: Cambridge University Press, 2010.
- R. Corbett, F. Jacobs, and M. Shackleton. *The European Parliament.* London: John Harper Publishing, 2011.
- F. Hayes-Renschaw, W. Van Aken, and H. Wallace. "When and Why the EU Council of Ministers Votes Explicitly." *Journal of Common Market Studies* 44, no. 1 (2006): 161–194.
- F. Hayes-Renshaw and H. Wallace. *The Council of Ministers.* New York: Palgrave Macmillan, 2006.
- S. Hix. *What's Wrong with the European Union and How to Fix It.* Cambridge: Polity, 2009.
- S. Hix and B. Høyland. *The Political System of the European Union.* London: Palgrave, 2011.
- G. Majone. *Dilemmas of European Integration.* Oxford: Oxford University Press, 2009.
- D. Naurin and H.Wallace, eds. *Unveiling the Council of the European Union.* New York. Palgrave, 2008.
- M. Pollack. *The Engines of Integration: Delegation, Agency, and Agency Setting in the European Union.* Oxford: Oxford University Press, 2003.
- A. Stone Sweet. *The Judicial Construction of Europe.* Oxford: Oxford University Press, 2004
- J. H. H. Weiler. *The Constitution of Europe: "Do the New Clothes Have an Emperor?" and Other Essays on European Integration.* Cambridge: Cambridge University Press, 1999.

9. The Single Market and Competition

- R. Baldwin, M. Cave, and M. Lodge, *Understanding Regulation.* Oxford: Oxford University Press, 2012.
- S. L. Greer. "Market Integration and Public Services in the European Union." *Journal of Common Market Studies* 50, no. 3 (2012): 530–531.
- J. Hoelscher and J. Stephan. "Competition and Antitrust Policy in the Enlarged European Union: A Level Playing Field?" *Journal of Common Market Studies* 47, no. 4 (2009): 863–889.
- D. Howard and T. Sadeh. "The Ever Incomplete Single Market." *Journal of European Public Policy* 17, no. 7 (2010): 922–935.
- M. Lodge. "Regulation, the Regulatory State and European Politics." *West European Politics* 31, no. 1/2 (2008): 280–301.
- M. Lodge and K. Wegrich. *Managing Regulation.* Basingstoke: Palgrave, 2012

- L. McGowan and S. Wilks. "The First Supranational Policy in the EU." *European Journal of Political Research* 28, no. 2 (1995): 141–169.

10. Regional Policy and Cohesion.

- M. Baun and D. Marek, eds. *EU Cohesion Policy after Enlargement*. Palgrave Macmillan, 2008.
- R. Crescenzi and A. Rodriguez-Pose. "Infrastructure and Regional Growth in the European Union." *Papers in Regional Science* 91, no. 2 (2012).
- T. Farole, A. Rogriguez-Pose, and M. Stopper. "Cohesion Policy in the European Union: Growth, Geography, Institutions." *Journal of Common Market Studies* 49, no. 5 (2011): 1089–1111.
- A. Kay and R. Ackrill. "Financing Social and Cohesion Policy in an Enlarged EU: Plus ça change, plus c'est la même chose?" *Journal of European Social Policy* 17, no. 4 (2007): 361–374.
- R. Leonardi. *Cohesion in the European Union*. London: Routledge, 2006.

11. The Common Agricultural Policy

- J. Bachtler and C. Mendez. "Who Governs EU Cohesion Policy? Deconstructing the Reforms of the Structural Funds." *Journal of Common Market Studies* 45, no. 3 (2007): 535–564.
- A. Burrell. "The CAP: Looking Back, Looking Ahead." *Journal of European Integration* 31, no. 3 (2009): 271–289.
- K. Knickel, H. Renting, and J. Douwe van der Ploeg. "Multifunctionality in European Agriculture." In F. Brower, ed., *Sustaining Agriculture and the Rural Environment: Governance, Policy and Multifunctionality*, 81–103. Cheltenham, UK: Edward Elgar, 2004.
- Swinbank and C. Daugbjerg. "The 2003 CAP Reform: Accommodating WTO Pressures." *Comparative European Politics* 4, no. 1 (2006): 47–64.

12. The Economic and Monetary Union

- M. Buti, S. Deroose, and E. Gaspar, eds. *The Euro: The First Decade*. Cambridge: Cambridge University Press, 2010.
- K. Dyson, ed. *The Euro at Ten: Europeanization, Power, and Convergence*. Oxford: Oxford University Press, 2008.
- J. Pisani-Ferry and A. S. Posen, *The Euro at Ten: The Next Global Currency?* Washington, D.C.: Peterson Institute for International Economics, 2009.

13. Justice and Home Affairs

- V. Guiraudon. "Immigration and Asylum: A High Politics Agenda." In M. Green Cowles and D. Dinan, eds., *Developments in the European Union 2*. New York: Palgrave Macmillan, 2004.
- G. Lahav. *Immigration and Politics in the New Europe: Reinventing Borders*. Cambridge: Cambridge University Press, 2004.
- J. D. Occhipinti. "Police and Judicial Cooperation." In M. G. Cowles and D. Dinan, eds., *Developments in the European Union 2*. New York: Palgrave Macmillan, 2004.
- M. Rhinard. "The External Dimension of Justice and Home Affairs." *Journal of Common Market Studies* 50, no. 2 (2012):362–363.
- K. E. Smith. "The Justice and Home Affairs Policy Universe: Some Directions for Further Research." *Journal of European Integration* 31, no. 1 (2009): 1–7.
- E. R. Thielemann. "Symbolic Politics or Effective Burden-Sharing? Redistribution, Side-payments, and the European Refugee Fund." *Journal of Common Market Studies* 43, no. 4 (2005): 807–824.

14. Common Foreign and Security Policy

- F. Bindi, ed. *The Foreign Policy of the European Union: Assessing Europe's Role in the World.* Brookings Institution Press, 2010.
- S. Lucarelli and L. Fioramonti, eds., "External Perceptions of the European Union as a Global Actor." *Political Studies Review* 10, no. 2 (2012); 293–294.
- K. E. Smith. *European Union Foreign Policy in a Changing World.* Cambridge: Polity, 2008.
- D. C.Thomas. "Still Punching below its Weight? Coherence and Effectiveness in European Union Foreign Policy." *Journal of Common Market Studies* 50, no. 3 (2012): 457–474.

15. Trade and the Common Commercial Policy

- M. Bungenberg. "Going Global? The EU Common Commercial Policy after Lisbon." In *European Yearbook of International Economic Law.* Berlin: Springer, 2009.
- S. Meunier. *The European Union in International Commercial Negotiations.* London: Routledge, 2007.
- S. Woolcock. "European Union Trade Policy: Domestic Institutions and Systemic Factors." In D. Kelly and W. Grant, eds., *The Politics of International Trade in the Twenty-first Century: Actors, Issues and Regional Dynamics.* Basingstoke, UK: Palgrave, 2005.

16. Environment

- A. Jordan, D. Huitema, H. van Asselt, T. Rayner, and F. Berkhout, eds. *Climate Change Policy in the European Union: Confronting the Dilemmas of Adaptation and Mitigation?* Cambridge: Cambridge University Press, 2010.
- A. Jordan and D. Liefferink. *Environment Policy in Europe: The Europeanization of National Environmental Policy.* London: Routledge, 2004.
- A. Lenschow and C.Sprungk. "The Myth of a Green Europe." *Journal of Common Market Studies* 79, no. 1 (2010): 133–154.
- P. Lund. "The European Union Challenge: Integration of Energy, Climate and Economic Policy." *Energy and Environment* 1, no. 1 (2012): 60 – 68.
- J. McCormick. *Environmental Policy in the European Union,* London: Palgrave Macmillan, 2001.

17. The Sovereign Debt Crisis in the Eurozone

- L.Tsoukalis and J.A.Emmanoulides. "The Delphic Oracle on Europe: Is There a Future for the European Union?" *Journal of Common Market Studies* 50, no. 4 (2012).
- B. Thorhallson and Peadar Kirb. "Financial Crises in Iceland and Ireland: Does European Union and Euro Membership Matter?" *Journal of Common Market Studies* 50, no. 4 (2012).

Index

Andreas Staab

is the founder and director of
EPIC—the European Policy Information Centre—
a UK-based consultancy on the European Union. He also
teaches for the London programs of St. Lawrence University,
the University of California, and Washington University
in St. Louis, and is author of *National Identity
in Eastern Germany.*